VICTORIAN LACE

VICTORIAN LACE

By

PATRICIA WARDLE

REVISED SECOND EDITION

RUTH BEAN

CARLTON : BEDFORD

1982

Originally published by Herbert Jenkins, London, 1968

This edition published by Ruth Bean, Victoria Farmhouse, Carlton,
Bedford MK43 7LP, England

Distributed in the U.S.A. by Robin & Russ, Handweavers,
McMinnville, Oregon, 97128, U.S.A.

Copyright © 1982

ISBN 0 903585 13 8

Plate negatives, Alpha Plates, Northampton
Printed in Great Britain at the University Press, Cambridge

PREFACE TO SECOND EDITION

This new edition has been inspired by the recent revival of interest both in lace collecting and lace making. The text has been reprinted from the first edition without alteration, but the bibliography has been brought up to date and the illustrations greatly improved. I would like to thank Signor Giorgio Calligaris of Florence for encouraging me to go ahead with this new edition and Miss Santina Levey, Keeper of Textiles and Dress at the Victoria and Albert Museum, for assistance with the bibliography. Grateful thanks are also due to Mrs Ruth Bean, the publisher, for her enthusiasm and efficiency in presenting the book to the public again in an improved form.

Patricia Wardle

May 1982

FOREWORD

By
HUGH WAKEFIELD
Keeper of the Department of Circulation, Victoria and Albert Museum

THE Victorian period was not the greatest in the history of hand-made lace, but it was a period of great activity and also of achievement. Lace was much used for Victorian costume and, once bought for the adornment of a dress or hat, it was rarely destroyed. It is not surprising that by far the greater part of the old lace found today should prove to be Victorian in date.

This was the period which saw the effects of the industrial revolution and the long drawn-out struggle between hand-made and machine-made laces. Ultimately hand-made lace survived as a luxury product, but for most of the nineteenth century the two methods were competing, often for the same market. The author of this book is much concerned with the effects of this struggle, and she does well to bring within her scope the products of mechanized industry as well as those of the handworker. It will be seen, too, that the subject is not by any means confined to the British Isles. The Victorian woman liked to wear foreign lace, and thus the story of Victorian lace is the story of the craft throughout Europe and beyond.

So far collectors and connoisseurs in the present century have paid little attention to Victorian lace. It is hoped that this book will do much to stimulate a revival of interest by focusing attention on the most significant and attractive laces of the period. In producing a scholarly work of this nature the author has necessarily assumed on the part of the reader a background knowledge of the nature and earlier history of the craft. An appendix has been added, however, to describe the basic techniques of lace-making, and those readers who are unfamiliar with the techniques and their terminology are recommended to read the appendix before embarking on the rest of the book.

Patricia Wardle, B.A. (now Mrs. Alan Griffiths), is also the author of *Victorian Silver and Silver-Plate*, first published in 1963. The present book is largely the outcome of working for several years in the Textiles Department of the Victoria and Albert Museum in London. More recently, however, living in Holland, she has had the further experience of studying at close quarters the fine collections in the Musées Royaux d'Art et d'Histoire in Brussels and in the Rijksmuseum in Amsterdam, which now houses the Dutch royal collection.

CONTENTS

LIST OF PLATES

LIST OF FIGURES

14

ACKNOWLEDGEMENTS

MOST of the work for this book was done while I was in the Textiles Department of the Victoria and Albert Museum, which afforded an unrivalled opportunity for the study of lace. I would like to thank all my former colleagues there who supported and encouraged my researches and also my successor, Miss Santina Levey, who has given me much help in looking up information and obtaining photographs.

Anyone who undertakes a project of this kind is invariably encouraged and assisted by like-minded enthusiasts in other museums. I am most particularly indebted to Miss Anne Buck, Keeper of the Gallery of English Costume, Platt Hall, Manchester, who most generously allowed me to read and use information from a study (unfortunately unpublished) she has made of the lace industry of the East Midlands; to Mme. Risselin-Steenebrugen of the Musées Royaux d'Art et d'Histoire in Brussels, who gave up much of her valuable time to discuss with me the magnificent collection of lace and designs there during a most informative week's visit; and to Miss Louise Erkelens of the Rijksmuseum, Amsterdam, who extended to me the great privilege of a close examination of the beautiful nineteenth-century lace in the Dutch Royal Collection recently placed on loan there. I would also like to say a special word of thanks to Miss Zillah Halls, formerly of the Castle Museum, Nottingham, and now of the London Museum, who showed me the fine collection of machine-made lace at Nottingham, and to Miss Bernardine de Neeve of the Museum Boymans-van Beuningen, Rotterdam, who has often allowed me to study the choice collection of lace there. All five also gave much help over photographs, and I am especially grateful for the excellent series of enlarged details supplied by the Rijksmuseum.

Other people to whom I am indebted for help in obtaining photographs are Mr. M. B. Herbert of Leicester Museum and Art Gallery, Mr. E. J. Laws of Nottingham Museum and Art Gallery, Mr. A. T. Lucas of the National Museum of Ireland, Mrs. N. Saporiti of the Metropolitan Museum of Art, New York, Mr. P.

Smith of Luton Museum and Art Gallery and Mrs. N. M. Sonley of Bowness-on-Solway.

I am very grateful to the editor of this series, Mr. Hugh Wakefield, who has read the book most carefully and thoroughly in typescript and eliminated various minor errors and inconsistencies, and who has given an enormous amount of help over the illustrations. My husband also read the book in typescript and contributed a number of helpful suggestions, as well as much sympathy and encouragement throughout the progress of the work.

PATRICIA WARDLE

INTRODUCTION

L ACE of the nineteenth century has been somewhat neglected by modern writers. In fact most people, rather hastily, dismiss it as being inferior in both design and quality to laces of earlier centuries and, thus, as lacking in interest in comparison with them. Yet probably there was no century in which lace was so much admired and used as in the nineteenth, and certainly more lace survives from this period than from any other. This latter phenomenon can be partly explained by the fact that the nineteenth century is so near in time to the present day, but it must also be conceded that Victorian ladies cherished their lace and took great pains to preserve it.

As a result there can be few families whose members have not, at one time or another, when going through the belongings of an old grandmother or great-aunt, come across an assemblage of lace which has obviously been treasured by its former owner. Often narrow borders are neatly wound round pieces of card to keep them flat and tidy, while large pieces are carefully folded, and all are shrouded in the familiar blue or black tissue paper and, perhaps, labelled in an old-fashioned hand. Instructions such as those given by "Myra" to her readers in 1872 have obviously been assiduously followed:

"Most of last year's bodices were trimmed with narrow Valenciennes lace; I advise this to be carefully removed from corsage and pouffs, and washed and ironed without starching. . . . An excellent plan is to keep a trimming box, in which our stores of trimmings are placed, lace wound on cards. . . . Black lace and net should be dipped in ale and ironed out between sheets of paper, and wound on cards until required." (*Young Englishwoman*, 1872, pp. 442–3.)

Thanks to such thriftiness it is not difficult to discover quantities of nineteenth-century lace hiding away in drawers or trunks, although it seldom finds its way into antique shops.

Anyone who examines the contents of such hoards soon discovers,

17

moreover, one of the main reasons why nineteenth-century lace has been comparatively neglected. The fact is that our forebears tidily put away not only the best but also the worst of their lace. In the seventeenth and eighteenth centuries plenty of cheap common lace was made but it did not last long and was mostly thrown away when worn out, so that we are left with only the best pieces from those periods. The nineteenth century is near enough to us for virtually every sort of lace, however cheap and ordinary, to have survived and, indeed, one sometimes becomes rather overwhelmed by the sheer quantity of such ordinary lace as opposed to the rarer fine pieces. However, the mere fact that the bad lace has survived alongside the good adds interest to the study of nineteenth-century lace in that it gives us a more complete picture than is possible for any earlier century.

It was, of course, the invention of lace-making machines in the late eighteenth and early nineteenth centuries that resulted in more people than ever before being able to trim their clothes with what had been previously an expensive luxury fabric. Not only was machine-made lace much cheaper than most hand-made lace, but its advent led lace-makers in many areas to turn to the production of types of lace that were quickly and easily made in a necessarily fruitless attempt to beat the machines at their own game. So the use of lace had become habitual for a much wider range of society by the end of the nineteenth century. Vast quantities of lace were made and sold, English buyers being just as avid for foreign laces as for home-produced goods. P. L. Simonds wrote in the *Art Journal* of 1872 (p. 295): "Besides the enormous consumption of our cheaper Nottingham lace and the pillow-lace of Honiton, we import foreign lace to the value of more than £750,000 sterling. The declared value of the imports in 1870 were pillow-lace of silk amounting to £82,401; of thread £164,207; and machine, or imitation lace, not made by hand, £265,313." Most of the imported lace came from France and Belgium, the two chief lace-making countries of Europe. Simonds added: "besides the large quantity of British-made lace used at home, nearly £1,000,000 in value of cotton lace and £297,000 of silk lace were sent abroad".

Apart from the wealth of lace of all kinds that has survived from the Victorian period, there is also a plethora of contemporary writing about it. The great changes in the manufacturing industries brought about by the Industrial Revolution made people aware of the interest to be found in the study of their history. This tendency was particularly marked, as far as lace is concerned, in the second half of the nineteenth century. From that period date many long, detailed accounts of lace industries, both past and present, hand- and machine-made, often written by manufacturers or people concerned in the industry in some way.

Many more useful facts are contained in the catalogues of the series of international exhibitions held during the century, beginning with the Great Exhibition held in London in 1851. Here may be found recorded the names not only of lace manufacturers who exhibited their products but also those of designers and sometimes even of actual lace-makers, together with detailed descriptions by experts of the current state of the industry. Thanks to the exhibitions there exists a far larger mass of information about the actual persons engaged in the lace industry in the nineteenth than in any previous century. With eighteenth-century lace, for example, much research is needed to discover the names of the manufacturers, let alone those of the designers, which are completely unknown to us. Furthermore, as some of the lace shown in the international exhibitions was illustrated in various catalogues, it is occasionally possible even to identify exactly a particular piece of lace and thus to discover its precise date and provenance, something virtually impossible with earlier pieces. A number of these illustrations are reproduced in the present book in the hope that more happy discoveries of this type may be made, while the names of the more important lace manu- facturers who showed in international exhibitions are also given, as these may sometimes turn up on old bills or labels.

One of the most fascinating aspects of the history of lace in the nineteenth century is, of course, the struggle between the hand- and machine-lace industries. Such a conflict, between a decaying hand industry and a rising machine competitor, is a typically nineteenth- century theme. The struggle was by no means a simple affair, for both industries had their ups and downs during the course of the century. The fragility of the finished product must, indeed, never be allowed to disguise the fact that lace-making was a serious industry, run by hard-headed men and women. If manufacturers wished to stay in business, they had to be adept in coping with the vicissitudes which afflict a luxury trade, heavily dependent on the changing dictates of fickle fashion, and machine-lace men found this just as difficult as their rivals in the hand-lace industry.

Looking back from the present day, when machine-made products are all too familiar, it is sometimes difficult to remember or to appreciate the delight taken by the Victorians, particularly in the first half of the century, in new machine-made goods. In its early days, in fact, machine-made lace was not despised but was rather welcomed as the product of a most lively and ingenious industry. It was felt to be an excellent thing that less affluent people should be able to enjoy at least an imitation of the luxury textiles which were the preserve of the wealthy. Indeed, it might be said that by the 1850s and 1860s a sort of balance had been achieved between the two industries. By this time hand-made lace, now fully recovered from the economic troubles of the early part of the century, had reached a peak of prosperity. Many of the pieces of this period are of superb quality, bearing rich, complex designs, completely contemporary in feeling, carried out with a skill and refinement which makes them fully worthy of being compared with the best laces of preceding centuries. At the same time the manufacturers of machine-made lace had perfected many of the chief methods of producing worthy imitations of such fine products.

On the other hand, quantities of cheap, inferior machine-made lace were also pouring on to the market, and some of the weaker hand-lace industries were already suffering severely from this competition. By the last third of the century, in spite of the fact that much good hand-made lace continued to be produced, machine-made lace had virtually won the day because of the multiplicity of varieties that could now be easily and cheaply produced. Even so, the history of the machine-lace industry of this time is not without crises. These, admittedly, were now caused more by competition within the machine-lace industry itself rather than from the hand-workers.

Finally, the triumph of machinery brought with it a general reaction against its products. This, coupled with a kindling of interest all over Europe in peasant crafts and industries that were discovered to be on the point of dying out, led in many areas to a revival of hand lace-making. In addition there grew up a great interest in the lace of past centuries. It became fashionable to wear old lace, particularly seventeenth-century Venetian lace. It also became fashionable to collect old lace. Many extremely fine collections were assembled at this period by wealthy ladies who paid enormous sums for sumptuous laces of the seventeenth and eighteenth centuries, many of which have since found their way into museums. Collections of this type, though they may include fine nineteenth-century pieces, are in general quite different in content from those referred to at the beginning of the introduction, which consisted mainly of contemporary, wearable lace. There is, however, no doubt that the very high prices paid for antique laces at this time made many women anxious to preserve all their scraps of lace in the belief that these, too, were of considerable monetary value, a belief not borne out by events, for the actual cash value of lace, at least in the British Isles, has declined steadily and rapidly throughout the present century.

In an effort to make the details of the complex story of nineteenth-century lace as clear as possible, each type of lace will be dealt with separately, after a preliminary chapter giving a survey of developments throughout the century as a whole. Hand-made laces, grouped according to their country of origin, are followed by two chapters on machine-made lace. Embroidered nets, which stand mid-way between hand- and machine-made lace, are dealt with in the chapters on machine-made lace, except for Limerick lace, which is discussed with the other Irish laces. It has been found essential to include information relating to the earlier part of the nineteenth century in many of the chapters, as it is impossible to understand later developments without some knowledge of this pre-Victorian period. A number of enlarged photographs showing technical details have been included among the illustrations in order to assist readers to identify specifically nineteenth-century types of lace. No technical details are given of varieties of lace, such as Lille or Mechlin, which preserved eighteenth-century techniques into the nineteenth century, as these have been fully dealt with in many previous books on lace, or of the types such as nineteenth-century Valenciennes and *point Duchesse* which are easy to recognize without minute examination of technique.

Students of lace of earlier periods will be familiar with the fact that types of lace are usually distinguished by the names of towns: Valenciennes, Brussels, Chantilly, Alençon, Honiton, etc., which, while they indicate the place of origin of the type, by no means define the area in which it was made. Thus, in the eighteenth century, for example, Alençon and Argentan lace were each made in each of the two towns as well as in surrounding country districts. In the nineteenth century this tendency becomes even more marked. Writing in 1869 (*History of Lace*, p. 138), Mrs. Bury Palliser noted that "within the last few years the immense development of the Belgian lace trade has overthrown the characteristic lace of each city. Lace, white and black, point and pillow, may at the present time be met with in every province of the now flourishing kingdom of Belgium." The trend had, in fact, begun even earlier and was common to most of the lace industry in the nineteenth century. Furthermore, it was by no means unusual for a type of lace formerly associated with one country to be imitated in another. Readers must, therefore, not be surprised to hear of Chantilly lace being made not only in Caen and Bayeux but in Belgium too, of Alençon lace in Brussels and Burano, of Venetian lace in Brussels and Bayeux, of Honiton lace in Ireland, to name but a few examples.

CHAPTER 1

FASHIONS IN LACE IN THE NINETEENTH CENTURY

THE following survey of the ways in which lace was worn during the nineteenth century, the varieties favoured at different periods and the changes in design, is not intended to be an exhaustive chronicle, but to serve as a background to the main part of the book in which different types of lace are treated separately. More information specifically related to costume is to be found in a companion volume of this series, *Victorian Costume*, by Anne Buck.

Knowledge of the part played by lace in costume is, of course, an invaluable aid to dating, since the shape of a piece may be as revealing as the design or technique. Collectors will therefore find it profitable to study nineteenth-century paintings, book illustrations and photographs, as well as the sections devoted to fashion in women's magazines of the period. The latter contain many descriptions of the way in which lace was used, although it is often difficult to be certain as to precisely what type of lace is meant, as fashion writers frequently used trade names or terms the significance of which is no longer clear.

Pre-Victorian

For much of the first two decades of the century light, slightly-patterned laces of the type familiar at the end of the eighteenth century continued to be popular. The severe classical styles and light materials then fashionable precluded the use of heavily-ornamented lace. Net-like laces with borders of leaves, flowers or simple scrolling motifs, with little spots or flowers dotted over the rest of the ground, were favoured. The motifs were often rendered lighter still in effect by the use of slight fancy filling patterns, or else they were carried out in a delicate linear style. Classical scroll or key motifs and, occasionally, designs incorporating vases and urns are found at this period too, while some of the more ambitious

23

French and Belgian laces, intended for hangings or bed-covers, were decorated with elaborate figure-subjects in the classical manner.

Border laces of this period were generally straight-edged. They were used to trim the low necks and hems of dresses, or perhaps to form a small gathered ruff round the neck of the wearer. In the second decade of the century there was a fashion for bodices, sleeves and caps made of alternate strips of muslin and lace insertion. Light laces such as silk blondes, Mechlin and Lille, or similar types produced in the East Midland counties of England, were popular for dress trimmings, while there also survive from these years Brussels application laces of extreme delicacy and refinement with a ground of bobbin-made mesh. Lace caps were worn indoors, and lace was used to trim bonnets and hats. Broader laces, black as well as white, were favoured as trimmings for pelisses and capes for outer wear, and sometimes a pelisse would be made entirely of lace or embroidered machine-made net.

Machine-made nets, made on variants of the stocking-frame, were already available in quantity by 1800. They were often ornamented with simple hand embroidery or used plain over self-coloured or contrasting silk in dresses. Eugenia Wynne, for example, described her wedding attire in 1806 as follows: "My *bridal array* consisted of a white satin underdress and a patent net over it, with a long veil", while in the following year her sister Betsey went to court dressed in "white satin and patent net drapery which looked very neat" (ed. Anne Fremantle: *The Wynne Diaries, 1789–1820*, London, 1935, Vol. III, pp. 291 and 309).

The use of nets, both plain and embroidered by needlerunning or tambouring, increased greatly after the invention in 1809 by John Heathcoat of a machine which could produce a fast, twisted net closely resembling a bobbin-made mesh. During the next two decades, before the advent of patterned machine-made lace, embroidered nets enjoyed a great vogue. They were used on a large scale for scarves (Pl. 76), veils, wide collars, and the many varieties of outdoor mantle or pelerine popular at the time. Embroidered net went under various trade names, such as British point lace, and it is often difficult to tell whether a fashion writer is referring to it or to "real" lace. Machine-made net was also used as the basis of another type of imitation lace, known as Carrickmacross work, which began to be made in Ireland in the 1830s.

About 1815 a new manner began to creep into lace design, when straight edges were gradually replaced by scalloped ones.   Vandyked or scalloped edges, often very precise and neat in execution, were characteristic of the 1820s, while in the following decade shallower, more open scallops were preferred.   These trends are clearly evident in silk laces in particular.   From about 1816, in fact, blonde lace became all the rage, especially for evening wear.   It was lavishly used to trim dresses, caps, pelisses and aprons, and sometimes whole dresses were composed of it (Pl. 19).   Such dresses were usually worn over an underdress of contrasting colour.

The favourite design motifs of the 1820s and 1830s were sprigs or sprays of flowers, drawn either with a delicate naturalism or, more often, in a stylized manner of Turkish or Persian inspiration (Pls. 1, 67).   They are to be found on scalloped borders, or arranged in rows at the ends of long lace scarves or veils (Pls. 20, 24).

1837–1870

By the beginning of Victoria's reign various other trends were becoming apparent.   Blonde and embroidered net still retained their popularity, but black silk lace had begun to come back into favour in the middle of the 1830s after a period of decline, and in fashion writings of the late 1830s there are many references to Brussels application and needlepoint laces.   The Belgian lace industry was, indeed, beginning to flourish again, thanks largely to the intelligent use made of machine-made nets as a background material as well as to the development of new types of lace.

Lace was particularly favoured for evening wear.   Often a single deep flounce round the bottom of the skirt of a dress was echoed round the low neck by a deep falling collar of the type which, by the end of the decade, had come to be known as a bertha (Pl. 2). Blonde lace caps with long, floating lappets were also fashionable for evening wear.   For day-time wear, mantles of black lace were now beginning to replace those of white embroidered net or muslin which had been popular for so long.   Black and white mantles alike were often lined with coloured materials, while those of embroidered muslin were usually finished off with a deep fall of embroidered net or airy lace.   Peignoirs for morning wear were often made of embroidered muslin trimmed with Valenciennes, a lace recently returned to favour in a guise quite different from the

Valenciennes of the eighteenth century (cf. Pl. 33). Morning caps, too, were often made of embroidered net bedecked with ribbons. Blonde, black silk lace and embroidered net were used to decorate bonnets, which at this period assumed very large brims, usually set off by a lace frill inside, and were frequently finished off with a long veil or curtain in front, made of embroidered net or blonde lace. Such veils, distinguished by a narrow hem and a draw-string at the top, often occur in assemblages of nineteenth-century lace.

The most notable public event in England in 1840 was Queen Victoria's wedding. The royal bride's attire was described in *The World of Fashion* (1840, Vol. 17, p. 67): "Her Majesty the Queen wore on her head a wreath of orange blossoms and a veil of Honiton lace, with a necklace and ear-rings of diamonds. Her Majesty's dress was of white satin, with a very deep trimming of Honiton lace, in design similar to that of the veil. The body and sleeves were richly trimmed with the same material to correspond" (Pl. 3). This inaugurated a revival of Honiton lace which had taken advantage of the possibilities of machine-made net as a foundation in the same way as Brussels lace. The revival of Honiton was, however, just one aspect of the general revival of interest in richer varieties of lace at this time. It may be noted, in fact, that, while Queen Adelaide and the Duchess of Kent both appeared at the wedding patriotically attired in English lace, Princess Augusta wore a gown of blue velvet richly adorned with Brussels needlepoint.

Brussels application, Mechlin and black Chantilly were among the most popular laces in the 1840s. They were still often quite light and delicate in design with small, naturalistic flowers interspersed with scrolls, vases and other motifs derived from the revived rococo style of the period (Pl. 47). But already, before the end of the decade, a more ornate style was coming into lace design, involving the use of strapwork and twining ribbons with more luxurious flower arrangements. These appeared first in French and Belgian laces (Pls. 11, 26) and were well established by 1850. Now, too, the richest and most expensive lace of all, Alençon needlepoint, emerged triumphant from a long period of stagnation, being mentioned again in English fashion writing in the early 1840s, although its high price put it beyond the reach of all but the most wealthy.

Dresses, particularly those meant for evening wear, were lavishly trimmed with lace at this time: a skirt might have a deep flounce round the bottom, or several narrow flounces, or lace arranged in zigzags or other formations, complemented by a wide bertha collar round the bodice, or a fall of one or two rows of lace, with sleeves trimmed with lace to match. Lace designers were adept at arranging their motifs in matching wide and narrow borders (Pl. 11), and berthas and border laces were often made *en suite*, too. Unfortunately, it is a rarity to find such a set still kept together today. Hand-made lace was an expensive luxury item which was re-used as often as possible, so that it was inevitable that most sets should become separated by being used for different purposes in the course of time.

Mantles, pelerines and peignoirs were usually edged with wide lace ruffles, and lace-trimmed aprons were popular too. Long lace scarves declined in favour; on the other hand, at the end of the 1840s, black lace shawls began to be much larger in size, while mantles made entirely of lace also came in. An extremely luxurious example was described in *The World of Fashion*, May, 1846 (p. 117): "Mantilla of superb lace, lined throughout with *tarlatane*, of a pale rose colour ... two rows of a broader lace, but of the same rich pattern set in very full, surround the mantilla; it is closed at the side with a *noeud* and ends of rose-coloured satin ribbon, a smaller one fastens it at the throat, and in the front of the arm, where the sleeves are attached, are three puffs of ribbon but no ends."

Such a description may serve as a reminder that in the nineteenth century, as in previous periods, lace was valued for its contrast not only of texture but also of colour with other materials. Most of the lace which survives today is no longer in its original make-up, and, consequently, the ways in which it might be enhanced by materials of contrasting colours tend to be overlooked. For example, black lace was frequently used to set off light-coloured silks for evening wear, while a touch of white lace was valued as a contrast to the colour of a gay or sombre dress. By the end of the 1840s it was customary for a chemisette trimmed with lace to be worn to fill in a low neck, and for full undersleeves gathered into a narrow cuff to be worn under the wide, open sleeves currently fashionable. Such pairs of sleeves are often found in assemblages of nineteenth-century lace. Mention must be made, too, of white muslin handkerchiefs, a favourite accessory for much of the century. The most luxurious examples, often elaborately embroidered or edged with rows of tucks and hem-stitching, with wide borders of Mechlin, Valenciennes or East Midlands lace, date from the 1840s and 1850s. Bonnets continued to be lavishly trimmed with lace and provided with lace falls, and lace caps were worn at all times of day. For evening wear small lace caps with lappets made all in one piece were popular, while evening head-dresses were also often composed of a lace lappet in combination with flowers or ribbons. Lappets were made with rounded ends just like those of the eighteenth century. In February, 1849, a writer in *The World of Fashion* noted (p. 22) that "Nothing can equal the rage for lace at the present moment, no costume being considered perfect unless it is accompanied by its lace chemisette, lace full sleeves and lace trimmings; or in full dress, the lace flounces, *berthe*, and lappets, giving grace, lightness and elegance to the whole costume."

Much hand-made lace remained very expensive and beyond the reach of all but the wealthy, but by the end of the 1840s patterned machine-made lace was already beginning to appear in quantity on the market to supply the demands of the less affluent. Good imitations of Buckinghamshire, Mechlin, Valenciennes and Chantilly lace were all available at this time, with constant improvements being made in their manufacture (Pl. 70). In 1849, at the Queen's Birthday Drawing-Room, "Her Royal Highness the Duchess of Kent wore a train of white watered silk, covered with Nottingham lace, trimmed with lace and white ribbons. The petticoat was white watered silk, also covered with Nottingham lace; the front of the petticoat was decorated with ornaments of brilliants, and the stomacher was of diamonds" (*The World of Fashion*, June, 1849, p. 61). Thus royal approval was given to a rising industry in which England was leading the world. At this period, indeed, great pride and satisfaction was felt in the products of machinery, which were regarded with enthusiasm and interest (lace machinery, as well as machine-made lace, was shown to an interested public at the international exhibitions of the middle of the century). Certainly, much of the early machine-made lace was of a very high standard in both design and execution.

The early 1850s brought various new trends in lace fashions. New types of lace, quite different in appearance from those current earlier in the century, now became popular, particularly for daytime wear. Prominent amongst these was Maltese lace, which is said to have become fashionable after examples were shown at the Great Exhibition of 1851. Whether this is strictly accurate or not, it is certain that this silk lace, made in both black and white, in designs reminiscent of the geometric bobbin laces of the late sixteenth and early seventeenth centuries, enjoyed a great vogue in the 1850s and 1860s (Pls. 6, 49, 63). It was soon being made in most Western European lace centres of any importance. Shawls and mantles were trimmed with it or made entirely of it, and Maltese collar and cuff sets remained in favour for most of the rest of the nineteenth century. Needless to say, it was not long before manufacturers of machine-made lace were able to make creditable imitations of Maltese lace. Heavy worsted lace made in similar geometric patterns also became popular at the same time (Pl. 50). This type of lace, which originated in the lace-making area centred around Le Puy in France, was made in colours as well as in black and white and was lavishly employed for trimming outdoor garments such as mantles. This fashion for trimmings of a heavier type is reflected, too, in a vogue for tatting collars and cuffs and in the popularity enjoyed by Irish crochet at this period (Pl. 4).

These heavier laces were liked not only for their rich texture and effectiveness, but also for their comparative cheapness. Maltese lace and coarse worsted lace were a good deal quicker and easier to produce than lighter laces of more complex workmanship, and in many instances the makers of bobbin lace turned to their production in an effort to compete with the increasing amounts of cheap machine-made lace which were coming on to the market. A tendency to coarsen and cheapen in the interests of speedy production was noticeable at the same time in those lace-making circles in Belgium, which, generally speaking, concentrated on laces of a more refined type. It was in the early 1850s that the variety of Brussels bobbin lace known as *Duchesse*, similar in technique to though coarser in texture than normal Brussels bobbin lace and with a background of bobbin-made bars instead of net, came into being. *Point Duchesse*, with its repetitive designs of stylized flowers, especially roses, and scrolls, echoes in a lower key the motifs of the finest laces of this period (Pl. 30).

The 1850s and 1860s were the heyday of Chantilly, of Brussels application and, for those who could afford it, of Alençon needlepoint. The leader of European fashion at this time was undoubtedly the Empress Eugénie, who fully appreciated the decorative qualities of such fine laces, as the many portraits of her in richly bedecked crinolines testify (though it may be noted that she also thought it worthwhile to patronize the machine-made lace of Calais). Perhaps Chantilly was the most beloved of all laces at this period. It has certainly survived in quantity, as have the machine-made imitations which reached a very high standard and are often difficult to distinguish from the real thing. Square or triangular shawls of Chantilly lace, made in large sizes to complement the spreading skirts of the crinoline, were popular throughout the 1850s and 1860s (Pls. 73, 77), as well as shaped mantles entirely made of lace (Pl. 21). Many superb examples have survived to the present day. Writing in the early 1860s, Hippolyte Taine particularly commented on "immense shawls of black lace falling to the heels" as a notable feature of the "sartorial excesses on the persons of ladies and girls belonging to the rich middle-classes" on Sundays in Hyde Park, which he considered "very shocking" (*Notes on England, 1860–70*). Chantilly lace was also popular for parasol covers (Pl. 22) and for fans (Pl. 35). In addition, quantities of border laces, flouncings and shaped berthas were used in the adornment of crinolines, particularly for evening wear. White Brussels application was almost as popular as Chantilly and was made for all the purposes listed above (Pls. 27, 28). In England, too, Honiton lace continued fashionable, though it was not generally so sumptuous in effect as contemporary Continental laces (Pls. 43–45).

For all these fine laces, and for the machine-made imitations, the favourite design motifs at this period were undoubtedly flowers. Large pieces of lace were invariably bedecked with great, luscious bunches of flowers, often drawn with a rich naturalism so that roses, lilac, irises and poppies, to name a few of the favourites, can easily be distinguished (Pl. 39). The naturalism was heightened even further by the introduction of effects of shading first into Alençon, Chantilly and Brussels laces and later even into Valenciennes. At the same time the Brussels needlepoint lace, *point de gaze*, which developed after 1850, began to show relief effects: roses or other flowers in the design were given several layers of petals, which were only partially attached to the ground (cf. Pl. 40). The contrast between this three-dimensional realism and the gossamer-light ground, which was so typical of *point de gaze*, epitomizes the general trend of lace design of the later 1860s.   Roses were the flowers most commonly found on *point de gaze*, as they were on *point Duchesse* and on Honiton lace.   Honiton lace, however, was in general much simpler and made little attempt to imitate the more formal aspects of French and Belgian lace design.   In Brussels, Alençon and Chantilly laces of the 1850s and 1860s the bunches of flowers were surrounded by, or entwined with trailing ribbons of more or less elaborate design (Pls. 14, 26), or framed by motifs borrowed from the repertoire of Gothic architecture, and, above all, by strapwork which was invariably enriched by complex patterning (Pls. 13, 21, 27, 28). These opulent designs, the quality of which is difficult to convey in words, were entirely nineteenth century in feeling and could have been produced at no other time.

If the most expensive Continental laces, such as Alençon needle-point, were beyond the reach of many Englishwomen, there were still plenty of types well within their means, both hand- and machine-made.   The catalogue entry for Haywards (Daniel Biddle) of 81, Oxford Street, at the International Exhibition of 1862 in London, gives a good idea of the range available at this time:

Brussels lace squares	from	10 gns.	Brussels lace, sets of collars and	
Imitation lace squares	,,	1 gn.	sleeves	fr. 24s. to 2 gns.
Brussels lace tunics	,,	11 gns.	Honiton lace, do.	fr. 10/6
Brussels lace double			Full trimmed sets of collars	
flouncings	,,	16 gns.	and sleeves in lace and em-	
Imitation do.	,,	45s.	broidery	fr. 12/6 to 5 gns.
Honiton lace squares	,,	3 gns.	Muslin and cambric embroi-	
Honiton lace flouncings	,,	7 gns.	dered sets	fr. 5/6 to 30s.
Swiss lace squares	,,	3½ gns.	Lace and muslin double-skirt	
Black real point lace			dresses	fr. 15/9
flouncings	,,	18 gns.	Embroidered cambric	
Imitation do.	,,	2 gns.	handkerchiefs	fr. 3/6
A large assortment of flounces,			Trimmed lace do. fr. 10/6 to 25 gns.	
squares, etc. in Limerick,			Black lace mantillas and shawls fr. 25/–	
point d'Angleterre [tam-				
boured net?], and other in-				
expensive laces.				

Amongst new types of lace which became fashionable in the 1860s may be mentioned Cluny, a geometric guipure lace in scalloped forms of sixteenth-century inspiration, and "Spanish" lace, a type of silk lace, usually black, patterned with heavy stylized floral forms, which was made both by hand and by machine (Pls. 5, 74).   Blonde lace was still used at this time to trim bonnets and hats and, to a lesser extent, dresses, but it was now almost entirely machine-made.

1870–1900

By the end of the 1860s, lace was so much in favour that lace-making had joined embroidery, crochet, tatting and other varieties of fancy work as a pastime for ladies.   Much of this amateur lace was of a coarse nature, such as the so-called "guipure d'art", a variety of darned netting, or "modern point lace", a type of lace made with tapes joined by needlepoint filling stitches.   Patterns for these laces were printed in many magazines and might be obtained from such well-known suppliers as Madame Riego de la Branchardière and Madame Goubaud.   More refined types of lace were attempted too, and in the early 1870s, books of patterns and instructions for making Honiton lace were published by experts like the famous Mrs. Treadwin or a lady whose identity was modestly concealed under the pseudonym of "Devonia".

Machine-made lace was now presenting a serious challenge to the hand-made variety, and the beginnings of a reaction in favour of "real" lace may already be noted.   A typical piece of advice was that given in *The Young Englishwoman*, July, 1870 (p. 374): "Laces of excellent quality may be had at far lower prices than is usually supposed; and I strongly advise young girls, instead of buying every mode in collars, ruffles and sleeves in common lace, to purchase a few lengths of *real* lace, which they can alter and arrange as the fashions change.   If a girl who has a limited sum to spend will examine her account book for the last year, she will find that neckties, collars, chemisettes and sleeves of 'patent lace', of imitation 'Point Duchesse', and other novelties, have cost as many pounds as would have purchased some *real* lace that would have been always elegant, *distingué*, and of value."   Such wise words came too late however, to save many hand-lace industries or to lure would-be purchasers away from products which looked just as good as hand-made lace from a short distance.

By the early 1870s weak hand-lace industries, such as that of the East Midlands of England which had always concentrated on cheap varieties, had been almost extinguished by machine competition, and more flourishing areas were also beginning to be affected. From the late 1860s, for example, machine-made Valenciennes in

1. Queen Adelaide, by Sir William Beechey, *c.* 1831. The Queen is wearing sleeves of embroidered net or of application lace on machine-made net. *National Portrait Gallery* (No.1533).

2. Mrs. Toller, by G. F. Watts, *c.* 1840. Mrs. Toller is wearing a bertha collar of blonde lace. *City of Leicester Museum and Art Gallery.*

3. Queen Victoria's Wedding Dress, white satin trimmed with Honiton bobbin lace, 1840. *The London Museum* (No. D.325).

4. "Good Morning, Mama", by S.B. Halle, *c.* 1860. The mother is wearing a collar of Irish crochet; her jacket and the child's nightgown are trimmed with narrow bobbin lace. *Victoria and Albert Museum.*

narrow widths was virtually indistinguishable from hand-made. In addition, the collapse of the Second Empire in 1870, with the resulting economic troubles and removal of royal patronage, was a blow from which certain sections of the industry never recovered. Handmade Chantilly, for example, ceased from this time to be anything more than a prestige product, made in comparatively small amounts, even though machine-made Chantilly and Spanish lace continued to be popular to the end of the century. The tide had, in fact, turned, for although lace as a trimming was never more in vogue than during the last three decades of the nineteenth century, the bulk of the lace used was now machine-made.

In the late 1860s and early 1870s, fashion often looked back to the eighteenth century for inspiration. References were now legion in fashion writing to "Marie Antoinette" fichus, often made of lace combined with velvet ribbons, or of muslin or net trimmed with lace. Dresses both for day and evening wear were still frequently trimmed with lace, often pleated or laid on flat rather than gathered, while wide sleeves were edged with deep ruffles or complemented by wide lace undersleeves. The dresses of the time were commonly double-skirted, and, for evening wear, the overskirt might be made entirely of lace. Black lace, such as Chantilly, Maltese or Yak (worsted lace), often further embellished with jet beads, was still extensively used to trim outdoor garments or to form the whole of such garments (Pl. 7). Caps were mostly rather small and tended to be perched on top of the head, but long, hanging lace lappets were worn on caps as well as on bonnets and hats. Bonnets, too, were now much smaller than they had been earlier in the century and were often finished off with a frill or fall of lace at the back. Small bonnets made entirely of lace were fashionable around 1870.

At the beginning of the 1870s, black and white laces were often used in combination as a dress trimming. During this decade, too, began the vogue for ecru lace, i.e. lace in the dark creamy colour associated with unbleached linen thread or in even deeper coffee colour. This fashion, which was to recur at intervals throughout the rest of the century, coincided with the growing popularity of heavier types of lace such as imitations of Venetian needlepoint of the seventeenth century.

In general, lace design during the 1870s shows both a tendency towards the adoption of historical styles and a falling-off from the exuberant richness of the two previous decades. Not only did the imitations of Venetian lace begin to come in, but careful copies of eighteenth-century rococo motifs appeared on Chantilly and Brussels laces (Pl. 35). Flowers were now more delicately drawn and more sparsely arranged, while the elaborate strapwork of the 1850s and 1860s was replaced by rather attenuated forms of a lighter type (Pl. 22). Designs were, on the whole, a little neater, more precise, less crowded and more insipid than they had been.

By this time the wearing of Brussels or Honiton lace had become more or less obligatory for wealthy brides, and it was considered proper, too, for the bride's trousseau to include at least one "set" of lace.   In her book on Honiton lace, published in about 1874, Mrs. Treadwin gave detailed advice on the design of such a set, which must include a veil, a flounce about 10 to 12 inches deep and 6 yards long, a garniture about 4 inches wide and 8 yards long to match the flounce, a pocket-handkerchief and a fan.   To this set might be added a lappet for an evening coiffure.   She quoted contemporary prices for Honiton lace:

Bridal veils, from 5 to 50 gns. and upwards.
Flounces, partially appliqué on net, 10 inches wide, from 15*s.* to 3 gns. per yard.
Honiton point ditto, from 10 to 15 inches wide, from 3 to 15 gns. per yard.
Garniture lace, 4 inches wide, made entirely of point, from 1 to 4 gns. per yard.
Pocket-handkerchiefs, from 1 to 10 gns.
Lappets, from 1 gn. upwards.
Fans, from 2 to 12 gns.
Parasol covers, from 4 to 20 gns.

She noted that similar articles in Brussels lace were roughly the same price.

The trousseau of a rich French bride was described for English readers in *The Young Englishwoman*, February, 1872 (p. 94).   It included "a tunic of Chantilly lace, and three flounces of the same; three flounces of point d'Alençon and three of Honiton lace; a Marie Antoinette fichu of Chantilly lace, and another of point lace; a sunshade cover of Brussels lace, another of white lace, and parures of lace more than I could describe; coloured guipures for dress trimmings, and unbleached Valenciennes lace". Valenciennes border and insertion lace was increasingly used during the last quarter of the nineteenth century to trim underwear, which had now become much more elaborate and luxurious than it had been earlier in the century.

Perhaps the most significant development of the 1880s was the swing of fashion to heavier, more showy laces. Now the revival of Venetian needlepoint really came into its own. Quantities of old seventeenth-century lace were hunted out and skilfully remodelled into trimmings and accessories of shapes currently fashionable, while excellent, if somewhat stiff and mannered, copies were produced in many lace-making centres (Pls. 16, 41, 52, 62). Soon after the beginning of the decade the manufacturers of machine embroidery in Switzerland and Germany discovered how to make "chemical lace", a close imitation of this heavy needlepoint (Pls. 81, 82). This new product accorded perfectly with contemporary taste and thus enjoyed an immediate vogue, almost eclipsing other types of machine-made lace for a time. Machine-made lace was by now, however, very firmly established as a trimming material and, though the industry might be temporarily unsettled by crises of this nature, it was never in really serious difficulty for long. Indeed, the machine-lace manufacturers, particularly in France, soon learned how to adapt their machines to produce imitations of "chemical lace". Another new development in the second half of the 1880s was the production of machine-made laces in widths equivalent to those of ordinary dress material.

In the 1880s, wide collars of lace and lace jabots and cascades falling from the throat became fashionable. Many lace cravats, too, survive from this time. They consist usually of a narrow band with ends splayed out in oval or lozenge shapes. The tailor-made fashions which came in during this decade precluded the use of lace as a trimming, but it was still used in profusion on evening dresses, wedding-dresses (Pl. 8) and on tea-gowns of light materials which came in about 1885. Delicate laces such as Chantilly, Mechlin and Brussels *point de gaze* were popular as well as the heavier varieties mentioned above, while lace was frequently embellished even further by the addition of steel or jet beads or sequins. Mantles were frequently decorated with jetted black lace, and lace-trimmed aprons again became fashionable. Caps for day-time wear went out of fashion for all but the elderly, but bonnets and hats were still bedecked with lace. Small summer bonnets were often made entirely of lace set off with flowers and ribbons, while the contrast of lace with straw, velvet or plush was much admired.

The major part of all the lace used at this time was, of course, machine-made, but the general passion for lace trimmings in the last two decades of the century, coinciding with a wave of enthusiasm for the revival of hand-crafts, enabled some of the hand-made lace industries to enjoy a period of renewed activity. Much hand-made lace of this period, however, tended to combine perfection of technique with lack of inspiration in design, somewhat lifeless and mechanical repetitions of well-tried formulas being all too prevalent. Combinations of roses or other flowers with stiff rococo scrolls or other carefully rendered rococo motifs were very common (Pls. 23, 40, while naturalistic flowers, with or without stereotyped strapwork or meticulously worked patterned oval or round medallions, were also popular (Pls. 29, 31). Flower designs of a delicate but rather vapid naturalism were typical of embroidered nets, which enjoyed a revival at this period. Much of the machine-made lace was also traditional or eclectic in character: imitation *point d'Alençon* with neat patterns of late eighteenth-century type, Chantilly in the rococo manner and black Spanish lace patterned with heavy stylized flowers all being very typical varieties in vogue. Some light machine-made laces were, however, patterned with bird, animal and figure motifs unlike anything previously seen in lace design (Pl. 79).

All these trends continued into the last decade of the nineteenth century, with no very marked changes, except that designs of flowers drawn in a stylized manner betraying the influence of the contemporary *art nouveau* occasionally occurred in both hand- and machine-made laces. But these were exceptions to the general rule, for, if anything, lace design was now even more eclectic than it had been in the two previous decades. Heavy needlepoint laces of seventeenth-century inspiration now enjoyed an even greater vogue than before. Deeply-scalloped borders and collars were patterned with designs adapted not only from Venetian *gros point* and rose point but even from the geometric designs of the late sixteenth century. Heavier bobbin laces of seventeenth-century type were popular, too. Copies were made of Milanese laces, and in many lace-making districts in France and Belgium the workers turned their attention to the production of tape laces with needlepoint fillings in vaguely seventeenth-century patterns (Pl. 37). These were quick and cheap to produce, enjoyed a vogue and enabled their makers to withstand machine competition for a while, although, at the same time, traditional fine skills were lost through concentration on coarse, easy work. Thanks to the fashion for solid, heavy lace, Irish crochet and Carrickmacross work now came back into favour too. These heavy laces were used not only for collars and trimmings but, by the end of the century, it became customary to mount them on backgrounds of coloured silk or velvet to form whole garments (Pl. 9). Deep lace bertha collars were again fashionable for evening wear, while short jackets or capes for outdoor wear were trimmed with, or made entirely of lace of this type.

In contrast to these heavy varieties, a profusion of light, gossamer laces, such as embroidered nets, Mechlin and Chantilly (Pls. 75, 81), were still used to set off the flimsy materials used for blouses, tea-gowns and underwear, which assumed a particularly luxurious aspect at this time. All types of lace, too, were in great demand for hat trimmings —a favourite mode of the period was a stiff upstanding frill of pleated lace combined with ribbons, flowers, or even stuffed birds, on top of a small hat.

By the end of Victoria's reign, indeed, lace seemed to be more fashionable and used in greater quantity than ever before in its history. The future seemed set fair for this luxury industry, for, in spite of the fact that by far the largest part of the lace in current use was machine-made, the renewed demand for "real" lace by those rich enough to buy it seemed likely to assure the success of the revived hand-lace industries. In an account of the lace shown at the Chicago Exhibition of 1893 (ed. Maud Howe Elliott: *Art and Handicraft in the Woman's Building*, Chicago, 1893, p. 281), it was stated that "the imitation or machine-made laces, which for some time threatened the existence of the real lace industry, have now been relegated to their proper sphere, and no more take the place of the real laces than the paste jewel takes the place of the diamond".

Time was to show, however, that machine-made lace resolutely refused to be "relegated to its proper sphere". Despised though it might now be by those lamenting the departure of old rural crafts, it easily won the allegiance of the vast majority, who were interested chiefly in obtaining an effect of luxury or lightness by the least expensive means, and whose eyes could not now make any distinction between hand- and machine-made lace, except perhaps that of regarding the latter as superior because of its more regular and precise appearance.

CHAPTER 2

FRANCE

THE French hand-made lace industry began to recover from the crippling blow of the Revolution during the First Empire. But then, around 1815–20, there came a further economic crisis, the result of the collapse of Napoleon's régime and the beginning of competition from machine-made lace. In spite of this, the industry persevered and by the middle of the century had entered on a period of almost unprecedented prosperity. It owed this success to a number of important factors.

First and foremost, French lace manufacturers had the advantage, common to all the luxury trades of France, of being in close touch with the contemporary centre of fashion, Paris. It was here that the principal lace designers lived and worked, following a tradition established in the eighteenth century. Like their predecessors, the nineteenth-century designers were, for the most part, anonymous, but two whose names have been recorded were E. N. Toussaint and J. H. Mereaux, both of whom worked in the rue de la Jussière in Paris and showed their designs at the Great Exhibition of 1851. It was in Paris, too, that most of the important lace firms, whether they were concerned with expensive laces like *point d'Alençon* or cheaper varieties like the guipures of Le Puy, had their headquarters. It was thus easy for the manufacturers to maintain immediate links with the designers, to keep well abreast of rapidly changing fashions and to obtain a constant flow of new designs.

The French manufacturers were, however, fully aware of the fact that a good design can all too easily be ruined by poor workmanship. This they were at great pains to prevent. The French industry was, in fact, the best organized in Europe. In all its branches from Normandy to Lorraine the manufacturers established and maintained a tight control over their workers, ensuring the production of lace of the highest quality by means of constant and strict supervision. Great attention was paid to training workers as well. In most of the lace-making areas, lace schools were set up in the nineteenth century, and very often schools of design were also established, for it was recognized that it was important for workers as well as designers to have some skill in drawing.

French manufacturers not only concentrated their energies on the home market, but they were also at pains to study the demands of potential overseas customers and, by supplying these demands, to build up a flourishing export trade which contributed greatly to the prosperity of the industry. Thus, by establishing Spanish and Spanish American markets in the second quarter of the century, Auguste Lefébure was able to expand the bobbin-lace industry of Bayeux, while later in the century the prosperity of the Lorraine industry was largely based on exports to the United States.

Thanks to all these factors, and to a renewed period of royal patronage under the Second Empire, the French lace industry enjoyed two decades of dazzling prosperity from 1850 to 1870, maintaining a flow of magnificent products of all types and competing successfully with the increasing flow of machine-made laces.

The end of the Second Empire in 1870, the resulting economic crisis and the increasing popularity of machine-made lace, all hit the industry severely. Some sections of it never really recovered from this blow. The black silk lace industry of Normandy, for example, fell into a decline which had reached a parlous state by 1900. In a petition to the French parliament in that year it was stated that the number of workers in Calvados, estimated at about 50,000 in the middle of the century, had now fallen to less than 1,000 and most of these were aged fifty or more. Manufacturers laid part of the blame on the reduction in aristocratic patronage and on the decline in apprenticeship since the education acts of 1881 and 1882, which had made full-time schooling compulsory for all children up to the age of thirteen. But the principal reason for the decline was the mass of cheap, machine-made laces now flooding the market.

Only two types of lace seemed able to put up any opposition to these machine-made products. One of these was the aristocratic and highly expensive needlepoint lace of Alençon and Bayeux, which still held its own to a certain extent because of its superb quality that machines could not imitate, and because of its prestige as a status symbol. The other, curiously enough, was the cheap guipure lace made at Le Puy and Mirecourt. Both these areas were able to maintain a reasonable degree of prosperity because great attention was paid by the manufacturers there to good design and excellent quality combined with cheapness. They exploited the skill and adaptability for which their workers were famed to produce a constant flow of novelties, ensuring a steady sale, leading rather than following the machine laces, and trading on the *cachet* that hand-made lace still enjoyed.

NEEDLEPOINT LACES

Point d'Alençon

It seems appropriate to start the discussion of individual types of lace with an account of the fortunes of *point d'Alençon*, because this needlepoint was not only the most expensive of all laces throughout the nineteenth century but also the most fully documented, at least two books having been entirely devoted to it. These are: Mme. G. Despierres, *Histoire du Point d'Alençon depuis son origine jusqu'à nos jours*, Paris, 1886; and Félix Boulard, *La Dentelle Alençon*, Alençon, 1924. The study of *point d'Alençon* is, indeed, a rewarding one, since a great deal can be learned from it about the organization of the lace industry in France, and about the fluctuations in fortune inevitable in a luxury trade.

Point d'Alençon was a rich, heavy lace, costly because of the infinite skill required to make it and because its manufacture was a complex process. Even the smallest piece represents the work of numerous different hands. Methods of work in the nineteenth century, remained, in effect, much the same as they had been in the eighteenth. The process of making a piece of Alençon needlepoint began with the preparation of the parchment pattern. This would vary in size according to the width of lace to be made and the type of design to be used, but invariably the design was divided into several sections, each of which would be given to a different worker. Before it could be used, the parchment, normally green in colour, had to be pricked with holes indicative of the design; an operation known as *le picage*. The next stage was *le tracé*: in this operation two pieces of cloth were attached to the underside of the parchment and the outlines of the design were marked out on the top of it by means of a thick thread, which was held in place by a thinner thread passing over it and through the holes in the parchment and the two pieces of cloth. At a much later stage these securing threads would be cut by scissors passing between the two pieces of cloth and the finished piece of lace thus released from the pattern. After *le tracé* came the working of the actual needlepoint stitches on the foundation thus prepared. It was at this point that the greatest division of work obtained, for, although all the workers were capable of making all the different stitches involved, each one, in fact, had her own speciality. This might consist of working the solid parts of the motifs, i.e. the closely arranged stitches of *le mat*; or of making the *réseau* ground, composed of light, even, rectangular meshes formed by twisted loops on each side (Pl. 10); or of working the numerous types of fancy fillings, *modes*, used to decorate parts of the pattern, fillings which were one of the chief glories of Alençon lace. These stages of the work being completed, the lace passed into the hands of the worker who specialized in working the firm raised edges of the motifs, *la brode*. This *brode* was a most important feature of Alençon lace, for it had to be stiff, well-shaped and carefully made, or the whole effect of the design would be ruined. The *brode* in Alençon lace was, of course, worked over a horsehair to give maximum strength and, indeed, the ensuing relief often made small elements of the pattern, such as round spots or small petals of flowers, assume a concave appearance. Next came *l'enlevage*, the releasing of the lace from the foundation, followed by *l'éboutage*, the cutting off of stray ends of thread. The two final operations, *le régalage*, i.e. the making good of deficient areas or of stitches damaged during *l'enlevage*, and *l'assemblage*, the joining together of the various sections to make the final finished piece of lace, were frequently entrusted to the same worker. This worker had to be the most highly skilled of all, for she had to be expert in all the stitches and on her depended the skilful blending of the work of so many different hands into a complete whole.

It is clear, then, that *point d'Alençon* demanded not only a uniform and very high level of skill, but also the greatest care in manufacture, with supervision at every stage. Such a product was necessarily a costly one and, indeed, throughout the eighteenth century the Alençon lace industry, which had been founded by Colbert in the 1660s, had remained an object of royal patronage. Even before the French Revolution its prosperity had begun to decline a little, because lighter, more delicate types of lace were beginning to be more fashionable, but the Revolution itself dealt the industry a grievous blow. Not only was royal patronage removed, but the important markets of Germany, Russia and other parts of northern Europe were ruined. The resulting state of the industry in the first decade of the nineteenth century can be gauged from gloomy reports published in *L'Annuaire de l'Orne*. In 1808, for example, it was noted that most former lace-workers had gone over to other occupations, while in 1809 it was stated that the industry was well-nigh extinct, for during the previous year the number of workers had decreased from 3,000 to 1,500, and even the remaining workers could hardly earn anything for their labours.

This state of affairs obtained even in spite of the efforts of a few devoted manufacturers to keep the industry going. Amongst these was M. Jacques Mercier (later M. le baron Mercier), who showed examples of Alençon lace at an industrial exhibition in Paris in 1806. These included an allegorical piece representing French maritime commerce triumphing over the English, which was much admired.

Still, Alençon lace was too expensive for the ordinary buyer, who preferred the currently fashionable light blondes and nets. It was a lace for the ladies of the court and of the nobility, and even for them it was fashionable only in winter. *L'Annuaire de l'Orne* noted the depressing effects on the industry of the absence of the Emperor from Paris for several successive winters.

In 1810, the state of the industry was brought to the notice of Napoleon, for by this time the number of manufacturers still in business had been reduced to five. The Emperor responded handsomely by offering the struggling workers his patronage. He ordered a magnificent set of bed-hangings and coverlet, ornamented with the arms of the Empire surrounded by bees (his symbol), to celebrate his marriage with Marie-Louise, and in 1811 he paid a visit to Alençon to be regaled with a display of lace-making organized by M. Charles Clérambault. Further commissions from Napoleon and Marie-Louise helped the industry considerably during the next few years.

The designs of this period mostly followed the mode set in the late eighteenth century, consisting of rows of motifs, such as small flowers or perhaps classical scrolls, arranged along the straight or scalloped lower edge of the lace, while the rest of the ground was powdered with spots or tiny flowers regularly arranged. In order to give more life to these somewhat rigid designs, there seems to have been some attempt to introduce effects of shading into the leaves and flowers, but this did not become a common practice until much later on.

With the fall of the Empire in 1815, depression set in again. Blondes were still all the rage and, worse still, net was now being produced in large quantities by the recently invented bobbin-net machine. Most of the Alençon workers went over in desperation to muslin and net embroidery, producing the whitework which was then enjoying a great vogue. A few manufacturers struggled on but most of these supplemented lace-making with embroidery, which was usually, in fact, the mainstay of their business. Their fortunes can be followed through a series of industrial exhibitions held in Paris in the 1820s and 1830s.

M. Mercier, for example, showed lace and embroideries there in 1819 and 1823, while in 1827 he is mentioned in the catalogue as showing embroidered muslin. M. Clérambault showed a similar range of goods in 1823 and 1827, and another firm, headed by members of the old lace-manufacturing family d'Ocagne, appeared at all three exhibitions. By their persistence these manufacturers managed to maintain a nucleus of good workers, whilst employing others on the more flourishing white embroidery. It may be noted that former lace-workers delighted to enrich parts of the white embroideries with the beautiful fancy fillings in needlepoint stitches remembered from earlier days.

Various attempts were made to improve the lace manufacture, too. Baron Mercier took the line that it might be better to try to bring the lace down in price, and he experimented with the use of machine-made net as a foundation for the lace, an idea which he patented in 1839. This proved unsuccessful, however, and he gave it up after 1846.

Another development at the beginning of the 1830s was the substitution of cotton thread for linen, an innovation which might perhaps be attributed to M. Beaumé, père, who had earlier intro-duced the manufacture of muslin into Alençon and whose wife was a lace-maker. The wisdom of this step was hotly debated, but the cotton thread was both cheaper and easier to work, and so it won the day in the end. It was, however, seldom used for the whole of a piece of lace, since the groundwork was very often still made of linen, which gave a greater firmness to the fabric.

Thanks to these determined efforts, the Alençon lace industry gradually began to revive during the 1830s, though for most of the decade embroidery remained the staple product of many of the manufacturers. One sign of increasing demand for needlepoint lace was the fact that M. Charles Clérambault was able to introduce its manufacture in about 1830 into the convent of La Providence, where the nuns had previously been making embroideries for him. He also established a lace school there. Most of the manufacturers relied on visits from Parisian or foreign merchants to sell their products, or, occasionally they might sell to a private customer. Only one of them, d'Ocagne, had a house in Paris, at 25, rue Neuve-des-Bons-Enfants.

At some time around 1840, a great lift was given to the industry by the appearance on the scene of an important Paris house, Videcoq & Simon, 35, rue des Jeûneurs. Representatives of this house, which had become interested in Alençon lace, came to the town to reconnoitre. They discovered that a nucleus of good workers still remained, thanks to the dogged persistence of the manufacturers who had carried on during the years of depression. A workshop was established under a Mlle. Hutin, and new, richer designs were introduced. The first results were displayed to the public gaze at an exhibition held at Alençon in 1842, which also included exhibits by several of the faithful manufacturers, Mercier, Clérambault and d'Ocagne. (The other two who worked through the depression were Mme. Amiot and Mme. Launay-Rattier.)

In its report the Jury at the exhibition paid particular tribute to M. d'Ocagne for his labours during the depression period, and noted that the firm was now producing Alençon lace on a reasonably large scale under the able direction of Mlle. Dupré. The most notable piece in the d'Ocagne display was a court mantle made for a German princess. Lace made by the firm of Baron Mercier was shown by the Paris house of Ferrières-Perona, and the Jury remarked on the fact that Mercier, like d'Ocagne, was obviously trying to produce a less costly type of lace which would find a more general market. Videcoq & Simon proved to have taken a completely opposite line. They were inspired no doubt by the feeling that *point d'Alençon* had always had the character of a heavy, costly lace, and that, now that the lighter types of design fashionable for so long were at last beginning to go out of favour, it was better to concentrate on these aspects of the lace, to produce even more splendid and ornate designs adapted to its peculiar nature. The Jury observed that the pieces shown by Videcoq & Simon were full of elaborate filling stitches of the most complicated type, which made them veritable "chefs-d'œuvre", although also extremely expensive. Similar pieces were shown by a Mme. Richier-Leveque.

Events were to prove that this approach to the manufacture of *point d'Alençon* was the most profitable one. Throughout the 1840s the prosperity of the industry steadily increased and, conversely, the embroidery side lapsed again, but, sadly enough, as their efforts began at last to be crowned with success, the old manufacturers dropped out, one by one. Mme. Launay-Rattier died in 1845, M. Clérambault in 1847 (after having the satisfaction of receiving a gold medal at the industrial exhibition of 1844 in Paris, as a reward for his labours in keeping the industry alive), and Mme. Amiot in 1848. Baron Mercier gave up the lace manufacture in 1850 and the only old firm to continue into the next decade was the Maison d'Ocagne, which seems to have come to an end in about 1858, after successful showings at the various exhibitions during the 1850s (their Paris address is given in the 1851 Catalogue as 3, rue de Grammont).

Nevertheless, by the time of the Great Exhibition of 1851, Alençon lace was back in a commanding position, which was to be strengthened still more by the return of royal patronage under the Second Empire. In the Jury Report, M. Félix Aubry noted that the Alençon lace displayed by Videcoq & Simon attracted general attention because of the richness of the designs, the regularity of the groundwork and the variety of filling stitches. The most notable piece was a flounce, 48 centimetres wide, which formed part of a complete set of dress trimmings. This had taken thirty-six workers eighteen months to complete at a cost of 2,200 francs. It was to form part of the trousseau of the Empress Eugénie.

Eugénie was to extend her patronage of the lace industry considerably during the next few years. In April, 1854, she summoned a meeting of French lace manufacturers, for she wished to order two sets of dress trimmings, one in *point d'Alençon*, the other in Chantilly lace. Twenty-five manufacturers submitted designs and samples and, when the final choice was made, it fell to the lot of Videcoq & Simon to undertake the manufacture of the Alençon set.

The scale of the undertaking was indicated by a description in the

Journal d'Alençon of 1855 of the design and dimensions of the pieces. The design consisted of branches of exotic trees surrounding bunches of *impériales*, skilfully adapted to suit the different parts of the trimming, the flounces, each 4½ metres long by 110 centimetres deep, the sleeve ruffles, and the *berthe*, no less than 6 metres long, which was divided for purposes of manufacture into at least 155 different pieces. The operation was a great challenge to the lace-makers, for the work had to be completed in a short time. But they proved equal to the task. The whole set was ready to be put on show at the Paris Exhibition of 1855, where it attracted great acclaim.

After having done so much to set the Alençon industry on its feet, the house of Videcoq & Simon did not survive for long to enjoy the triumph. It is next heard of, under the new name of MM. Simon, père et fils, at an exhibition held in Alençon in 1858, where, once again, the lace shown excelled both from the point of view of design and execution. This was to be the last appearance of the house, which was not heard of again. Mlle. Hutin, supervisor of the workers in Alençon, died in 1860.

However, following the lead given by Videcoq & Simon, other houses made important contributions to the Alençon industry during the 1850s, which was a period of great expansion and prosperity. Prominent amongst the innovators was the son of the M. Beaumé mentioned earlier, M. Jules-Pierre Beaumé, who had set up in business with his mother. M. Beaumé, fils, turned his attention to the perfecting of those rich fillings which were one of the chief features of *point d'Alençon*, and around 1855 he tried to ensure a greater precision of workmanship by issuing parchments known as *moniteurs*, which were actually printed with the outline of the area of filling required in each part of the design and the dimensions of the pattern to be used. It was M. Beaumé, too, who was responsible for the further enrichment of the lace by the re-introduction of effects of shading. These were achieved by varying the closeness of the stitches in the *mat* or solid part of the pattern. In this way three-dimensional effects were often introduced into the designs. These had a particular appeal in the 1850s when luxuriant naturalism was one of the principal features of design.

Some critics complained that such effects were mere chasing after novelty, and that three-dimensional shading was a denial of the true character of the lace, which should depend on the skilful blending of stitches and fillings for a rich effect. Such critics also noted with disapproval that the old use of *brides* (bars) and other elaborate backgrounds, formerly characteristic of Alençon lace, had now been given up in favour of the uniform *réseau* of rectangular meshes. The whole effect of the lace now depended on the design itself, which usually consisted of bunches or garlands of flowers (Pls. 11, 13) united by twisted ribbons or by winding strapwork, in which fancy fillings were deployed to great advantage. Three-dimensionalism was sometimes carried to its logical conclusion; charming bunches of lace flowers occasionally survive from this time (Pl. 12).

M. Beaumé's activities were specially commented on by the Jury at the Alençon exhibition of 1858, when it was noted that his laces showed not only the new shading effects but also a much greater regularity of workmanship than hitherto. The Jury was charmed by M. Beaumé's generous acknowledgement of his best workers by name, something not commonly done. They came not only from Alençon itself, but from nearby villages such as Damigny and Lonrai. Beaumé's laces were made entirely of cotton. He ceased production in 1860 and was not followed by any successor.

At the 1858 exhibition, equally rich laces were shown by the Paris house of Pigache & Mallet, which had a business in Alençon under the direction of Mlle. Zélie Guèrin. Their work, however, was not considered so fine as that produced by M. Beaumé or by another exhibitor, Mlle. Mary, *dite* Lépine. This lady succeeded to the management of the old lace firm of Launay-Rattier in 1845 and she was known to have bought parchments and designs from Mme. Amiot on her retirement in 1848. Mlle. Mary was, in fact, a believer in tradition. She preserved the old designs and techniques with great faithfulness and was the only one of the lace manufacturers to continue making needlepoint entirely in linen thread. She never entered into a direct association with any Paris house, although for a while she supplied the Maison d'Ocagne, but, instead, she relied on selling to visiting merchants and private buyers. She seems to have remained in business until her death in 1871.

The most important development of the 1850s, though, was the advent of the two Paris houses which were to dominate the Alençon needlepoint industry to the end of the nineteenth century. First in the field was M. Auguste Lefébure, the successful Bayeux lace manufacturer who had established a house in Paris (see pp. 66–7). In

5. Victorian Photography of a Lady wearing a large shawl of black silk lace of Spanish type, *c.* 1862-5. *The Gallery of English Costume, Platt Hall, Manchester.*

6. Lady Shand, by R. Herdmann, 1867. Lady Shand's dress is trimmed with wide bobbin lace of Maltese type. *National Gallery of Scotland.*

7. Fashion-plate showing a black lace paletot with wide sleeves, 1870. *The Young Englishwoman,* 1870, p.533.

8. Wedding-dress, grey poplin trimmed with white machine-made lace, 1884. *The Gallery of English Costume, Platt Hall, Manchester.*

1851 M. Lefébure included a fine scarf of *point d'Alençon* in his display at the Great Exhibition. During the 1850s he set up a model workroom in Bayeux for the manufacture of needlepoint lace (see pp. 62–5), and he also came to control a large section of the industry in Alençon through intermediaries who acted as supervisors for him. One of these was Mme. Donville, who had worked first for Baron Mercier and later set up in business on her own. It was she who supervised the execution of an order given to Lefébure in 1856 by Baron Haussman, for a robe and cushion in *point d'Alençon* to be presented to the Empress for the Prince Imperial by the city of Paris. M. Toussaint-Constant Roussel also worked for Lefébure in Paris, after setting up in business there in about 1855. Both Mme. Donville and Roussel continued to make lace on their own account as well as working for Lefébure.

The second Paris house was the Compagnie des Indes, whose fortunes were originally based on the importation of Kashmir shawls. By 1851 they had come to take a leading interest in the Belgian lace industry, including a number of splendid shawls of Brussels application in their display at the Great Exhibition. A few years later, the firm, which was headed by several partners, MM. Geffrier, Walmez and Deslisle frères, began to take an interest in French lace too. In 1854 they entered into a business agreement with a Mme. Besnard (*née* Couhier) at Alençon, who had been working on her own behalf since about 1843. Like Lefébure the Compagnie des Indes took the lace manufacture very seriously and endeavoured to improve and expand it. Their efforts in this direction included the establishment of a lace school in 1857 in the grounds of the Château de Lonrai, near Alençon, under the direction of Mme. Besnard. Later on, in 1865, they also re-established the lace school in the Community of La Providence, which had originally been started by M. Clérambault.

Thanks to the efforts of these two houses, Alençon lace enjoyed a remarkable period of prosperity in the 1860s. Lefébure, who had taken his sons Ernest and Anatole into partnership in 1857 and 1864 respectively, and the Compagnie des Indes, known after 1865 as Verdé-Delisle & Cie., received the highest accolade of the nineteenth century: medals awarded at the international exhibitions. The work of both houses may be seen at its best in the pieces shown at Paris in 1867, which epitomize all the features of Second Empire design. The poppies and convolvulus of the Verdé-Delisle design (Fig. 1) are highly typical of this period, as is the arrangement of intertwined swags and lighter garlands. But perhaps even more accomplished was the design shown by Lefébure (Pl. 14), in which a fluted, richly-patterned lace frill and an equally rich border of lozenge-shapes set off bunches of flowers and ferns. This lace was reckoned by many, including Mrs. Bury Palliser, to be the finest lace in the whole exhibition. It was designed by Alcide Roussel. Both Lefébure and Verdé-Delisle were unusual in having special designers working solely for them, something smaller houses were not able to afford.

Fig. 1. Alençon needlepoint lace shown by Verdé-Delisle Frères (Compagnie des Indes) at the Paris International Exhibition of 1867. (*Art Journal Catalogue.*)

Roussel is the most important lace designer of the nineteenth century whose name has come down to us. A little information about him may be gleaned from a small catalogue of an exhibition held in Paris in 1865. He was born in Saint-Maximin (Oise) and studied design under a M. Feuillette. He seems to have entered the service of Lefébure in the 1850s, for his first recorded success was the winning of a prize medal, the first of many, at an exhibition in Brussels in 1856. His skill in design is demonstrated not only by the piece already referred to but also by a design for a parasol cover shown at the same exhibition in 1867, which combines a regular arrangement of large leaves and small flowers with bands of more formal ornament of classical type (Pl. 15). Other designs by

Roussel are illustrated in E. Lefébure's *Broderies et Dentelles*, published in Paris in 1887.

The extent to which *point d'Alençon* had returned to favour at this period may be gauged from the fact that in the 1860s it began to be produced in Belgium too. Belgian Alençon, while less sophisticated in design as a rule, generally rivalled the French product as far as technique was concerned (Pl. 42). Furthermore, *point d'Alençon* could be produced more cheaply in Belgium than in France, the wages of the Belgian lace-workers being much lower than those of the French.

The collapse of the Second Empire in 1870 and the resulting economic crisis in France were a blow to the Alençon lace industry, although by no means such a grievous one as the French Revolution had been. The lace had been re-established in fashionable favour so well that it was now able to survive. But there can be no denying that its peak of prosperity was past.

In 1873 the only French firm to exhibit lace at the Vienna Exhibition was Verdé-Delisle & Cie. and it is significant that their main exhibit was a complete *toilette* which had been ordered by the Empress Eugénie before the collapse of the régime. This was, incidentally, an indication of the direction fashion was taking, for it was a copy of a design originally made for Madame de Pompadour. The parasol which formed part of this *toilette* was exhibited again by Verdé-Delisle at Philadelphia in 1876 and the whole *ensemble* was eventually sold to an American lady. The house of Lefébure, now Lefébure Frères, still pressed on with the manufacture of *point d'Alençon*, too, and, indeed, in 1874 turned its attention to a new line with a revival of Argentan lace (see pp. 61–2). The manufacture of Alençon needlepoint was also introduced at Burano after the revival of lace-making there in the late 1870s (see p. 207).

Another indication of the continuing popularity of this lace in the 1870s and 1880s is the fact that the first imitations of it by machinery were made in 1879. It is noteworthy, however, that those imitations, which were favoured throughout the 1880s, were mainly in the style of the early years of the nineteenth century, and there is no doubt that there was a renewal of interest in such designs at this time. It seems likely that many such designs had continued to be made throughout the nineteenth century on a limited scale.

In 1887, during a tour of lace-making centres in France and

Belgium on behalf of the Irish industry, James Brennan, of the Cork School of Art, and Samuel Murphy, of the Waterford School of Art, visited Lefébure. Both were impressed by the very great skill of the Alençon workers and by the very high quality of the lace. They particularly commented on the subtlety of the shading effects introduced into the designs. In his report, of which the manuscript is preserved in the Library of the Victoria and Albert Museum (Brennan's report may also be seen there), Murphy wrote, "M. Lefébure showed us a quantity of flat needlepoint lace made at Alençon, comprising borders from 5″ to 10″ wide and flounces up to 18″ wide, ranging from £5 to £40 the metre."

Even in the enthusiastic reports of Murphy and Brennan, however, may be detected signs that the Alençon lace industry was entering its last slow decline. It, too, now had to face machine competition. The challenge was met in various ways. Now it was more necessary than ever to study the demands of consumers; Murphy noted, "when there are no special orders to hand, M. Lefébure thinks that it is well to keep the workers engaged on borders from 5″ to 10″ wide as these articles are most likely to find a ready sale". Attempts were also made to produce rather "fancy" types of lace, which might appeal by their novelty. Brennan thought "one piece of *Point d'Alençon* was very charming, the price £10 the metre, the ground was a small meshed net of yellow thread, on which the ornament was worked in white". He further notes that this piece was of a floral design "very graceful and light, the fillings were used with good effect and very much varied".

In the attempt to compete with machine-made lace, too, great emphasis was placed on the maintenance of an extremely fine, correct technique. This, combined with the use of somewhat stereotyped designs, is, in fact, one of the common features of many declining hand-made lace industries at the end of the nineteenth century. In trying to defeat machine products by superiority of hand technique the workers only succeeded in imparting a somewhat hard and mechanical finish to their work, albeit this was often of a standard of skill only rarely attained hitherto.

Mme. Despierres, writing in 1886, notes that about five businesses were still functioning at that time : Mlles. Taunay, successors to the Mme. Donville who worked for Lefébure; M. Huignard, who succeeded Mme. Besnard in working for Verdé-Delisle & Cie., and who was in turn succeeded in 1886 by M. Georges Martin; M. Roussel, director of lace manufacture for Lefébure in Alençon; Mlle. Hurel and her sister, Mme. Lerenard, who had established a business in 1876, working for the Grands Magasins du Louvre; and the widow, Mme. Alfred Lambert, who set up her business in 1877. In fact, however, the number of workers, which had risen to 8,000 in 1862, had dropped again to 2,000 by 1886 and their wages had fallen too. Furthermore, the lace school founded by Verdé-Delisle & Cie. at Lonrai ceased to exist in 1885 because of the lack of apprentices.

So, although Mme. Despierres hopefully suggests that business appeared to be improving gradually, and although it seems clear that *point d'Alençon* was reaching a rather wider public as more people could now afford to buy it, there seems little doubt that at the end of the nineteenth century the industry had returned to a condition perilously near to that it had occupied at the beginning. None the less, Lefébure Frères continued to attract a certain number of important commissions: such as wedding veils for Princesse Amélie, daughter of the Comtesse de Paris, in 1878; for Princesse Hélène, who married the Duc d'Aosta in 1896; and for Arch-duchess Marie-Dorothée, bride of the Duc d'Orléans, in 1896. Both they and Verdé-Delisle & Cie. continued to show *point d'Alençon* in the various international exhibitions, particularly at the Chicago World's Fair in 1893 and at Paris in 1900. At the latter exhibition Lefébure showed a typical novelty: a lace with a new type of *réseau* composed of little scrolls resembling oriental gold filigree work.

Point d'Argentan

In the eighteenth century the needlepoint lace of Argentan was made in the same way as that of Alençon, except that it usually had a stronger *réseau*, a network of regular hexagons covered on all sides by buttonholing and sometimes further decorated with *picots*. In fact, both types of lace were made in both centres.

At the French Revolution, Argentan lace virtually disappeared. A few pieces were shown at an industrial exhibition in Paris in 1806. These were allegorical in design and were made by Mmes. Lainé and Guérin of Argentan. After this episode, however, nothing more is heard of Argentan lace until very much later in the century.

In 1874 the Mayor of Argentan asked the firm of Lefébure to try to revive the lace manufacture of the town. The story goes that several old, half-finished pieces of Argentan lace were discovered, by a fortunate chance, in the attics of the Hospice of St. Louis. These were handed over by Lefébure to Mlle. Desirée Hamel, one of the best of the Bayeux needlepoint lace-makers, who was instructed to study them and learn the technique. Not only did she succeed in this but she also established herself in a community of Benedictine nuns at Argentan, set up a workshop there and brought about the revival of the manufacture.

Point d'Argentan continued to be produced in small amounts to the end of the century. It was characterized by a general insipidity of design, based mainly on the floral elements of mid-eighteenth century *point d'Argentan*, and by a certain rigidity of execution, in which it betrays its Bayeux origins. This lace nearly always has a hexagonal mesh ground, worked with a meticulous and somewhat mechanical regularity. The skilled technique but lifeless design and end product are typical of late nineteenth-century lace. Good examples of this type of *point d'Argentan* are illustrated by A. Carlier de Lantsheere (e.g. *Trésor de l'Art Dentellier*, 1922, Pl. 69: 5).

Point Colbert

When M. Auguste Lefébure turned his attention to the manufacture of needlepoint lace in the early 1850s, the revival of interest in the heavier laces of the seventeenth century, Venetian needlepoint and *point de France*, had hardly begun. He felt, none the less, that it would be valuable to promote the revival of such handsome old types of lace, for these would almost certainly find favour in current fashion. He determined, therefore, to establish the needlepoint lace manufacture at Bayeux. At first he tried to persuade Alençon workers to leave their native town and come to Bayeux. These efforts proving unavailing, however, he was obliged to look elsewhere for assistance.

He had been struck at the Great Exhibition of 1851 by a charming display of three-dimensional bouquets of flowers worked in needlepoint lace. (A bunch of flowers of this type is illustrated on Pl. 12.) A patent for those flowers had been taken out by a Mme. Joséphine Hubert of Mondeville, near Caen, who, it seems, had learned lace-making during a period of residence in Alençon. She had set up a workshop in Mondeville with four sisters, the Mlles. Bernard, to whom she had taught the technique. M. Lefébure bought up the patent and brought three of the Bernard sisters to Bayeux to establish a workroom. In 1854 he showed a selection of needlepoint flowers at an exhibition held at Avranches. He also got the workers to unravel old specimens of needlepoint and to study them carefully in order to learn the secrets of their technique. Their studies and efforts resulted in the creation of a new type of needlepoint lace, christened *point Colbert* in honour of Colbert, the founder of the French lace industry in the 1660s.

The manufacture of *point Colbert* began in about 1855, but it does not seem to have excited much attention until the Paris exhibition of 1867. Some idea of what this lace was like may be formed from an example selected for illustration in the *Art Journal Catalogue* (Fig. 2).

FIG. 2. Border of needlepoint lace, *point Colbert*, designed by Alcide Roussel for Auguste Lefébure & Fils and shown at the Paris International Exhibition of 1867. (*Art Journal Catalogue.*)

It was much heavier in style than *point d'Alençon*, and had a ground of *brides picotées*. Although it took its inspiration from seventeenth-century Venetian lace, M. Lefébure wisely resisted the temptation to make slavish copies of seventeenth-century designs. The design shown in the catalogue, by Alcide Roussel (see pp. 58–9), shows characteristic flower forms, with neatly curling tendrils, some of which curl back over the main stem—rather different from the freer baroque forms of the seventeenth century. It is also notable that the repeat of the design is rather small, much smaller, in fact, than that found in Venetian lace. These characteristics were even more marked in wider designs. Furthermore, the lace stitches are not so closely worked as those of Venetian lace, although they present a very even and regular appearance. The lace is often rather yellowish or greyish in colour. Similar designs are illustrated by Mrs. Bury Palliser in her *History of Lace*.

Point Colbert was used for furnishing purposes as well as for costume.

A curtain shown in 1867 had a wide border of scrolling branches enclosing flowers and birds, edged by a leaf design, in which full and effective use was made of shading effects of the type introduced into *point d'Alençon* in the mid 1850s.

This type of lace seems to have become really popular in the later 1870s, when heavier laces of seventeenth-century type came back into favour. In 1877, in fact, Mme. Alfred Lambert successfully introduced its manufacture into her newly-founded business at Alençon itself. In 1878 at the Paris Exhibition the firm of Lefébure showed a whole *toilette* in *point Colbert* made for the Duchess of Santona, as well as a lace cover for the volume containing the Papal Bull of the Immaculate Conception. For this display M. Ernest Lefébure was awarded the Legion of Honour and twenty-eight of his workers were given medals.

James Brennan was most impressed by the *point Colbert* he was shown on his visit to Lefébure in 1887. M. Lefébure considered, he said in his report, "this is a success—and no doubt it is—for, whilst bearing all the characteristics of rose point, it gives no idea of heaviness. This, I think, is due to the open and vigorous nature of the design, and the sparing manner in which ties were used. A good gradation is carried out in the embossed parts, the fullness always occurring about the centre of the curve, and this embossment is generally found at one side of the leaf. The effect of light and shade is carried out in this also by means of perforations, and ornamental fillings are used."

Two examples of contemporary *point Colbert* are illustrated in E. Lefébure's book, *Broderies et Dentelles*, published in 1887 (pp. 242 and 244). One is a collar in the Venetian-inspired manner, the other is a border in the style of early seventeenth-century *reticella* lace but again showing the curvilinear forms beloved of Lefébure's designers and highly characteristic of the taste of the period.

Point Colbert maintained its popularity to the end of the century, and Lefébure steadfastly kept to his policy of commissioning new designs. A typical example of the turn of the century is illustrated on Pl. 16. The products of this house should therefore never be confused with the many more literal copies of Venetian lace made at this time, for by careful study it is possible to distinguish them.

By the end of the nineteenth century the needlepoint lace-makers of Bayeux had developed considerable versatility. In 1904, A.

Lefébure (*Dentelles et Guipures*, 1904, p. 226) noted that the main types of needlepoint being made there were *point Colbert* and another needlepoint lace known as *point de France*, distinguished by a background mesh of large, regular hexagons ornamented with *picots*, and by delicate floral motifs. Another observer (E. Van Loon: *De Kantindustrie in Frankrijk en Italië*, 1904) wrote that, in fact, the needlepoint-workers were the only lace-makers still in regular employment in Bayeux and that they could imitate any type of needlepoint required.

BOBBIN LACES

Chantilly lace and blonde lace

The name Chantilly is given to a black bobbin lace made of silk, usually a type of silk known as *grenadine* which is not shiny. Chantilly lace is characterized by its light, airy appearance, produced by the combination of grounds worked in a six-pointed-star mesh (*fond chant*), or by the simple, open *réseau* used in Lille lace, with flowers and decorative motifs worked in the open half-stitch or *grillé* technique (Pl. 17). These motifs are given clarity by being surrounded by a thick silk thread. In the eighteenth century, Chantilly lace was made not only at Chantilly itself, but also in the neighbouring areas round Paris and at Caen and Bayeux in Normandy. Little black silk lace survives from this time, however.

Laces made in a similar way with black or white linen (later cotton) thread were also produced in the same centres, as were the silk laces known as blondes which are allied in technique. It is thus convenient to take all these types of lace together.

Blonde lace is usually ivory or cream-coloured, hence the familiar name. But black blondes were made too. Several new varieties of blonde were introduced during the nineteenth century, including *blonde de Caen* and *blonde mate*, or Spanish blonde. *Blonde de Caen* is described by Mrs. Bury Palliser (*History of Lace*, p. 224) as a lace "in which the flower is made with a different silk from that which forms the réseau and outlined with a thick silk strand". This blonde has a light *réseau* of Lille type to enhance the contrast between motifs and ground (Pl. 18). Spanish blonde was specially developed for export to Spain and the Spanish American colonies, and was usually much heavier in design.

White blondes were specially noted for their beautiful lustrous appearance and pure colour, effects not achieved without difficulty, as Mrs. Palliser goes on to explain: "Not every woman can work at the white lace. Those who have what is locally termed the 'haleine grasse', are obliged to confine themselves to black. In order to preserve purity of colour, the lacemakers work during the summer months in the open air, in winter in lofts over their cowhouses: warmed by the heat of their animals they dispense with fire and its accompanying smoke." Blonde was, however, she adds, usually made in the summer months.

The lace manufacture of Chantilly, being considered a royal undertaking, was especially heavily visited at the time of the French Revolution in consequence. However, a revival began under Napoleon. The Emperor was particularly interested in the lace industries of Alençon and Chantilly and he issued an edict that only these two laces should be worn at court. This caused no distress whatsoever to fashionable ladies of the time, for blonde lace was then all the rage. Writing about French lace in the light of the Great Exhibition of 1851, Félix Aubry noted (*Rapport sur les dentelles, etc., 1851*, Paris, 1854), that bands of white blonde lace formed the major part of the production of Chantilly around 1805. Blonde lace was, in fact, to be the staple production of Chantilly and Caen for several decades. Black silk laces were also made at the beginning of the century, mainly for export, and so were laces in black and white linen thread which were the staple product of Bayeux.

During the second decade of the nineteenth century the black and white thread laces suffered very much from the fall of the Empire and the advent of machine-made lace. Blonde, however, was so high in the public favour that it was able to survive the crisis almost unimpaired. Classical motifs in design, such as key patterns or arrangements of formalized plants, gave way in the 1820s and 1830s to the large flowers, usually arranged to form the scalloped edge so beloved of the "Romantic" period (Pl. 2). Whole dresses might be made of blonde (Pl. 19) as well as borders, fichus and veils (Pl. 20).

In Bayeux the manufacture of silk blonde had lapsed since the eighteenth century, but in 1827 it was re-introduced, to supplement the black and white thread lace industry, by Mme. Charpentier. She was succeeded two years later by the redoubtable Auguste

Lefébure. He was the one who introduced the manufacture of *blondes mates* for export to Spain and Spanish America and succeeded in building up a very flourishing trade based on a careful study of the types of design fashionable in those countries. Lefébure also effected great improvements in the lace schools. These had formerly been run by somewhat superannuated old lace-makers, but now young forewomen, *au fait* with the latest methods, were put in charge of the pupils.

In spite of all this flourishing activity, however, the blonde lace manufacture was not destined to survive much longer. Lace of this type was very easy to imitate by machinery, and cheap machine products, often very little inferior to the hand-made lace, soon began to flood the market, with the result that the hand industry began to decline at the end of the 1830s.

Luckily for the manufacturers, though, black lace came back into fashion in the middle of that decade and, indeed, entered on a period of prosperity that was to last for a considerable time. Up to the middle of the nineteenth century the very best Chantilly lace was produced at Chantilly itself. Aubry noted in his 1851 report that it might be distinguished from similar lace made at Caen and Bayeux by its very fine *réseau* and the closer weaving of the flowers.

But although the manufacture of Chantilly lace began to prosper at this period, it needed constant attention from the manufacturers to keep it at boiling point. Being a luxury article, lace had to keep abreast of fashion to preserve its place in public favour, and this meant a never-ending flow of new designs had to be produced. Furthermore, the machine-lace industry speedily discovered how to make very passable imitations of Chantilly lace as well as of blonde lace. The hand-made lace manufacturers replied to this challenge not only by the continual production of new designs, but also by speeding up methods of manufacture. One innovation, for example, was the introduction of an easier type of *réseau* of oblong meshes, known as *fond d'Alençon*, which was widely adopted. Very large scarves and shawls of lace became increasingly popular during the 1840s, and their production was made possible by another technical innovation, which involved making the lace in narrow bands. These were then joined together most ingeniously and invisibly by a stitch known as *point de raccroc*. This technique is said to have been invented by a lace-worker named Cahanet and perfected under the direction of M. Violard, an inventive manufacturer whose head-quarters were in Paris (*Report of the Jury, Paris Exhibition, 1867*, p. 241, note). It was speedily adopted in all the centres where Chantilly lace was made. In 1851 the Jury of the Great Exhibition noted (*Report*: p. 1021) "The women of Calvados are remarkably quick at this work, and by means of a stitch called *raccroc*, which is used in joining several parts in one entire piece, so that the seam is imperceptible to the eye, even with a glass, they are able to perform in less than a month, with nine or ten persons, what formerly occupied a workwoman one whole year." This type of "mass-production" in fact enabled the hand-workers to compete with the machines. It may be noted in passing, that surviving Chantilly lace is often worn along those seams so that the narrow bands are, once more, clearly visible.

The *Report of the Jury* of 1851 gives a clear picture of the state of the industry in the middle of the century. Caen had, by this time, virtually given up the blonde lace manufacture and, with Bayeux, was devoting its energies to the production of Chantilly lace "piece goods, such as veils, scarfs, berthas, mantles, ladies' robes, shawls, etc., etc." Chantilly itself was now noted only for the best class of lace: "fewer hands are employed than at Bayeux, but the improvements of the latter have been regularly adopted. The articles manufactured are less intended for general use than to satisfy the desires of the luxurious, being laces of the very finest textures and most beautiful patterns." Still, some blonde laces figured in the exhibition. L. Randon, of Caen and 9, Passage des Petits Pères, Paris, showed white silk lappets and lappets of silk and gold, another of Caen's specialities. A. Delcambré, of 6, rue de Choiseul, Paris, showed similar products alongside black lace, while A. Duval of Caen showed yellow and white silk yarn for making blonde lace. Other firms who showed Chantilly lace were G. Violard, 4, rue de Choiseul, Paris, whose name has already been noted, the large Paris house of Videcoq & Simon, 35, rue des Jeûneurs, and of course, A. Lefébure of Bayeux and 42, rue de Cléry, Paris. His display included a counterpane in white thread (now cotton) lace, a reminder that white thread lace in the Chantilly technique was produced throughout this period, albeit in far smaller quantities. It was, indeed, highly thought of, and even compared to Mechlin lace for fineness and delicacy.

Imitation is a sure sign of the success of a luxury product. Lace of Chantilly type was by this time being produced at Grammont in Belgium (see pp. 114–6) and even in Buckinghamshire in England (see pp. 158–9). A more sinister note, however, was struck by the Jury's mention of the successful production of black lace by machinery in both England and France: "admirable imitations of the beautiful black lace of Caen and Chantilly, the patterns of which are most correctly copied, while the difference in price is 75 per cent". No wonder the manufacturers of Chantilly and Normandy had to provide a constant flow of new designs. Their success in doing so may be gauged by the numbers of beautiful shawls and mantles surviving from the 1850s and 1860s, showing endless variations on the theme of bunches of naturalistic flowers, swags, patterned strapwork and ribbons, the favourite design motifs of the period (Pl. 21).

Machine competition began to tell in the 1850s. The manufacture at Chantilly itself began to decline as manufacturers moved further into the country in the effort to secure workers who would not demand such high wages. Now Caen and, above all, Bayeux took the lead. At the Paris exhibition of 1855, the town of Bayeux was awarded a *Grande Médaille d'Honneur* for its lace export industry and M. Lefébure was honoured, too, for his contributions to the prosperity of the lace industry. Videcoq & Simon, likewise, received a medal for their Chantilly lace equally with the Alençon; they seem to have had a workroom at Chantilly itself. Other firms awarded medals for their Chantilly laces were M. Pigache & Mallet, M. Delcambré, M. Violard and M. Lecyre, all of Paris.

The middle of the 1850s saw the beginning of a new phase of imperial patronage. The story of Empress Eugénie's first orders has already been told (see p. 50). In 1854, in fact, she ordered a shawl of Chantilly lace from Lefébure and a flounce of the same from Pigache & Mallet. These were only the first of a long series of orders, for, as may be seen from her portraits, Eugénie was very fond of Chantilly lace.

By 1862 there were said to be 50,000 women making Chantilly lace, while the blonde lace manufacture had been entirely given up. The Jury of the International Exhibition in London of that year felt that the heights of perfection had now been reached in Chantilly lace. Caen was specially noted for borders, flounces, etc., for trimming dresses and for small pieces of lace in general, while

Bayeux specialized in large pieces such as shawls of the highest quality.   A design by Verdé-Delisle Frères (Compagnie des Indes), shown at the Paris exhibition of 1867, shows the typical very beautiful naturalistic flower style of this period, much enhanced by delicate effects of shading, an innovation which increased the effect of almost three-dimensional reality.   The design, illustrated in the *Art Journal Catalogue*, is the same as that of the piece of Brussels lace by the same firm shown on Pl. 39.   The Compagnie des Indes entered into this branch of the lace business in the early 1850s. Mrs. Bury Palliser, writing in the *Art Journal Catalogue*, noted that the manufacture of Chantilly lace, although almost defunct at Chantilly itself, was by now the most flourishing in the whole of France.   A typical design of the end of this decade and the beginning of the next is the parasol cover shown on Pl. 22.

But these years proved to be the high point of the industry for, in 1870, the Second Empire came to an end, royal patronage disappeared, the fashion for large shawls likewise ended, and the lace manufacturers could no longer successfully pursue their attempt to compete with similar products poured forth by the lace machines. Beautiful though it was, Chantilly lace still had not quite the prestige and *cachet* of Alençon and, unlike the latter, it could be imitated all too successfully.   It is true that a few manufacturers, notably the unquenchable firm of Lefébure, continued to make Chantilly lace and to show it at exhibitions, and a few aristocratic ladies continued to buy it.   Lady Harcourt's lace (Pl. 23), part of a set bought from Worth for her marriage in 1899, is a typical example of late nineteenth-century floral design, but perhaps it is significant of the change in fashion that she never actually wore it.

The Chantilly lace produced in the remaining years of the century after 1870 is most beautiful in design—delicate naturalistic flowers, often combined with perfectly delineated rococo ornament—and superlative in technique.   But it was made for prestige purposes only and the industry was no longer viable; indeed at the Paris exhibition of 1889, the making of Chantilly was truthfully described as now more of an art than an industry.   E. van Loon, visiting Bayeux in 1904 to make a report for the Dutch government on the lace industry (*De Kantindustrie in Frankrijk en Italië*, The Hague, 1904), noted that the firm of Lefébure more or less monopolized all the lace industry there.   But it was subsisting on the products of the needlepoint lace-makers and almost no Chantilly lace was being produced any more.

Valenciennes

After the French Revolution the manufacture of Valenciennes bobbin lace virtually passed from France to Belgium, and, indeed, lace of this type eventually ceased to be made at Valenciennes itself, in spite of attempts made, particularly by Napoleon, to revive the industry. According to Mrs. Bury Palliser (*History of Lace*, p. 235), "The last important piece made within the city walls was a head-dress of 'vraie Valenciennes' presented by the city to the Duchesse de Nemours, on her marriage in 1840. It was furnished by Made-moiselle Ursule Glairo, herself an aged lady, who employed the few old lace-workers then living, with the patriotic wish of exhibiting the perfection of the ancient manufacture."

However, a certain amount of Valenciennes lace of inferior quality was still made in France during the nineteenth century. The principal centre of this manufacture was Bailleul, a town on the Belgian frontier. Here were made narrow edgings of Valenciennes lace. These were not nearly so fine or light in texture as the Belgian Valenciennes; they had a very thick, round-meshed *réseau* and were soft to the touch. On the other hand, they were renowned as being the whitest and cleanest Valenciennes made and they had the further advantage of being very solid, strong and cheap. They were thus much sought after as trimmings for linen, and quantities of such lace found a ready export market in England, America and India. Care was taken to adapt designs to changing taste; Mrs. Bury Palliser notes (*op. cit.*, p. 241), "In 1832 the scalloped edge was adopted, and from this period dates the progress and present pros-perity of the manufacture."

Prosper it certainly did. Félix Aubry noted (*Rapport sur les dentelles, etc., 1851*, Paris, 1854) that while there were 2,500 workers in 1830, the number had risen to nearly 8,000 by the 1850s. A Bailleul manufacturer even achieved the honour of a second-class medal at the Paris exhibition of 1855. According to the *Jury Report of the International Exhibition of 1862* in London, there were at that time no less than 10,000 lace-workers in and around Bailleul and, indeed, the industry seems to have enjoyed its greatest prosperity at this point. But Valenciennes lace was easily imitated by machinery and the hand-made lace industry could not hope to hold out long against this ever-increasing competition. Still, the Bailleul manufacture managed to survive to a limited extent to the end of the century. Pierre Verhaegen noted that a small number of local factors were still in business in 1902 (*La Dentelle et la Broderie sur Tulle*, Brussels, 1902).

Simple Valenciennes lace was also made at Le Puy (see p. 80) and at Dieppe. In 1826, a lace school was established in Dieppe under the direction of two nuns from the Community of La Providence in Rouen. The school was patronized by the Duchesse de Berri and later by the Empress Eugénie, and at the Paris Exhibition of 1855 it was awarded a medal for its Valenciennes with square-meshed *réseau* and was complimented on the progress it had made. It prided itself on using linen thread and yet producing cheap lace. None the less Dieppe was never more than a very minor lace centre in the nineteenth century and by the end of the century the school was defunct.

There is no way now of distinguishing French Valenciennes from the cheaper varieties made in Belgium.

Lille and Arras

Lille lace was very popular during most of the first half of the nineteenth century. It resembled Mechlin lace, but had a much finer and lighter mesh-ground (cf. Pl. 18). The Lille mesh was, in fact, an easy one to make and as such it was the first to be imitated by the bobbin-net machines. As well as the Lille mesh, the old *fond Chant*, the six-pointed-star mesh used in Chantilly lace in the eighteenth century (cf. Pl. 17), was employed. Such light grounds resulted in few threads being available for working the solid part of the pattern. This, therefore, was very flimsy in texture and was given form by a thick outlining thread. In the nineteenth century this *cordonnet* was formed of an even thicker thread than before, while even fewer threads were used for the rest of the lace, for thread had greatly increased in price and every expedient was adopted to economize on it.

In the earlier part of the century, straight-edged borders were made, usually with a very simple design of a repeating motif, such as a patterned oval, along the lower edge. The ground was often powdered with small square spots (*points d'esprit*). In the 1820s and 1830s a scalloped edge was adopted and patterns with borders of

9. "Toilettes de Casino", from *The Queen* of 1899. "On the left is a Princesse tunique of lace or white crêpe, with appliqués of black lace, jet embroidered, over an accordion pleated underskirt of lemon silk muslin. The coral-pink canvas dress has overskirt and boléro of écru guipure, whilst the remaining dress of heliotrope crêpe de Chine is enriched with a scrollwork of black spangles and bands of guipure and white taffetas yoke." *The Queen*, Vol. CVI, I, p.252.

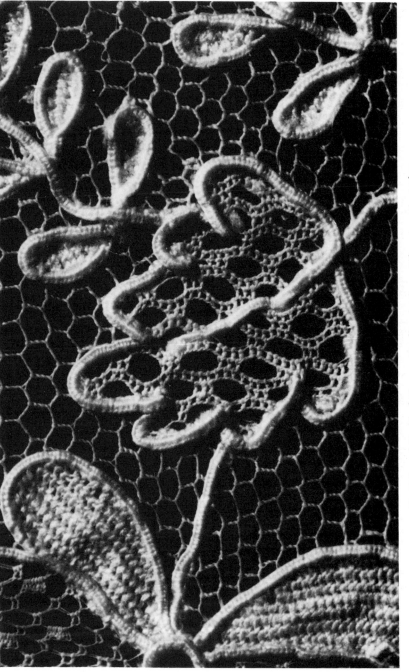

10. Enlarged Detail of Alençon Needlepoint Lace. *Rijksmuseum, Amsterdam.*

11. Matching Wide and Narrow Borders of Alencon Needlepoint Lace, French, c. 1850. *Rijksmuseum, Amsterdam.*

10. Spray of Flowers in Alençon Needle-point Lace. French, mid 19th century. Musées Royaux d'Art et d'Histoire, Brussels (No. 903)

13. Border of Alencon Needlepoint Lace, French, c. 1850-60. *Victoria and Albert Museum* (No.31.1880).

14. Border of Alençon Needlepoint Lace, part of a matching set designed by Alcide Roussel for A. Lefébure & Fils of Paris and Bayeux, c. 1867. Lace of this design was shown at the Paris International Exhibition of 1867. *Victoria and Albert Museum* (No. T.59-1949).

small flowers in the Mechlin style were favoured. However, heavier, richer laces were now rapidly coming into fashion and the industry began to decline. In 1851 there were only about 1,600 lace-workers left in Lille and by the end of the next decade the industry was virtually extinct, the lace-makers having mostly turned to other, more lucrative forms of employment.

A similar type of lace was made at Arras. It was less fine than that of Lille but much stronger, and the workers prided themselves on its whiteness. During the first decade of the nineteenth century, Arras lace was popular and it continued to prosper until the 1830s. Then, as in most other lace centres, cotton thread was substituted for linen, and this, paradoxically, made it more difficult for the hand-made lace to compete with the machine-made in quality. In addition, both Lille and Arras laces had to face competition from similar laces produced more cheaply in Mirecourt (see pp. 82–3). In 1851, however, 8,000 workers were still employed in Arras and the surrounding district. As prosperity declined, production became stereotyped, and the industry was thus even less able to hold its own against machine competition. By 1881, there was only one firm left in business. In 1883, the Académie of Arras made an attempt to revive the industry, but this came to nothing and by the end of the century it had vanished altogether.

OTHER LACE-MAKING CENTRES

So far in this chapter we have been considering specific types of lace, named after their town of origin and made in well-defined districts. In this last section two important large areas of lace-making, each producing lace of several different types, are described as well as a few smaller lace industries which do not fall into any of the categories already dealt with.

Le Puy

In the nineteenth century, Le Puy was the centre of a very considerable area of lace-making in the Auvergne. This was a poor agricultural region and lace-making, therefore, offered a source of income which was eagerly seized on by all the womenfolk of the area. Mrs. Bury Palliser included in her article in the *Art Journal Catalogue of the Paris Exhibition, 1867* (p. 112) a translation of a

significant passage from a French account of lace-making in Le
Puy (Turgan: *Les Grandes Usines*, VI, Paris, 1867, pp. 237–68),
which is worth quoting again: "The whole of the women are lace-
makers from their cradles.   As soon as the infant can use her hands,
instead of a doll, a small lace pillow, with three threads fixed upon a
nail, is given to her as a toy, and her tiny fingers are taught to plait
the threads.   As she grows older a more complicated frame is
substituted, and she begins to fabricate a narrow lace: a child of six
years old has been known to earn a half-penny a day.   Lace-making
at Le Puy is not only a trade, but a passion.   It is the infant's
plaything, the woman's support, and, when old and obliged to
return to the simple laces of childhood, the aged workwoman will
ply at her pillow so long as her eyes can distinguish, or her fingers
move the bobbins.   When their twirling is no longer heard in a
house, it is a sure sign that the end of its occupant is at hand."

The article in Turgan's compilation gives much valuable information about the history of this industry.   It flourished in the eighteenth century on the production of simple laces of Lille or Valenciennes type, which were mostly sent to Cadiz for export to Central
America.   By the end of the century finer varieties of lace were in
demand and the lace-makers, giving the first sign of the versatility
that was to be the source of their prosperity in the nineteenth
century, turned to making them in both linen and silk with equal
success.   The French Revolution caused a considerable set-back
in the industry, but by the early years of the nineteenth century a
revival was well under way.   Cheap lace with small-scale designs
was made with sufficient success to secure an honourable mention at
the industrial exhibition held in Paris in 1806.   Turgan gives a list
of those who were most instrumental in assisting the revival of the
lace-industry at this time: Messieurs Guichard-Dorval, Roland
père, Assezat deuxième, Robert cadet, Hedde Martin, Jacques-
Robert Laurenson and Champagnac, and la veuve Dulax.   In
spite of devoted efforts, however, the industry suffered severely in
the next decade from the competition of machine-made laces.   Also,
in view of the similarity between Le Puy laces and those of Saxony,
the Le Puy industry was particularly hard hit when, in 1816, heavy
duties were laid on French laces entering Germany, while German
laces were admitted into France on favourable terms.

Matters remained at this pass until the early 1820s when several manufacturers began to make serious attempts to put the industry on its feet again. Prominent among these was M. Robert Faure, who succeeded in obtaining honours at exhibitions held in 1825 and 1829. In 1823 he had taken on a new designer, M. Théodore Falcon, who soon began to turn his energies to reviving the prosperity of the industry. Falcon realized that radical reorganization was necessary. Up to that time it had been customary for lace-makers to buy their own thread or silk and to go on making their own favourite pattern in their own way. At the end of a week they would cut off what they had made and take it into Le Puy to sell it for very small sums to shopkeepers in la rue Chaussade and la rue Raphaël. These shopkeepers sold them, in return, silk and thread and, sometimes, pricked patterns. These methods, perhaps suitable enough for a minor cottage industry, were more than insufficient if the workers were to have any hope of competing successfully with machine-made products.

Falcon, and others like him, realized that it was essential for the workers to be kept in touch with the centres of fashion, to be stimulated to produce lace of the highest quality and to be supplied constantly with new designs. He thus began to go out himself into the country districts, controlling and supervising the workers, issuing designs and collecting up the finished work. By this means he not only built up a body of workers supplying him exclusively, but he was also able to get orders carried out more speedily and to make it more difficult for novel patterns to be copied by rival manufacturers or, worse still, by the machines. He studied old laces and contemporary laces to get ideas for new designs and often pricked the parchments or cards himself.

His silk and cotton laces, often in floral patterns, began to enjoy a great vogue in France itself as well as being exported. The industry began, in fact, to be very prosperous in the 1830s, as others followed this lead, and in 1839 M. Falcon, who had established his headquarters in Craponne, north of Le Puy, was awarded the only silver medal given to lace at the industrial exhibition held in Paris, in recognition of the immense progress he had made. He had by this time established a lace school where twenty picked workers were trained for three months and then sent back to their country homes to teach improved methods to their neighbours. In 1844, at a further exhibition, the Jury again commended M. Falcon and also singled out M. Seguin of Le Puy for special mention.

During the 1840s the industry expanded with great rapidity and, at the time of the Great Exhibition of 1851, M. Félix Aubry (himself a very considerable lace manufacturer at Le Puy) noted (*Rapport sur les dentelles, etc.*, *1851*, Paris, 1854) that there were 125,000 to 130,000 workers in the four *départements* of Haute-Loire, Cantal, Puy-de-Dôme and Loire. The repertoire of the lace-makers had been considerably increased by this time and their versatility was becoming almost legendary. In addition to simple laces of Lille type and Valenciennes, they made very fine black silk guipure laces. Black guipures incorporating pearls or jet in their design were also made, while another new line just beginning was a coarse white lace in imitation of the Maltese guipures. Since 1849, moreover, woollen laces, both black and polychrome, had been made and enjoyed a tremendous vogue. Coloured cotton laces were also made. All these novelties, M. Aubry noted, enabled Le Puy to compete with the greatest success against the similar laces of Saxony, for the German manufacturers were reduced to copying Le Puy's designs at second hand.

Amongst the most important firms exhibiting in 1851 were that of M. Aubry himself: Aubry Frères, of 33, rue des Jeûneurs, Paris; M. Robert Faure, 25, rue de Cléry, Paris, who showed worsted lace of all colours as well as silk guipure; and Joseph Seguin, 40, rue des Jeûneurs, Paris, who showed silk lace. Blondes and cheap laces were also shown by a Mlle. Marguérite Julien of Le Puy, presumably a representative of the older tradition of lace-making in the area which still survived to a certain extent.

From this time on, the industry went from strength to strength. Further honours and commendations were heaped on the heads of manufacturers in 1855 at the Paris International Exhibition. M. Seguin received a first-class medal, while second-class medals were awarded to M. Julien & Cie., B. Robert and Célina Balme, and more than twenty individual workers were honoured. M. Robert Faure received a first-class medal for his attempts to introduce needlepoint lace into the area. He showed a handkerchief and a piece of lace made in a style reminiscent of Venetian needlepoint of the seventeenth century. This manufacture never caught on very much in Le Puy, however, as the technique proved more difficult to master than those of the simpler types of bobbin lace made there. M. Falcon, too, received an accolade, the highest there was: the

Legion of Honour. This, however, was to be his final honour, as
he died in 1856.

Black and white guipure laces of Maltese type became the staple
product of Le Puy during the 1850s and the workers there easily
outstripped likely competitors as far as quality was concerned. A
school of design was set up at Le Puy in 1859 to assist in the maintenance of high standards. In 1862 the Jury of the International
Exhibition in London noted (*Report*, p. 4): "There are several
articles of great beauty in the present Exhibition, particularly a
black guipure shawl, remarkable for its excellence of workmanship,
having been made with different kinds of silk which enabled the
manufacturers to introduce a group of natural flowers, and give it
the appearance of sculptured lace." This piece was no doubt
produced expressly for the exhibition, but it gave a true picture of
what the workers were able to achieve. The shawl was exhibited by
M. Robert Faure, who received a medal for it and his other laces,
polychrome as well as black. J. Seguin was also honoured for
"real lace, black and white, all evincing great taste in design and
excellence in manufacture".

By this time Le Puy had the biggest export trade of any lace
industry in France. The workers were able to maintain their
prosperity by their adaptability to new techniques and materials.
As soon as one set of designs and materials went out of fashion they
turned to a new, rapidly altering their products and securing new
favour. This must be the classic example of a cottage industry
exploited as a luxury trade with the utmost skill by astute manufacturers.

Turgan noted that by 1867 the staple product of the industry
was the type of guipure, most commonly made in white cotton, which
was known as Cluny lace. This was a development of Maltese lace,
and took its name from the fact that the original designs were
inspired by sixteenth- and seventeenth-century scalloped bobbin
laces in the Cluny Museum in Paris. In addition numerous types
of coarse lace in worsted were still made, as well as simple cotton
laces which the workers always turned to making when there was
nothing else on hand as there was a permanent market for them.

The organization of the industry had now assumed a regular form.
Turgan gives a roll-call of the large manufacturers—Falcon Frères,
Vinay, Séguin, Chevallier-Balme, Bernard-Mazandier, Breysse-

Langier, Chastel-Gravier, Experton, Philippe Bonnet, Robert Faure, Bandon, Rocher-Blanc, Sauret, Joseph Seguin—who, as he says, had established what almost amounted to a feudal hold over all the country districts. They arranged for orders from Paris to be carried out by their workers or else introduced designs and novelties of their own. In addition, there were a number of small firms which bought up the ordinary types of lace noted above directly from the workers or from local factors. Sometimes these small merchants would themselves make a tour of the villages to buy lace. The best quality laces were made in the northern parts of Haute-Loire, the more ordinary ones in the south, and the workers' wages showed a corresponding discrepancy.

After the end of the 1860s it becomes more difficult to follow the history of this industry in detail, but it seems to have been able to maintain its prosperity pretty well unimpaired to the end of the nineteenth century. Some typical guipure laces of the 1880s from Le Puy are illustrated by E. Lefébure in his *Broderies et Dentelles*, Paris, 1887, pp. 279 and 281. Pierre Verhaegen noted in 1902 (in his survey, *La Dentelle et la Broderie sur Tulle*, published in Brussels) that guipure laces, mainly in geometric patterns were still being produced in quantity, and that Le Puy was one of the most important of the lace centres which still survived. Quantities of cheap torchon lace were made there, too. The workers were still able to produce lace in any material, from linen, silk and worsted to goat's hair and even the fur of angora rabbits. They made gold and silver lace too. A. Lefébure, writing in 1904 (*Dentelles et Guipures*), confirms Verhaegen's statements and notes that the laces of Le Puy were much in demand for trimming linen and for furnishing purposes. He attributes the continued success of these laces to their high quality and notes that care had been taken to keep them competitive by reason of their cheapness.

Mirecourt

Mirecourt was the centre of lace-making in Lorraine, a very extensive industry with many similarities to that of Le Puy. Like Le Puy it had specialized in the eighteenth century in the production for export of cheap laces of Lille type. In the early nineteenth century, however, this type of lace began to be more popular in France itself. By dint of improving their designs and the quality of lace while maintaining its cheapness, the manufacturers of Mirecourt succeeded in building up a very flourishing industry by the 1840s. Their workers, like those of Le Puy, were able to adapt themselves readily to new techniques and the late 1840s saw a number of important innovations in the industry.

The Jury of the Great Exhibition of 1851 noted in its report that Mirecourt's speciality was Lille lace, which was constantly produced in new designs. The *Report* then went on (pp. 1021–2): "They also produce a lace very much resembling Honiton, called 'guipure'. Within the last four or five years flowers have been made and sewn upon that extremely fine net termed 'Brussels net'. This fabric has, in two years, been so much improved that it now bears close affinity to the Belgian, at Binche and at Brussels, and is greatly esteemed for its admirable whiteness, its fine quality and moderate price." Mrs. Bury Palliser noted (*History of Lace*, p. 252): "The Lorraine application possesses one advantage over those of Flanders, the flowers come from the hands of the lace-makers clean and white, and do not require bleaching. The price too is most moderate."

At the Paris Exhibition of 1855, a M. Colnot, aîné, of Diarville (Meurthe), was awarded a first-class medal for his display of laces, all of which came from Mirecourt. These included a large piece of so-called Honiton lace, which was regarded as a masterpiece. It was noted that M. Colnot was one of the manufacturers principally responsible for the innovations of the 1840s. Unfortunately, few other names of Mirecourt manufacturers seem to have been recorded.

During the 1850s the making of black and white guipure laces of Maltese type, similar to those of Le Puy, was started at Mirecourt. Mirecourt concentrated on the production of white lace and did not go in for the many varieties of colour and texture for which Le Puy was famous. To the production of this type of lace too, the Mirecourt manufacturers brought the same *savoir faire* that had given them prosperity in other varieties; great attention was paid to design and to quality of work.

In the 1860s the industry was in a highly flourishing state; Mrs. Bury Palliser noted in her *History of Lace* that there were nearly 25,000 workers by the end of the decade. It seems that guipure laces had now come to be the main product of the industry. Indeed, according to the *Jury Report of the Paris Exhibition of 1867* (p. 243), the so-called "Cluny" lace, a variety of guipure, was an invention of Mirecourt. Apparently in about 1861 or 1862 a Mme. Gaudillot had conceived the idea of employing the Mirecourt lace-makers on the production of old, long-forgotten types of bobbin lace current in the late sixteenth and early seventeenth centuries. These laces had an immediate success and it was from them that Cluny lace, a kind of scalloped *passementerie*, had developed. This, notes the Report, was less artistic than the direct copies of old lace, but more commercially viable. It was, indeed, enormously successful and greatly enhanced the prosperity of the industry. The Report commented that the Mirecourt industry was the most militant in the fight against competition from machines, and it was also the most productive in the whole of France. The lace-makers were very quick at their work and very adaptable and, under intelligent direction, they were able to keep up a constant flow of new designs. Their laces were always remarkably cheap and in very good taste and, as a result, were immediately accepted by the public and slavishly copied by foreign lace-makers.

These qualities enabled the workers to maintain a considerable prosperity right up to the end of the nineteenth century. A. Lefébure noted that the industry was still flourishing in 1904. By this time the manufacture of Lille laces, flowers for application and imitation Honiton had long since been given up. It seems likely, in fact, that they were abandoned during the economic crisis of the early 1870s in favour of concentration on the more profitable guipure laces. Lefébure says (*Dentelles et Guipures*, 1904, p. 265) that the guipures of Mirecourt might be distinguished from those of Le Puy by the fact that the flowers were generally surrounded by a thick *cordonnet*, giving a relief effect, which made the laces very popular for furnishing purposes. As well as floral designs, arabesques were popular and this latter lace was, indeed, sometimes known as "dentelle arabe". These laces enjoyed a very considerable export trade to the U.S.A. where they were much admired for their cheapness, their decorative qualities, and the fact that they were very strong and hard-wearing and easy to wash and bleach.

Paris

In the nineteenth century, little or no lace was made in Paris itself apart from gold and silver *passementerie*. In the middle of the

century, however, there existed in Paris a considerable industry
devoted to applying bobbin-lace motifs to machine-made net to
make a variety of application lace.   The motifs were obtained from
Binche and Mirecourt.   At the Paris Exhibition of 1855, for example,
a M. Robillaud was awarded a first-class medal for a magnificent
court mantle made of bobbin-lace flowers from Binche applied to
net in Paris.

Courseulles-sur-Mer

At this small centre in Normandy bobbin-lace flowers for application were made in the middle of the nineteenth century.   Later on,
at the end of the century, it was the scene of an attempt to produce a
new type of lace that it was hoped would have some chance of
competing with the by now ubiquitous machine laces.   This
innovation, invented by Georges Robert and Félix Aubert, was
described by Fernand Engerand, then *Député* for Calvados, in an
article on the lace industry of that area in *Revue des Deux Mondes*,
April 1st, 1900.   The new lace was a polychrome bobbin lace which
demanded much skill in execution.   It was intended to be a product
of high luxury, appealing to a market machines could not cater for
and made in a way machines could not copy.   Each piece was
unique, with its own special design and method of manufacture.
Great care was taken over the blending of the colours, each thread
usually consisting of three differently coloured strands twisted
together.   Only a few lace-makers were possessed of sufficient
skill to be able to make this lace, but none the less it did secure
a certain success around the turn of the century.   Examples of it
are illustrated by A. Carlier de Lantsheere in his various compila-
tions.

La Haute-Saône

In his survey of the French lace industry in 1904 (*Dentelles et
Guipures*, 1904, p. 265), A. Lefébure noted that at that time there
existed a considerable industry in this area for making the so-called
"dentelle renaissance".   This consisted of machine-made tapes or
lacets of various kinds worked into patterns and joined together by
means of very simple needlepoint stitches executed in rather thick
cotton thread.   This type of lace, popular because it was cheap but
of very little merit otherwise, began to be made in Belgium on a

commercial scale in the 1880s (see pp. 127–8), so that it may be presumed that the French industry came into being at around the same time.   The area was also a centre for darned netting and for embroideries in imitation of old cutwork.

CHAPTER 3

BELGIUM

THROUGHOUT the nineteenth century the Belgian lace industry was as important as the French both for quality and quantity of production. But it was not in quite such a strong position; it was on the whole rather more loosely organized, and it also depended heavily on France for designs. Nevertheless, like the French industry, it managed for most of the century to cope with changing fashion and economic crises by being sufficiently resilient and resourceful in inventing new types of lace to meet or stimulate new demands.

Though perhaps not so heavily hit as French lace by the French Revolution, the Belgian industry still suffered a considerable recession. It was, however, much assisted in its recovery by the patronage of Napoleon, who made personal visits to Brussels as First Consul, with Josephine, and later, as Emperor, with Marie-Louise. On the latter occasion, according to Mrs. Bury Palliser (*History of Lace*, pp. 123–4), the Emperor ordered some lace albs, which he intended to give to the Pope, while the city of Brussels presented the Empress with a collection of application lace on a ground of real bobbin-made net. As a result of this gracious patronage the industry enjoyed a reasonable period of prosperity until the collapse of the Empire and the advent of machine-made net and lace caused a new recession after 1815. The beginning of the machine-net industry in France in 1819 was a particularly hard blow.

There followed a period of decline which, owing to political and economic troubles in Belgium, lasted until the end of the 1830s and gave rise to much distress and pauperism in country districts where lace-making was the main support of many of the inhabitants. In the towns, new industries grew up which absorbed many former lace-makers. Fashion, too, was against Belgian lace at this time. After 1819, European markets were flooded with machine-made net, both plain and embroidered, which enjoyed a great vogue, while blonde was the most popular hand-made lace until the late 1830s.

By 1840, however, hand-made lace of richer, heavier types was beginning to become fashionable again and, furthermore, to appeal to a wider public, for the rising middle classes were now prosperous enough to afford such luxurious finery. Steps were taken to rejuvenate the Belgian industry by introducing new types of lace and by reorganizing the apprenticeship system, which had declined during the recession. Many new lace schools were established, at least two-thirds of them run by convents, which played a very important role in the industry. At the same time the United States became an important new export market, a highly encouraging factor for the Belgian industry, which always depended very heavily on exports, home consumption being necessarily limited by the small size of the country.

During the 1830s in Belgium, as elsewhere, an important change in the manufacture of lace had occurred: the fine linen thread employed hitherto began to be replaced by machine-spun cotton. The renowned linen-spinners of Belgium were, in fact, gradually disappearing and much of the flax grown there was now sent to England to be spun by machinery. From this time on linen thread was used only for the choicest Brussels or Valenciennes bobbin lace, and for the finest needlepoint laces in the Venetian manner.

By the later 1840s the industry was, once more, in a flourishing state and, like its French rival, it was to enjoy a period of great prosperity for most of the third quarter of the century. France, however, was the leader of fashion and it was to her that the Belgian lace manufacturers turned for designs. Parisian designers charged a high price for their drawings and great care was taken by the Belgian manufacturers to safeguard the designs from copying or piracy. When James Brennan of the Cork Municipal School of Art visited Mme. Augustinus, a lace manufacturer of Bruges, in 1887, she told him, as he noted in his report, that "when the designs are given out to the workers who make needlepoint lace in the vicinity of Brussels, the designs are so cut up that the worker is unable from the portion handed to her to complete the original design, which otherwise she might do, and then dispose of the lace privately. . . . The designs are obtained from Paris, and for a design for a flounce from 10 to 15 inches deep forty francs may be paid, or more, should the design be a rich one. The designs are drawn in outline only, the fillings being arranged by the person who gives out the lace to the workers."

There is, in the Musées Royaux d'Art et d'Histoire in Brussels, a collection of designs formerly belonging to the Maison Patte-Hannot. Many of them are clearly intended for *point de gaze* and they bear on them the lines drawn by the manufacturer indicating how the work should be divided up. Although the work of several different hands may be detected among these drawings, there is rarely anything on the design to indicate who the artist was or whence it came. One of them, however, is marked with the name of a Parisian designer, Victor Le Clère, and dated October 10th, 1858. Furthermore, amongst the French lace designers who exhibited their work at the Great Exhibition of 1851 was J. F. Ragot, of 89, Boulevard

FIG. 3. Brussels application lace, bobbin and needlepoint motifs applied to machine-made net, designed by P. Bonnod of Brussels, shown by Debenham & Freebody at the International Exhibition of 1862. (*Art Journal Catalogue*, p. 47.)

St. Martin, Paris, who showed "Design for a white lace counterpane, Brussels application, without trimmings."

But it must not be supposed that there were no lace designers in Belgium itself, for this was far from being the case. In 1851, G. Violard and F. Polak, both of Brussels, showed designs for lace at the Great Exhibition. At the International Exhibition of 1862, P. Bonnod, B. J. van der Dussen d'Habbeeck and A. J. Houtmans were awarded medals for their designs, while C. C. Houtmans and J. Naeten also exhibited. All five worked in Brussels. One of Bonnod's designs was illustrated in the *Art Journal* catalogue of the exhibition (Fig. 3) and, indeed, there seems to have been at this time an attempt to bring the Belgian designers into greater prominence. On page 5 of the *Report of the Jury*, it is stated that "the

Jurors of Class XXIV, having been requested to examine the designs for lace of the Belgian designers, were much pleased with their graceful, elegant and easy styles, and their peculiar adaptability to the purpose for which they are intended. This shows at once that the Belgian artists understand both how to produce beautiful and effective designs, and to adapt them to the special sort of lace articles for which they are intended, besides knowing how they should economically and effectively be carried out; considerations not understood or mostly lost sight of by some designers."

On the whole, though, Belgian designers seem to have confined their attentions mainly to the less expensive types of lace. Amongst the designs from the Maison Patte-Hannot referred to above, for example, are two for Duchesse bobbin lace stamped with the name of a Belgian designer, P. Goossens. This impression is confirmed by Pierre Verhaegen in his valuable account of the Belgian lace industry: *La Dentelle et la Broderie sur Tulle*, published at Brussels in 1902. Verhaegen states that at the time of writing there were still one or two lace designers in Brussels, but they worked only for the manufacturers of secondary importance, producing cheaper types of lace. He also notes that several manufacturers were currently trying to free the industry from its reliance on French designs by training artists locally. The firm of Minne-Dansaert at Haeltert had, indeed, a considerable success in this endeavour. But of course, many of the smaller manufacturers in country districts dispensed with the services of designers altogether, making their own patterns, which relied heavily on tradition, or were copies of more sophisticated originals at several removes. In the collection of the Musées Royaux d'Art et d'Histoire in Brussels are some examples of such designs, for *point de Lille* by E. van Migem of Antwerp, and for *point de Paris* by Marie Parkussen of Turnhout.

The Belgian industry seems, in general, to have been more loosely organized than the French. There were far more middlemen, i.e. local factors, between the manufacturer and the worker. These factors were usually women who had been lace-makers themselves, for it was essential that they should have a good technical knowledge. It was the factor who collected the designs from the manufacturer, often pricking the pattern in preparation for the worker where necessary, and the factor who was responsible for giving out the work to the lace-makers according to their capacity, for supervising it, collecting it when done, and putting the final touches to the finished lace. Quite often the manufacturer would have little or no contact with the workers themselves, everything being done through this intermediary, who could normally be relied upon to drive a hard bargain with the workers. Indeed, as far as the workers were concerned the system was full of disadvantages, one of the main ones being that they had to buy the raw materials of their trade from these same factors, who also frequently operated the so-called "truck" system of payment in kind. Some of the factors operated on a very small local scale, making weekly rounds of the workers to buy up the lace produced since the last visit. Others had the workers come to them once a week or once a month to deliver their lace. Most of them supplied one firm only; others, less scrupulous, bargained amongst different firms or even sold lace in the designs of one firm to another. In 1896, at a time when the lace industry was far from being as flourishing as it had been earlier, a census showed there to be no less than 976 lace factors in Belgium. Quite often there were as many as five or six of these intermediaries between the worker and the eventual buyer of the lace. The workers were, in effect, very much in the hands of the factors and they had little or no redress against abuses. Indeed the only thing a skilled worker could hope for was to become a factor in her turn.

In some areas convents played an important part. Mention has already been made of the part played by religious houses in encouraging the lace industry in the middle years of the century by setting up lace schools and reorganizing a system of regular apprenticeship. Workers usually ceased to work on the convent premises after finishing their apprenticeship or after marriage, but, nevertheless, the convent still tended to occupy the role of the factor in its own area and for its own workers. Of course the dealings of the convents were, on the whole, much more geared to assisting the workers than those of secular factors, and where a convent conducted the business it was generally established on a much more stable basis.

The firms supplied by the lace-makers and factors were concentrated mainly in the towns that formed the nuclei of the lace-making areas. They varied greatly in size, scope and importance, but as the century progressed there was a marked tendency towards amalgamation and centralisation of the industry, with the greatest number of firms being concentrated in Brussels itself. It was the manufacturers who had to choose the design and sell the finished product. Some confined themselves to one type of lace only: these were mostly situated in local centres of production and often worked on a small scale, catering for the tourist market. A large number of medium-sized firms, mainly situated in Brussels, dealt in several types, but only a few of the largest firms could handle all the different types of lace produced in Belgium.

Throughout the second half of the nineteenth century the principal lace-exporting house in Brussels was the Compagnie des Indes, or Verdé, Delisle & Cie., of 94, rue Royale. This firm, as has been noted in the previous chapter, played an important role in the French lace industry, too. Indeed, at the International Exhibition of 1862 in London it won two medals, one for its Belgian laces, one for its French. Its Paris house at this time was at 80, rue Richelieu, while its London agent was M. Séguy, 2, South Street, Alexander Square, Brompton. From the *Catalogue of the Great Exhibition of 1851*, it is clear that another Brussels firm, Van Eeckhout & Co., also had a branch in Paris, at 38, rue Nôtre-Dame des Victoires, while yet another firm with two such branches was Normand et Chandon of 21, rue de Malines, Brussels and 82, rue Richelieu, Paris, who showed lace at the Paris Exhibition of 1867. Many manufacturers, however, were content to rely on links with a French fashion shop such as Les Grands Magasins du Louvre. Some also had links with London firms. From the 1862 catalogue, for example, we learn that Bruyneel Sen. of Grammont and J. Strehler of Brussels both had connections with Daniel Biddle of the London house of Haywards of Oxford Street.

In the middle of the century the great French firm of A. Lefébure & Fils established its own workshop at Destelberghe for the making of Brussels application and *point de gaze*. The reason may have been the difficulties involved in obtaining careful and adequately supervised work. It was noted in the *Reports of the Jury of the Paris Exhibition of 1867* that the workshop was a model one of its kind, producing designs of great artistic value and perfect taste. Amongst work by the firm's leading designer, Alcide Roussel, illustrated by E. Lefébure in his *Broderies et Dentelles*, 1887, are two designs for Brussels needlepoint lace, a shawl and a lappet, which were probably products of this workshop.

15. Parasol Cover in Alençon Needlepoint Lace, designed by Alcide Roussel for Auguste Lefébure & Fils and shown at the Paris International Exhibition of 1867. *Art Journal Catalogue.*

16. Part of a Border of Needlepoint Lace, *point Colbert,* made by A. Lefébure of Bayeux, French, late 19th century. Reproduced from A. Carlier de Lantsheere: *Tresor de l'Art Dentellier,* Pl. 61:4.

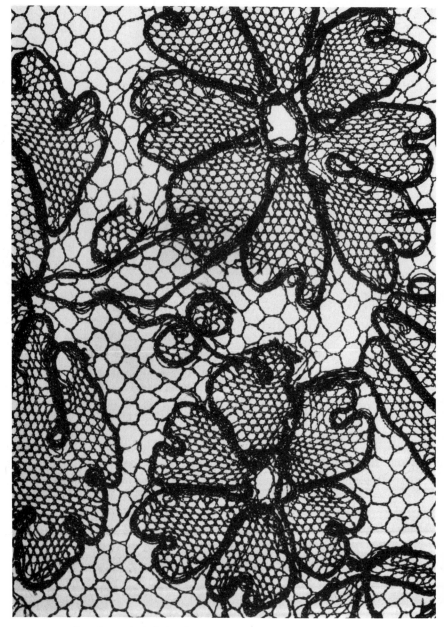

17. Enlarged Detail of Black Silk Chantilly Bobbin Lace. *Rijksmuseum, Amsterdam.*

18. Enlarged Detail of Blonde Bobbin Lace. *Rijksmuseum, Amsterdam.*

19. Dress of Blonde Bobbin Lace, French, *c.* 1820. *Rijksmuseum, Amsterdam* (No. N.M.14105).

20. Veil of Blonde Bobbin Lace, French, *c.* 1830-40. *Victoria and Albert Museum* (No. 906-1875).

21. Mantle of Black Silk Chantilly Bobbin Lace, French, c. 1860. *Dutch Royal Collection on loan to the Rijksmuseum, Amsterdam* (No. R.B.K.J.251).

22. Parasol Cover of Black Silk Chantilly Bobbin Lace, French, *c.* 1870. *Rijksmuseum, Amsterdam* (No. **R.B.K. 16115**).

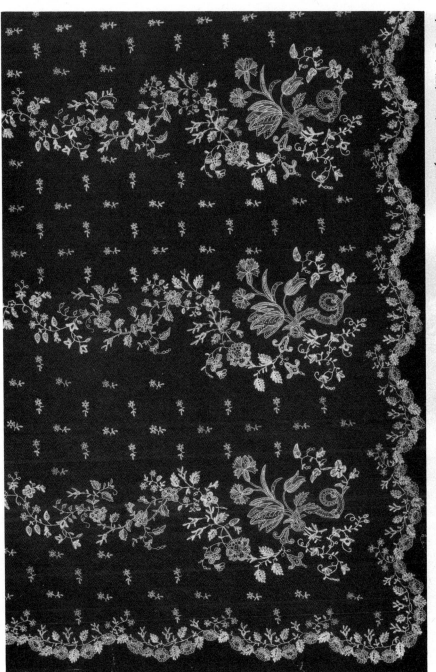

24. Veil of Brussels Needlepoint Lace applied to a bobbin-made mesh ground (*vrai drochel*), Belgian, c. 1830. *Musées Royaux d'Art et d'Histoire, Brussels* (No. 501).

25. Enlarged Detail of Brussels Bobbin Lace applied to machine-made net. *Rijksmuseum, Amsterdam.*

The third quarter of the nineteenth century was a period of great prosperity for the Belgian lace industry. New types of lace were introduced with much success, while older types were equally successfully modified to meet the demands of current fashion. Cumbersome though the organization of the industry was, there was no doubt that it could adapt to new demands with rapidity while continuing to maintain a high standard of workmanship. These powers of adaptability had, of course, been acquired through long years of experience starting in the middle of the sixteenth century. But the current prosperity could not easily be maintained against the increasing competition of machine-made lace and against the constant loss, increasing as the century progressed, of workers to other less demanding and more highly paid occupations. The fact that the industry was badly hit by economic troubles arising out of the Franco-Prussian War of 1870 showed on what a tenuous basis its prosperity now rested. It is noteworthy that those areas where convents controlled the industry rode the crisis more successfully than the others.

By the last two decades of the century, the industry had come to depend almost entirely on workers in the countryside. Indeed, one important firm, Minne-Dansaert, transferred its headquarters from Brussels to Haeltert in 1889 in order to maintain a better liaison with its workers. The only town which retained a considerable number of lace-workers was Bruges. Alan S. Cole gave an account of lace-making in Bruges during one of his Cantor lectures on lace-making to the Royal Society of Arts in 1881: "In the summer you may look down long and wide back streets of the town, and see hundreds of women in groups of three, four and five outside their cottages plying their bobbins most industriously. It is estimated that there are over 4,000 lace-makers at Bruges. The laces made are collected for the merchants, whose agents, on market day, sit in little boxes, like ticket offices, in the market places. To these the makers bring their laces, which are received and paid for by the agent. At the same time, the agent gives to the workers fresh orders, and serves out the pattern to be done. Every pattern, after it has been worked, has to be brought back to the agent, under penalty of a heavy Government fine, which thus is a protection for designs." (*Journal of the Royal Society of Arts*, 1881, p. 802.)

The lace produced at the end of the century shows a great divergence in quality. Work of outstanding technical skill existed side by side with cheap, coarse laces in the production of which speed was the key factor. Many workers turned in the 1890s to making the latter which did, indeed, enjoy a brief fashion, bringing back a degree of prosperity to the industry at the end of the century, but presaging its eventual decline when the vogue should have passed.

LACES OF MIXED TECHNIQUE

Brussels application

Brussels application, consisting of motifs made by bobbin or needle sewn or sometimes stuck to a net ground, was one of the most important and popular products of the Belgian lace industry throughout the nineteenth century. The manufacture of this type of lace began in the late eighteenth century when cobwebby laces, adorned only with small scattered motifs, were fashionable and it was deemed quicker to make the mesh ground separately and to apply the motifs to it, rather than working the mesh round the finished motifs as had been done formerly. This bobbin-made net, known as *le vrai drochel*, was worked in strips about one inch wide which were sewn together invisibly by the stitch known as *point de raccroc*, also used in Chantilly lace (see pp. 67–8). The method had one great advantage: it enabled much larger pieces of lace to be made very much more easily than had been possible before. Indeed, throughout the period of the First Empire, application was used not only for costume purposes, but also for large items such as bed-covers for which one might have thought this delicate fabric too fragile. The favourite design motifs at this time were classical scrolls, medallions and similar ornament, delicate floral forms and figures from classical mythology.

The making of application lace was a complex task involving a considerable number of specialized workers. Prominent among them was the *drocheleuse* who made the bobbin net strips for the ground. A very high degree of skill was demanded of the *drocheleuse* for it was essential that the finished ground should have a uniform appearance and not betray the work of different hands. The finished strips of *drochel* were joined together by a worker known as the *jointeuse* or *attacheuse*. The heading at the top of the lace was made by a worker known as the *dentellière*. Flowers for application were made in needlepoint by the *pointeuse* and the *brodeuse* who worked the relief portions, while the bobbin motifs and flowers were also divided between two workers: the *platteuse*, who made the *plat* or solid parts of the flowers, and the *formeuse*, who made the fancy fillings. It may be noted at this point that in nineteenth-century Brussels bobbin lace the raised lines within motifs are nearly always formed of a number of threads bound together at intervals, rather than being an extension of the woven *toilé* as they had been previously.

Motifs and flowers were made in many villages throughout Belgium, but the final task of applying them to net was carried out in Brussels, in special workrooms run by the various lace manufacturers, by workers known as *striqueuses* (Fig. 4). Their task was a highly skilled one and demanded great neatness and precision: even the tiniest spot had to be sewn on by hand or stuck down exactly in the right place if the harmonious effect of the finished design were not to be spoiled. All too often the work was injurious to their health also. Usually the flowers and motifs coming from the villages were not absolutely white, but had acquired a reddish tinge from the hands of the workers. Before applying them to the net ground, the *striqueuse* had to place them in a packet of lead carbonate which she beat with her hand or the heel of her shoe to work the powder into the lace and whiten it. The motifs emerged a brilliant white but, as Mrs Bury Palliser noted (*History of Lace*, p. 121), this was all too likely to turn black if the lace was, for example, "laid in trunks or wardrobes in contact with flannel or other woollen tissues bleached with sulphur". Mrs. Bury Palliser goes on to say that "bottles containing scent, the sea air or a heated room will produce the same disagreeable change, and the colour is with difficulty restored".

The beginning of the manufacture of machine-made net seemed at first to be a grave threat to the lace industry, but Belgian manufacturers did not take long to realize that in one respect at least the products of the machines might be turned to the advantage of the hand-made lace workers, for the net could be utilized as a background for application. This change to a machine-made ground did not at first oust the skilled work of the *drocheleuse* completely. A considerable number of pieces of application of the 1820s and 1830s, including veils as well as borders and flounces, still have a ground of

FIG. 4. *Les striqueuses.* (Turgan: *Les Grandes Usines,* Vol. V,
1867, p. 242.)

the beautiful *drochel* (Pl. 24), which was prized for its great delicacy
and suppleness far surpassing those of machine-made net. But its
days were inevitably numbered. Although it continued to be
made to a limited extent in the middle years of the century and was
shown as a prestige item in exhibitions in the 1850s and 1860s,
its great costliness placed it out of the reach of all but the richest
buyers. Mrs. Bury Palliser noted that in the late 1860s it was made
for royal orders only, and by the end of the century it was extinct.

It seems to have been in the 1830s that machine-made net, by then
being produced in quantity by a firm in Brussels itself (p. 257), began

to be used on a really large scale for application. The machine-net was, of course, made of cotton and it was at this time, too, that cotton began to replace linen as the main material of which the motifs were made. Characteristic design motifs of the second quarter of the century—the delicately drawn sprays of flowers which often had a rather Turkish flavour—were arranged in rows to form borders to the favourite bonnet-veils of the period, or flounces and border lace. The actual edge of the lace was often composed of a row of leaves or flowers and similar motifs might be arranged over the rest of the field. An enlarged detail of Brussels application on a machine-net ground is shown on Plate 25.

In the 1840s these motifs began to give way before bolder designs of flowers often entwined with ribbons or arranged amongst strap-work (Pl. 26). By the end of this decade the manufacture of application was expanding rapidly. It was about then, for example, that the lace-makers of Binche went over to making lace flowers for application, a more profitable line than their traditional product. The flowers made at Binche, with those of Liederkerke, were reckoned to vie with those of Brussels as the most beautiful and some Binche flowers were sent to Paris to be made up (see p. 85).

In 1851 the Jury of the Great Exhibition noted (*Report*, p. 1024): "Since the great improvements which have been made in producing this beautiful lace at so considerable a reduction in price, the demand for it has become very general and it is now worn by nearly all ladies of rank and fashion." A typical design of the early 1850s was shown by A. Delahaye (Fig. 5), while the more elaborate style of the second half of the 1850s is illustrated by the beautiful mantle from the Boymans Museum, Rotterdam (Pl. 27), which displays to perfection the precision and delicacy of these complex designs produced on such a large scale. In addition to such impressive pieces, quantities of more ordinary lace were produced, notably flounces and borders of all widths, handkerchief borders, caps, and so on. All too often the design of smaller borders is banal and uninspired, but the fact that lace of this type has survived in such large quantities shows how successful the Belgian manufacturers were in appealing to a wide market.

Two shawls shown by the Compagnie des Indes at the Paris Exhibition of 1867 exemplify the most sophisticated designs of the Second Empire (Pl. 28). There can be no doubt that they were the work of French designers.   In its report on this exhibition the Jury noted that though the production of application lace was being constantly improved, it was, in fact, beginning to decline a little in public favour, and not so much was produced as formerly.   The collapse of the Second Empire in 1870 and the cessation of the fashion for large shawls and mantles of lace were both serious blows to the application lace trade.   To quote the example of Binche again, Verhaegen notes (in *La Dentelle et la Broderie sur Tulle*, 1902) that after 1870 the making of flowers for application dwindled rapidly

FIG. 5. Brussels application lace shown by Delahaye at the Great Exhibition of 1851. (*Art Journal Catalogue*, p. 208.)

there and the workers became absorbed by other industries.   An attempt to revive the lace industry in Binche in 1893 came to nothing.

Nevertheless, application continued to be made to the end of the century.   Narrow borders, handkerchiefs and lappets or neckties of application are often found bearing the rather stiff designs borrowed from the eighteenth century which were characteristic of the 1880s and 1890s.   Another favourite use for application was for large wedding veils; Brussels lace was, indeed, the favourite choice of rich brides to the end of the century.   Such veils are often exceedingly sumptuous (Pl. 29).   In design they unite the patterned strapwork derived from mid-nineteenth-century design with bunches of flowers, often more delicately drawn now, or with tightly-drawn rococo ornament. Their technique is usually of a well-nigh incredible *finesse*, while the contrasting effects of bobbin- and needle-made motifs are exploited most subtly to give light and shade to the design. Though the quantity of application produced at this period may have been much diminished, the best of it cannot be surpassed in point of quality.

A study of the catalogues of the international exhibitions held in London and Paris in the 1850s and 1860s reveals that a large number of firms were engaged in the manufacture of Brussels application lace. The majority, situated in Brussels itself, are listed below, with an indication of which exhibitions they contributed to (addresses are given where known):

Buchholtz & Co., 3 rue Léopold.	London, 1862, 1874; Paris, 1867.
Ed. Clément-Lambin & Eugénie Eggermont, 1 rue des Charbonniers.	Paris, 1867.
Compagnie des Indes (Verdé, Delisle & Cie.) 94 rue Royale and 80 rue Richelieu, Paris.	London, 1862; Paris, 1855 (as Geffrier-Valmez **et** Delisle Frères), 1867.
C. Coppin, 18 rue du Progrès	Paris, 1867.
J. Custodi-Besme, 41 rue du Pepin	London, 1862.
Damières-Petitjean, 52 rue Ruysbroeck	London, 1862; Paris, 1867.
Sophie Defrenne, 58 rue de Laeken	London, 1862 (as C. Reinheimer); Paris, 1855.
A. Delahaye (successor to A. Ducpetiaux & Son)	London, 1851
B. Duhaijon, Brussels and Ypres	London, 1851; Paris 1855 (as Duhaijon, Brunfaut & Cie.).
Everaert Sœurs, 12 rue des Dominicains	London, 1851, 1862; Paris, 1855, 1867.
Francfort et Élie, 23 rue Neuve	Paris, 1867.
V. Ghysels, 18 rue de la Madeleine	London, 1862.
N. J. Gregoir-Geloen, 66 rue Fossé-aux-Loups	London, 1862.
Hensscheun, Van Eeckhout & Co., Brussels and 38 rue Notre-Dame des Victoires, Paris (*See also* under Rosset & Normand)	London, 1851; Paris, 1855 (as Van Eeckhout & Co.).
Houtman & Christiaens, 19 Boulevard de l'Abbattoir	Paris, 1867.
Hutellier, 21 rue de la Chancellerie	London, 1862.
H. Keymeulen, 22 rue Neuve	London, 1862.
C. Minne-Dansaert, 3 rue du Béguinage	London, 1862.
Naeltjeus, Brussels	London, 1851.
L. Robyt, Brussels	London, 1851.
Henri Roosen (Maison Seclet-Vancutsen), 99 rue Neuve	London, 1862.

Rosset & Normand, Brussels	Paris, 1855, 1867 (as Normand & Chandon, 21 rue de Malines and 38 rue Nôtre-Dame des Victoires Paris).
Épouse P. F. Sasse, 2 rue de l'Infirmerie	London, 1862.
Schuermans & Ibro, 8 rue du Boulevard	London, 1862.
J. Strehler, 24 rue du Poinçon	London, 1862; Paris, 1867.
Eugénie Van Caulaert-Stienon, 44 rue de Ligne	London, 1862.
Van der Haegen Van Overloop, 61 rue Neuve	London, 1851, 1862.
Van der Kelen-Bresson, Brussels	London, 1851; Paris, 1855.
V. Van der Smissen, 14 rue du Jardin Botannique	London, 1851, 1862.

In addition, a few firms outside Brussels also exhibited application lace:

Léon Lefebure, 37 rue Neuve, Alost	Paris, 1867.
Van der Smissen-Van der Bossche, Place Impériale, Alost	London, 1862; Paris, 1867.
Eykens-Mendés (firme T. Mendés), 2 Maaldery Straat, Antwerp	Paris, 1867.
Mme. Mabilde Plettinck, Ghent	London, 1851.
J. T. Haeck, Destelberghe, nr. Ghent	London, 1851.

Point Duchesse

Application was one of the most luxurious and expensive products of the Belgian lace-makers; the lace known as *point Duchesse*, on the other hand, was developed to meet the demands of a wider and perhaps less discerning public. *Point Duchesse*, which has survived in extremely large amounts, consists of rather coarse leaves, flowers and other motifs joined together by *brides* (bars) without any mesh ground. Sometimes the motifs were composed of a bobbin-made tape (*lacet*), twisted into shape and secured by sewing, sometimes they were made to shape on the pillow. The latter show the usual characteristics of Brussels bobbin lace: the use of a close (whole-stitch) or more open (half-stitch) *toilé* and the emphasis of edges and details by a raised edge or by a line of thick threads bound together at intervals. Two different varieties of *point Duchesse* may be distinguished: *Duchesse de Bruxelles*, which is of finer quality and incorporates panels of needlepoint lace of *point de gaze* type, and *Duchesse de Bruges*, consisting of bobbin-made lace only. As these names imply, production of *point Duchesse* was centred on Brussels and Bruges, particularly the latter.

Point Duchesse seems to have been developed in the 1840s. In its early stages the lace was commonly made of bobbin-made *lacets*, as Verhaegen notes (*La Dentelle et La Broderie sur Tulle*, p. 165). These were arranged to form patterns of scrolls and flowers of a rather crude type. The lace, being comparatively quick and easy to make, was also inexpensive and thus achieved a quick success. Its hard-wearing qualities no doubt also endeared it to careful purchasers as well as ensuring its survival to the present time.

This initial success encouraged the manufacturers to develop the lace by improving the technique, i.e. making the motifs on the pillow instead of from *lacets* and adding portions of needlepoint lace. The name *Duchesse* was given to the lace in the 1850s in honour of Marie-Henriette, Duchesse de Brabant, who later became Queen of the Belgians. The manufacture seems to have spread to other centres at this time. In 1855, M. Paridant of Aerschot was awarded a medal at the Paris Exhibition for "dentelles, dites *duchesses*", an indication that the name was a recent invention. In the following decade a Ghent firm, Delphine Beels & Sœurs, showed "nouvelle duchesse de Gand, point breveté", at the Paris Exhibition of 1867. Typical borders of the third quarter of the century are illustrated on Pl. 30.

Point Duchesse went on to enjoy great popularity during the rest of the nineteenth century. It was sometimes spoken of as being similar to Honiton lace and it does, indeed, resemble it in technique (cf. Pl. 44), but it is generally much coarser in execution. The lace was particularly well adapted to coarser designs of the revived rococo type which became so very popular in the last quarter of the century. Its rather heavy appearance also found favour at that time, so that the manufacture of *point Duchesse* of both types was in a very flourishing state right to the end of the century. There were, of course, very considerable differences of quality in these laces. Some of the best pieces reach a high standard and, though their designs may be stereotyped, they are nonetheless attractive for their boldness (Pl. 31). At the other end of the scale are the banal repetitions of coarse rose-like flowers and trefoil leaves to be found on innumerable handkerchiefs and collars.

Duchesse de Bruges was, on the whole, rather less fine in quality than *Duchesse de Bruxelles*, but even at its worst it should not be confused with *dentelle de Bruges*, a very coarse form of bobbin lace made of thick threads in designs of crudely-drawn flower motifs sewn together to form a pattern.

Point Duchesse, not being one of the finest of Belgian laces, is mentioned only rarely in exhibition catalogues. All the large firms in Brussels dealt in it, but generally did not choose to give it any great prominence in their entries in the catalogues. It was made, too, by numerous small concerns which seldom figured in exhibitions. Two such have already been mentioned. In the *Catalogue of the Paris Exhibition of 1867* two more firms are specifically stated to have shown *point Duchesse*: Palmyre Mabesoone & Sœurs, Saint-André-les-Bruges, whose display consisted entirely of this lace, and Eykens-Mendés of Antwerp, who showed it with other cheaper laces and a little needlepoint.

Point d'Angleterre

This name was commonly applied in the eighteenth century to Brussels lace in order to conceal its place of origin for smuggling purposes. It lingered on into the nineteenth century, when Brussels application is sometimes referred to as "application d'Angleterre". In the second half of the century, manufacturers of application and *point de gaze* revived the name again and gave it to a new kind of lace of mixed technique. This *point d'Angleterre* consisted of bobbin-made motifs, often enriched the needle-made fillings, united by a needle-made mesh ground of *point de gaze* type. It was expensive to make and was normally reserved for small, rather choice articles such as handkerchiefs, small neckties and so on. One firm at least, Minne-Dansaert, is known to have made a speciality of this kind of lace (Pl. 32). There is, in the Musées Royaux d'Art et d'Histoire in Brussels, a wide flounce made by this firm which was offered to Pope Leo XIII on the occasion of his jubilee in 1887. The designs of *point d'Angleterre* seem to have been mainly floral in character.

BOBBIN LACES

Valenciennes

Brussels application and *point de gaze* were the prestige products of the Belgian lace industry, with the cheaper *Duchesse* laces following them closely in style. More important commercially than any of

these was Valenciennes bobbin lace, which was, in fact, the chief
branch of the Belgian lace trade in the third quarter of the nineteenth
century. A certain amount of Valenciennes had been made in
Ypres in the eighteenth century, but it did not assume any importance until the nineteenth century, when Belgium took the lead in
this manufacture after it had been given up in Valenciennes itself
and reduced to an industry of very minor proportions in France as a
whole (see pp. 71–2).

The Valenciennes technique was quite different from that of
Brussels bobbin lace. In the latter the flowers and decorative
motifs were made separately and the mesh ground was worked
afterwards in the spaces between, the threads of the mesh being
carried in bunches across the back of the motifs. In Valenciennes,
on the other hand, the lace was made all in one piece, motifs and
ground together, exactly the same number of threads being used all
the way through the process of making the lace. It was distinguished
by a very white, closely-woven *toilé*. For this a great many threads
were needed and, in order to use them up in the ground, a very
strong mesh was evolved with plaited strands on all four sides
forming a diamond-shape, with a round hole in the middle of each
diamond. The lace was always very expensive as its manufacture
was a slow and difficult process.

Lace of this type in the favourite patterns of the late eighteenth
century, small flowers scattered over a mesh ground above a narrow
border of scrolls, flowers or similar motifs, continued to be made
around Ypres and in other parts of both East and West Flanders up
to the 1830s. According to M. Félix Aubry (*Rapport sur les dentelles,
etc., 1851*, published at Paris in 1854), it was M. Félix Duhaijon-
Brunfaut of Ypres who, in 1833, decided that the time had come to
revitalize this industry. The changes he introduced were radical:
new designs more in accordance with the taste of the nineteenth
century for bolder floral effects were carried out in an adapted
version of the old technique. It was deemed necessary not only to
give the lace a greater appeal by emphasizing the contrast between a
densely white pattern and a cobwebby ground, but also to make its production both quicker and cheaper. To achieve this the practice was
adopted of adding threads to form the *toilé*. These would be carried
over at the back of the work, like those of the mesh ground in Brussels
bobbin lace, while the work was in progress, and the redundant

threads cut away after the lace was finished. This also meant that a lighter type of ground could be made and it was at this period that the airy diamond-shaped meshes, by which nineteenth century Valenciennes can easily be distinguished from that of the eighteenth-century, came into being (Pl. 33).

The new technique became popular at once, both with the workers and the public, and a wave of prosperity swept through the industry, gathering more and more momentum during the 1840s. In *L'Exposé de la situation de la Flandre orientale*, published in 1851 (quoted by Verhaegen: *La Dentelle et la Broderie sur Tulle*, 1902, p. 110), it was stated that since 1840 no less than 301 new lace schools had been founded there, and that more than half of these were devoted exclusively to teaching the Valenciennes technique. In Western Flanders the increase in the size of the industry and the number of workers was even more marked. Enormous quantities of Valenciennes lace were exported to France, particularly the better varieties. England and Germany were good markets too and the United States began to be exploited as a market in the 1850s.

In the *Report of the Jury of the Great Exhibition of 1851* there appeared a description of this by now extremely flourishing industry. The principal centres were Ypres, Menin, Courtrai, Bruges, Ghent and Alost, each town producing a slightly different type of lace. The best laces, i.e. those with the finest mesh and closest *toilé*, came from Ypres. There Valenciennes was made in greater widths than elsewhere, the most expensive types costing, at that time, up to £50 a yard. In 1851 there were about 20,000 lace workers in and around Ypres, most of their products being intended for the export market. Bruges specialized in laces of "good, useful quality, suitable for trimmings and much sought after by English buyers". Ghent made good quality laces mostly in narrow and medium widths, and Menin and Courtrai also produced laces of medium quality. The Jury noted that the Alost designs were inferior to those of Ypres and the lace was not of such a good colour.

Among the firms who exhibited were Duhaijon-Brunfaut of Brussels and Ypres (it may be noted here that in 1855 M. Duhaijon-Brunfaut was awarded a medal at the Paris Exhibition for his services to the lace industry), P. H. Hammelrath of Ypres, S. Soenen of Ypres, Beck & Son of Courtrai, John Denblauu-Peel of Courtrai,

Bernaert & H. de Cuyper of Courtrai and Van Straelen, Director of the Poor School at Bruges.

The designs of the 1840s and 1850s echo those of Brussels laces, the main elements being swags, ribbons, strapwork and flowers. (Pl. 33). They are often of a less complex character owing to the exigencies of the technique used. As well as the beautiful wide borders, quantities of narrow edgings and insertions were turned out and Verhaegen notes (in *La Dentelle et la Broderie sur Tulle*, 1902) that for these favourite traditional designs were often used. These were distinguished by old names such as "la Tulipe", "la Croix de Courtrai", "le Grain de Blé", "la Grappe de Raisin", "le Chapeau de Curé". Verhaegen notes too that an important part of the export trade to France was the peasant market of Normandy and the south of France around Arles and Perpignan, and it was no doubt laces of this kind that adorned the headgear of peasant women in these areas.

In the 1850s some fresh innovations were made in the Valenciennes technique. The open net-like half-stitch of Brussels lace was introduced into the solid parts of the design in order to create the effects of light and shade that played such an important part in all lace design at this time. The lower border on Pl. 33 shows the use of this technique. A final stage in the borrowings from Brussels bobbin lace was the adoption of the method of making the motifs first and working the net ground round them afterwards. Lace of this type, distinguished by the greatest possible contrast between pattern and ground, was known as *Valenciennes de Gand* (Ghent) or *Valenciennes de Brabant* (Pl. 34).

The industry continued to flourish throughout the 1860s. At the International Exhibition of 1862 in London, Valenciennes lace was shown by Buchholtz & Co. of Brussels, P. Mullie-Truyffaut of Courtrai, Van der Smissen-Van den Bossche of Brussels, A. J. Boeteman of Bruges, N. J. Gregoir-Geloen of Brussels and Ypres and Vanderplancke Sœurs of Courtrai. The Jury Report noted that this was still the most prosperous and important branch of the Belgian lace industry. During the 1860s great progress was made by the manufacturers of Courtrai in improving their Valenciennes lace. Writing of the Valenciennes shown at the Paris Exhibition of 1867, Mrs. Bury Palliser noted (*History of Lace*, p. 131) that the widest borders came from Courtrai and Ypres. The display included a piece in process of manufacture in which there were no less than 1,200 bobbins on the pillow. Even this was exceeded by a parasol cover shown by a Courtrai firm at the South Kensington Exhibition of 1874, in which there were 8,000 bobbins. Such exhibition pieces were, of course, fantastically expensive and far beyond the reach of ordinary buyers. At Paris in 1867, all the manufacturers of Ypres united to put on a joint display. A Courtrai firm which first appeared on the exhibition scene at this time was J. Vandezande-Goemare.

But the prosperity of the Valenciennes manufacture was not destined to last. It was an easy lace to imitate by machinery and throughout the third quarter of the century imitation Valenciennes was appearing on the market in ever-increasing amounts and gradually ousting the more expensive hand-made edgings and insertions. The collapse of the Second Empire affected the industry most adversely at the time when competition from machine-made lace was becoming really serious. Valenciennes of all qualities went on being made until the end of the nineteenth century, but in ever-diminishing quantity. In 1902 Verhaegen noted (*op. cit.*) that, except for in Bruges, the Valenciennes industry had retreated from the towns to country areas. Only the old workers were able to make Valenciennes of really good quality, the younger ones making narrow insertions and borders which had little hope of competing with machine products for much longer.

Chantilly lace

Ample evidence has already been given of the great adaptability of Belgian lace manufacturers to changes in fashion. The introduction of the manufacture of Chantilly lace into Belgium is another success story on the same theme. According to Mrs. Bury Palliser (*History of Lace*, p. 134), the manufacture of black silk bobbin lace was introduced by a M. Lepage into Grammont and Enghien in the years before 1840. Formerly cheap white lace in linen thread had been made there. The new manufacture took hold rapidly and by the time of the Great Exhibition of 1851 a Grammont firm, Stocquart Frères, was able to show "shawls, half-shawls and scarfs of black silk lace. Mantilla. Veils. Berthe. Parasols, head-dresses, etc." The lace was produced very cheaply and was thus able to compete with French Chantilly though it was actually of inferior quality. Heavier black silk laces of "Spanish" type were also made.

The manufacture prospered very much in the 1850s and 1860s and more or less ousted the older types of lace. Verhaegen states (*La Dentelle et la Broderie sur Tulle*, p. 142) that in 1851 forty-nine of the lace schools in Grammont were teaching the Chantilly technique exclusively. During this period the manufacture spread to Oudenarde as well. Examples of Belgian Chantilly were shown at the International Exhibition of 1862 in London by Bruyneel aîné, J. G. Lepage-Kina, Stocquart Frères, and Saligo-Van den Berghe, all of Grammont, and by Sœurs Everaert of Brussels. At Paris in 1867 all the firms in Grammont joined together to put on a display of black Chantilly lace. In addition to those already mentioned were included: Brecx-Van Bockstaele, Charles Bruyneel, Byl Frères, Auguste Caron, Bernard de Groote, J. Dekeyzer-Weyenberge, Denis de l'Arbre (formerly de l'Arbre Vrancx), Delil-Pieret, P. Demeulemeester-Decrick, Victor Demoyer, F. De Moyer-Ghysselink, De Ruyter-Vanderdonckt, Adrien Deschauwer, Veuve d'Hont, Veuve J. B. Diericx, A. Fontaine-Liottier, Ghys-Bruyneel, Graven-Buyserie, Veuve Leclerq, Désiré Lefebure, Maillet Frères & Sœurs, P. J. Pacquay-De Ruyter, Adolphe Pauvels-van Belleghem, Rosalie Rens, Robyn-Stocquart, Roemart-Ghysbrecht, Amédée van Belleghem, Van Caenegem-Declerq, Louis van Caezeele, C. van Cranbrugghe-Vandenberghe, T. Vanderdonckt, Veuve Van der Snickt-Devos, V. Vansteendamme, Van Wette & Sœurs, P. van Wymersch, H. Wittocx.

The various Jury Reports note a continuing improvement in quality; indeed, the Jury at Paris in 1867 magnanimously stated that the Chantilly of Grammont had improved out of all recognition as well as having increased its trade five times over since 1855, mainly by developing the American market. Although in quality Belgian Chantilly was still inferior to French, its grounds being coarser and the general effect of the lace flatter and less lively as the relief threads were not so carefully put in and less attention was paid to effects of shading, nevertheless it was able to be competitive because of its cheapness and the regularity of the work, the good quality of silk used and the careful choice of designs. An example of Grammont lace of about 1870 is a fan mount (Pl. 35) in the Boymans Museum in Rotterdam. This is illustrated by A. Carlier de Lantsheere

(*Les Dentelles à la Main*, p. 56) as by Ghys-Bruyneel of Grammont. Without some clear indication of this sort it is not possible nowadays to distinguish the Chantilly of Grammont from that made in France.

If Belgian Chantilly shared the prosperity of that of France, it was destined also to suffer the same fate. The collapse of the Second Empire and increased machine competition were both severe blows in the early 1870s. Most merchants were left at this time with huge stocks on their hands and many of them went bankrupt. The industry never recovered its former prosperity, although a few firms continued to produce black silk lace, in spite of the fact that most of the workers either changed over to making other types of lace such as *point Duchesse* or else left the industry altogether. Some comments by Samuel Murphy of the Waterford School of Art, who visited Mme. Lepage-Depape of Grammont in 1887, show how dependent the industry was on France: "The designs are made in simple outline by professional designers in Paris. . . . The payment for designs is at the rate of 3 francs (2/6) for a repeat of about 4″ × 3″." Efforts were still directed to producing work of the highest possible quality: "The workers are under the supervision of Madame Lepage, who does not hesitate to reject work which she considers below proper standard" (MS Report in Victoria and Albert Museum Library).

Towards the end of the century a modest revival occurred in the Grammont industry. Merchants found a market for their old stock and even began to produce new pieces. But few workers now remained in the industry and it was never again possible for the lace-makers of Grammont to compete with the machines.

Mechlin lace

Mechlin bobbin lace, like Valenciennes, was made all in one piece on the pillow. Its characteristic features were a six-sided mesh ground, similar to that of Brussels bobbin lace, and a delicate *toilé*, the motifs being outlined by a thicker thread or *cordonnet*. Mechlin was greatly favoured in the eighteenth century for its lightness and delicacy. The industry suffered heavily at the time of the French Revolution, however, and never really recovered its former vitality.

Mechlin was just as difficult to make as Valenciennes and even more costly, two factors which told against it in the nineteenth century. In the earlier part of the century the workers carried on making the old designs—borders edged with a line of flowers and

26. Two Borders of Brussels Application Lace: *top,* bobbin lace applied to machine-made net; *bottom,* needlepoint and bobbin lace applied to machine-made net; Belgian, mid 19th century. *Dutch Royal Collection on loan to the Rijksmuseum, Amsterdam* (Nos. R.B.K.J.309, 232, 21; R.B.K.J.230).

27. Mantle of Brussels Bobbin Lace applied to machine-made net, Belgian, *c.* 1855-60. *Museum Boymans-van Beuningen, Rotterdam.*

28. Shawls of Brussels Application Lace shown by Verdé-Delisle Frères (Compagnie des Indes) at the Paris International Exhibition of 1867. *Art Journal Catalogue.*

29. Detail of Wedding Veil, Brussels bobbin and needlepoint lace applied to machine-made net, Belgian, *c.* 1890-1900. *Musees Royaux d'Art et d'Histoire, Brussels* (No.3397).

30. Two Borders of Bobbin Lace, point Duchesse, Beligian, second half of the 19th century. *Dutch Royal Collection on loan to the Rijksmuseum, Amsterdam* (Nos. R.B.K.J.174 B and C).

31. Panel for the Front of a Dress, bobbin and needlepoint lace, *Duchesse de Bruxelles*, Belgian, late 19th century. *Musées Royaux d'Art et d'Histoire, Brussels* (No.3454).

32. Handkerchief, bobbin and needlepoint lace, *point d'Angleterre,* made by Minne-Dansaert, Belgian, late 19th century. *Musées Royaux d'Art et d'Histoire, Brussels* (No.979).

33. Two borders of Valenciennes Bobbin Lace, Belgian, second half of the 19th century. *Dutch Royal Collection on loan to the Rijksmuseum, Amsterdam* (Nos. R.B.K.J.262, 265).

34. Handkerchief of Valenciennes Bobbin Lace, *Valenciennes de Gand,* Belgian, late 19th century. *Musees Royaux d'Art et d'Histoire, Brussels* (No.1534).

35. Fan Mount of Chantilly Black Silk Bobbin Lace, made by Ghys-Bruyneel of Grammont, Belgian, c. 1870. *Museum Boymans-van Beuningen, Rotterdam* (No.227).

36. Border of Mechlin Bobbin Lace, Belgian, second half of the 19th century. *Musées Royaux d'Art et d'Histoire, Brussels* (No. 1743).

with other flowers dotted about on the mesh ground—in ever narrower widths. Mrs. Bury Palliser noted (*History of Lace*, p. 125) that in 1834 there were only eight firms left making Mechlin lace.

Nevertheless, in the late 1840s and the 1850s it enjoyed something of a revival and even made an appearance at the Great Exhibition of 1851, where a Miss Van Kiel of Mechlin showed a head-dress, collar and veil in this lace, and a M. P. Pasteyner of Louvain showed a scarf. It is clear from the nature of these exhibits that the workers had by this time adopted the method which was to enable them to produce objects of considerable size. They made the lace in narrow bands which were joined together by the stitch known as *point de raccroc* used in Chantilly and Brussels lace. These joins are usually made with such care that it is impossible to detect them with the naked eye. Mechlin lace of the nineteenth century has the same technical characteristics as that of the eighteenth, but is generally much slighter and flatter in appearance owing to its being made of cotton thread. It often seems rather characterless as a result, although frequently quite fine in execution. The designs tended to preserve the old floral tradition with only a few echoes of current taste (Pl. 36). The lace was made at Turnhout as well as at Mechlin itself.

The revival was very shortlived, however. At the Paris Exhibition of 1867 a collection of Mechlin lace was shown by Jean Van Loco of Turnhout, but this was more a reminder of past achievements than an indication of present prosperity. The Jury noted, indeed, that the renewed interest in this lace had already died away and that very little was now being made.

By the end of the century the lace-industry at Mechlin itself had disappeared, in spite of an attempt to revive it in 1873. A certain amount of Mechlin lace was still being made at Turnhout, but Verhaegen notes (*La Dentelle et la Broderie sur Tulle*, p. 131) that it was generally of inferior quality and doomed to extinction, as only three workers remained who knew how to make working patterns of new designs for the lace-makers.

Point de Lille and Point de Paris

These two bobbin laces are very similar in technique and style to Mechlin lace, though less fine and quicker to produce. In both cases the mesh grounds were much easier to make than that of

Mechlin: Lille having a simple hexagonal mesh (cf. Pl. 18) and *point de Paris* an open mesh of six-pointed star shapes (cf. Pl. 17). Both were made in the areas around Antwerp and Turnhout where some Mechlin lace was also made. The manufacture was introduced in the eighteenth century and continued throughout the nineteenth mainly because these laces relied for the most part on a stable and unchanging market.

At Turnhout were made narrow borders in best-quality lace, usually in traditional patterns, which found a market in France. Otherwise these laces were designed expressly for the Dutch peasant market, indeed the workers sometimes referred to the lace as "Dutscheslag" (Dutch net). The designs bore no relation to current fashion for it was their unchanging, traditional aspect that endeared them to their purchasers and ensured a steady sale. They were usually rather coarse and countrified, featuring large floral motifs. Typical patterns were derived from the favourite vase of flowers motif of coarse eighteenth-century laces known as "pottekant". In the Musées Royaux d'Art et d'Histoire in Brussels is a collection of lace of this type from the firm of E. Van Miegem of Beveren-Waes. A characteristic example is illustrated in M. Risselin-Steenebrugen's *Dentelles Belges, 19ᵉ–20ᵉ Siècles*, Pl. XXXI.

Away from the traditional centres of manufacture of this type of lace, some crude narrow borders in similar technique were made in the province of Namur and in Luxembourg. *Point de Paris* was occasionally produced in black silk, but white cotton was the material most commonly employed. Verhaegen notes (in *La Dentelle et la Broderie sur Tulle*, 1902) that towards the end of the nineteenth century, M. Carlier, a Brussels lace merchant, introduced into these areas the making of a lace of *point de Lille* type in coarser thread to use for furnishing purposes.

Guipure de Flandre and related laces

Guipure de Flandre began its career in the late 1840s like *point Duchesse* which bore some resemblance to it in its early stages. According to Verhaegen (*La Dentelle et la Broderie sur Tulle*, p. 161), it was the invention of a Mlle. Marie van Outryve d'Ydewalle and it arose out of her wish to copy an old guipure lace of the seventeenth century which she had seen on an altar-cloth in Bruges. By studying the old lace she developed a version of the technique which she taught to the nuns of a convent at Ruddervoorde in about 1846. She made the designs herself with the aid of her brother-in-law, Baron Béthune. The lace consisted of flowers and other motifs made of bobbin-made tapes which were united by *brides* (bars) and decorated with fillings either bobbin or needle made. The lace was generally made in designs of a distinct seventeenth century flavour. It was not difficult to make and it was, therefore, easy enough to keep the price low.

The new lace soon caught on in the public favour and the manufacture spread to all the regions round Bruges, Iseghem and Thielt. The technique had improved sufficiently by 1867 for the lace to be accorded a special mention by the Jury of the Paris Exhibition of that year (*Report*, p. 240), which noted that, although the designs were rich and heavy, yet the lace preserved an appearance of lightness and a graceful elegance.

This type of lace enjoyed a great success in the last quarter of the century when heavier laces began to be really fashionable. Indeed, many imitations of seventeenth-century laces of Milanese type were made at this time which it is virtually impossible to distinguish from the originals, so refined is their technique. Other less imitative designs in this technique often have a certain boldness which can make them quite attractive (Pl. 37).

At the other end of the scale were types of lace that were quick and easy to make but coarse and unattractive in appearance. A type known as *Dentelle Renaissance* was made with a thicker *lacet* which was very often machine-made and sometimes slightly patterned. Another type of lace made with machine-made *lacets* was ornamented with reliefs and fillings coarsely worked in bottonhole stitch in thick threads. This was known as *Luxueil*. Both these varieties were made in great quantities in the 1880s and 1890s when they had a considerable vogue. The workers liked to make them because the work was easy and brought in quick returns. Indeed, they felt able to compete with the machines by producing these crude laces, which yet preserved some of the *cachet* attached to the word "hand-made". But the vogue was shortlived, as any such vogue must be, and by the time it was over many of the workers had partially lost their old skills and were unable to return to making finer types of lace. It may be noted, however, that a debased form of *Luxueil* still figures prominently among the productions of the remaining lace-makers in Belgium at the present time, and that this type of lace has always enjoyed a considerable success in the American market.

Verhaegen notes (*La Dentelle et la Broderie sur Tulle*, 1902, pp. 162–3) that in 1899 and 1900 *guipure de Flandre* made in linen thread or in ecru-coloured cotton enjoyed a tremendous vogue, to the extent that whole dresses were sometimes made of it. The lace was given a raised appearance by the addition of a very thick *cordonnet* to some parts of the design. It owed its success at this time to the fact that from a short distance it looked like the Venetian needlepoint currently enjoying a great vogue, while being, in fact, very much cheaper.

Torchon and Cluny laces

Torchon is the easiest of all types of bobbin lace to make and, indeed, it was usually made by children and apprentices at the start of their training. Cluny guipure (see pp. 83–4) was an innovation of the second half of the nineteenth century and represents an equally simple type of technique. Both laces were made in all the lace-making areas of Belgium, but especially in Bruges, Ypres, Courtrai, Ingelmunster, Aeltre, Beveren, Tamise and Turnhout. Specially good varieties were made around two villages in the Ardennes, Aye and Marche, the productions of the former serving mainly for the decoration of church furnishings and vestments in the neighbourhood. Sometimes torchons of coloured threads were made in these areas.

By the end of the nineteenth century these simple types were the most commonly made laces in Belgium, but the manufacture was declining and the prices paid for the lace rapidly becoming lower and lower. It is not possible now to distinguish torchon and Cluny made in these areas from that in production elsewhere, although it seems that it was on the whole less fine than that of Le Puy in France.

NEEDLEPOINT LACES

Point de gaze

In the first half of the nineteenth century fine needlepoint was used in combination with bobbin lace in Brussels application (Pl. 24).

In the *Report of the Jury of the 1851 Exhibition*, however, there
occurs for the first time a mention of "the new kind of real Brussels
(the 'gaze point')". Mrs. Bury Palliser gives a good description of
some of the main features of *point de gaze* (*History of Lace*, p. 123),
noting that it was "the most filmy and delicate of all point laces.
Its forms are not accentuated by a raised outline in buttonhole
stitching, as in *point d'Alençon* and *point d'Argentan*, but are simply
outlined by a thread. The execution is more open and slight than
in early lace, and part of the toilé is made in close, part in open-
stitch to give an appearance of shading." Another characteristic of
point de gaze was the variety of delicate filling stitches. One type, a
series of tiny round dots or *perles*, was almost invariably used to
ornament the centres of flowers, especially the roses which are so
characteristic of this lace. These roses were often accentuated by
being given a double or triple layer of partly detached petals,
creating a relief effect as well as a white highlight. The cobwebby
effect of *point de gaze* was further enhanced by the extremely delicate
needlepoint mesh used for the ground. This was composed of semi-
circular loops of thread, each hanging from the one above (Pl. 38).
The loops were never strengthened by the addition of a second
thread such as was used to produce the characteristic rectangular
mesh of *point d'Alençon* (Pl. 10). Mrs. Bury Palliser notes (*op. cit.*)
that: "It is made in small pieces, the joining concealed by small
sprigs or leaves, after the manner of the old point, the same lace-
worker executing the whole strip from beginning to end." These
small pieces were joined together when completed. It has already
been noted (p. 88) how the designs were cut up and handed out to
the workers.

Once introduced, *point de gaze* enjoyed an immediate success. In
design it followed Brussels application, with perhaps more emphasis
on the floral aspects. With its fragile appearance, combined with
delicate shading and realistic relief effects, it was calculated to
have the maximum appeal to the fashionable public of the nineteenth
century. By the end of the 1860s, Mrs. Bury Palliser was able to
write (*op. cit.*): "Point gaze is now brought to the highest perfection
and the specimens in the Paris Exhibition of 1867 were remarkable
for the precision of the work, the variety and richness of the 'jours'
and the clearness of the ground." The Jury of 1867 noted that
while Brussels application was beginning to decline, the production

of *point de gaze* was still expanding rapidly and gaining in prosperity. In the Metropolitan Museum of Art, New York, there is a piece of *point de gaze* of this period which illustrates the floral style to perfection (Pl. 39). Another piece of the same design is in the Hermitage Museum, Leningrad. This lace is of the same design as a piece of black Chantilly lace shown at Paris in 1867 by Verdé, Delisle & Cie. (Compagnie des Indes), showing that French designs could on occasion serve equally well for very different types of lace.

Like application, Brussels needlepoint continued to be made to the end of the century, albeit on a reduced scale after 1870. Although Brussels itself had previously been the principal centre of manufacture of *point de gaze*, in the last two decades of the century, lace-making gradually died out there and manufacturers were forced to rely more and more on workers in country districts. As with application, however, the quality of the lace was by no means diminished at this period, as is clear from a splendid fan mount in the Musées Royaux d'Art et d'Histoire at Brussels (Pl. 40). This design by Leon Sacré won a prize at an industrial exhibition in Brussels in 1883–4. It shows the characteristic revived rococo style of the period in its most perfect and accomplished form.

Most of the principal firms making Brussels application (see pp. 107–8), also made *point de gaze*, but in the various exhibition catalogues are mentioned other firms which seem to have specialized in it. These were: Mme. C. de Clippèle, 148 rue Royale, Brussels, who exhibited at Paris in 1855, where her display included a shawl in black *point de gaze*, and at London in 1862; E. J. Hoorickx, 5 and 6 rue de la Chancellerie, Brussels, who showed coloured *point de gaze* at London in 1862 and Paris in 1867; Mlle. Reallier of Brussels and C. F. Roy of Brussels who both exhibited at London in 1851; and J. B. van Bossum, 62 rue de Mons, Hal, near Brussels, who appeared at London in 1862 and Paris in 1867.

Venetian needlepoint and other imitations

Up to the middle of the nineteenth century, Brussels itself had always been considered the source of the very best needlepoint lace in Belgium, although it was also made in the south and west of Brabant and in the area of eastern Flanders bounded by Ghent, Oudenarde, Grammont, Alost and Termonde. After the middle of the century the emphasis shifts to these areas with the gradual decline of lace-making in the capital itself.   Indeed, Verhaegen (*La Dentelle et la Broderie sur Tulle*, 1902, p. 81) notes that there were in 1902 only about 200 lace-makers left in Brussels itself and that some of these made laces other than needlepoint.

It was in the environs of Alost, Wetteren and Ghent that the production of imitations of Venetian seventeenth-century needlepoint was developed to such a high point of perfection.   That this manu-facture was well-established by the 1860s is clear from a sentence in the *Report of the Jury of the International Exhibition of 1862* (p. 4) in which "Venice Point" is included in a list of the best known types of Belgian lace shown in the Exhibition.   Two firms specifically mentioned as including it in their display were Buchholtz & Co., 3 rue Léopold, Brussels and J. Strehler of 24 rue du Poinçon, Brussels.

All types of Venetian lace, including *gros point* and *point plat*, were imitated.   Belgian imitations are notable for the excellence of their technique, which frequently stands up to a most rigorous comparison with the work of seventeenth-century lace-makers, and by their closeness in design to the models they copied.   Often the nineteenth-century laces are betrayed only by a certain rigidity and monotony of design which only becomes apparent when one has studied a very large number of pieces (Pl. 41).   In their imitations of rose point, the Belgian workers often outdid their seventeenth-century predecessors in exuberant flights of fancy, adding an incredible number of frothy ornaments to the lace while never detracting from its lightness.   None the less this nineteenth-century rose point is still often rather mechanical in appearance.   The superb technical skill of the workers could not disguise the fact that their designs were based on a tradition now no longer vital and vigorous.

These laces increased in popularity towards the end of the century and were produced in ever-increasing amounts.   Indeed, it was not unknown for wily Venetian merchants to order such laces in Belgium and sell them in Venice labelled *point de Venise* with no other com-ment, or even for unsuspecting Belgian tourists to buy them as genuine Venetian work.

The lace-makers' skill in imitation was turned to other uses at this time too.   Very careful copies of late sixteenth- and early

seventeenth-century designs, in pattern books such as those of
Vinciolo and Vecellio, were turned out in great lengths, and other
types of seventeenth-century needlepoint of French inspiration were
also copied.   Linen thread was often used for these laces, but it is not
uncommon to find such work made of cotton too, in which case it is a
comparatively simple matter to detect the nineteenth-century date
of the lace.   Cotton was not used until the 1830s for lace and it may
be distinguished from linen by inspection under a microscope,
though not by the naked eye.   Of course, nineteenth-century work
may often be detected, too, by the form it takes.   Collars, cuffs,
corsages, panels for skirts and even whole dresses of Venetian and
other imitation seventeenth-century laces are frequently of shapes
unknown in the seventeenth century.

It was not only to old needlepoint laces that the Belgian workers
applied their imitative skill, for in the 1860s they began to produce
more than passable imitations of contemporary French *point
d'Alençon* (see p. 59 and Pl. 42).   These laces, too, were characterized by a certain rigid and mechanical appearance which again
betrays their imitative character.

CHAPTER 4

ENGLAND

COMPARED with the French and Belgian hand-made lace industries, the English was of minor importance. Far smaller and much less well organized than them, it was mainly concerned with supplying the home market for, although considerable quantities of English lace were exported to the U.S.A., it could not hope to compete with French and Belgian products in most continental markets. Indeed, the more fashionable and wealthy customers in England itself also preferred to buy French and Belgian lace which was generally superior both in design and workmanship.

The story of English hand-made lace in the nineteenth century is, for the most part, that of an industry in decline, for, although at times a renewal of prosperity seemed to be beginning, such resurgences were usually shortlived and by the end of the century it was plain that the lace industry in England, if not actually extinct, was no longer a viable commercial proposition. The main cause of this collapse was, of course, the rise of the machine-made lace industry. English lace-makers had never been noted for lace of a quality equal to the finest productions of France and Belgium and therefore machine competition hit them very hard, for the machines were soon able to produce inexpensive kinds of lace much more quickly, efficiently and cheaply than the hand workers. Some hand workers attempted for a time to compete with the machines on these terms, but the effort was hopeless and foredoomed to failure.

The English lace industry was the less able to meet the challenge of machine competition because of weaknesses inherent in its organization. The industry was centred on two not very large areas of the country which were widely separated from each other. Furthermore both areas were in only indirect contact with London. There seem to have been two firms in London in the nineteenth century which concerned themselves exclusively with the lace trade. These were Groucock, Copestake, Moore & Co. (later Copestake, Moore, Crampton & Co.) of 5 Bow Churchyard, and Daniel

Biddle (later Haywards) of 81 Oxford Street. Both began as machine-made lace concerns in Nottingham and both dealt in all kinds of lace, foreign as well as English. They seem to have had no direct connection with the actual lace-workers but to have relied on local firms for their supplies. Some department stores in London, such as Howell & James and Debenham & Freebody, also handled lace in the same way. The only lace merchant actually engaged in direct manufacture who had a headquarters in London seems to have been Esther Clarke of 18A Margaret Street, Cavendish Square, who showed Honiton lace in London at the exhibitions of 1851 and 1862 and at Paris in 1855.

The hand-made lace trade was, in fact, largely in the hands of local dealers in the main towns of the two lace-making areas: the East Midlands and Devonshire. It seems, too, that in the nineteenth century many of these dealers had ceased to have any very firm control over the actual lace-makers, for numbers of middlemen had crept into the industry in the form of small agents and dealers who handled the lace of a very restricted area. These latter came in the nineteenth century to take over much of the lace business from the larger firms and they conducted it without much real knowledge of the craft, being concerned only with buying and selling at the most advantageous rate. In his evidence to the Select Committee on Arts and Manufactures in 1836, James Millward, a prominent lace manufacturer of Olney in Buckinghamshire, stated (*Minutes of Evidence*, para. 202): "The persons at present engaged in lace manufacturing or rather in lace-dealing, are quite another class from what they were 20 years since. . . . [The trade] has been taken up by shopkeepers and travellers, and other persons who know very little about it. Instead of manufacturing, it is generally lace dealing." These dealers either had the workers come to them once a month with what they had made during the past month, or they travelled round to collect lace from the workers. It was these small dealers who then supplied larger firms.

Often the dealer was a local shopkeeper. A typical example at Beer in Devon was described by Alan S. Cole, in his *Report to the House of Commons on the Present Condition and Prospects of the Honiton Lace Industry* in 1887 (p. 2), as a small grocer: "His daughters understand how to prick patterns, join lace together and make pillow-lace. He buys sprigs from the lace-makers, and has them joined together and made up into collars, cuffs, etc., by his daughters. He employs some 30 workers or so, from time to time." Such dealers as this would frequently sell the raw materials and patterns for the lace to the workers, although quite often, too, the workers were left to their own devices. This usually meant repeating traditional patterns or perhaps endeavouring to compose a new one of their own inspired by what they saw around them. Lace-dealers frequently operated the truck system, i.e. they forced the workers to take payment in goods. Cole described a dealer at Colyton (*op. cit.*, p. 3): "He ... keeps a very limited general store shop, and gets his lace in by bartering goods for it." Small wonder that in such poor circumstances of work and with trade declining: "Many lace-makers have now taken up with putting bristles into handles for the brush manufactory at Axminster" (*ibid.*). It was the same in the East Midlands: as soon as any more lucrative activity, such as straw-plaiting, presented itself, workers immediately gave up lace-making. Few and far between were enterprising workers like the one in Beer, Devon, whom Cole visited, who had tried to set up in business on her own account (*op. cit.*, p. 3): "She tries to sell her lace direct to customers, because, when she takes it to the dealers, they offer tenpence for a shilling's worth, and make you take the tenpence in goods."

It is not surprising that in these circumstances English lace lagged far behind French and Belgian in point of design and much of it steadily deteriorated in quality too. The only really good work done was obtained by dealers such as E. Godfroy of Buckingham or Mrs. Treadwin of Exeter, who themselves kept a certain measure of control over the workers. Even they found increasing difficulty in obtaining really good-quality work. Mrs. Treadwin's methods and views were reported by Cole (*op. cit.*, p. 2): "Mrs. Treadwin produces standard pieces up to which her workers have to work. She rather complained that taste in the worker had not been cultivated for the benefit of the manufacture. The wholesale trade has encouraged hastily-produced laces of poor quality."

When such conditions prevailed, even the most energetic efforts of a few devoted persons to improve the standard of design and workmanship could accomplish little more than to secure a temporary period of comparative prosperity in the middle years of the century, when the fashion for lace was at its height. The industry was too small and ill-organized to have any influence in official circles and it could not, therefore, prevent import duties on foreign laces from being lowered in 1826, 1842 and 1846 and eventually removed altogether in 1860. This, coupled with a decline in the American market owing to the Civil War and the imposition of import duties on lace there, hastened the inevitable decline of an industry which could not hope to compete with either foreign or machine products.

The gradual dwindling away of the lace-schools was another symptom of the decline, not a cause of it as some disgruntled dealers suggested. These schools seem to have been mainly a nineteenth-century phenomenon and there were always many more of them in the East Midlands area than there were in Devonshire. The schools, usually sited in pokey cottage rooms, were run by lace-makers who taught the children the rudiments of reading and writing as well as lace-making. The children, who were taken from the age of five, paid a small fee and in return received part of what was gained from selling the lace they made. These schools had begun to close down even before the Workshops Act of 1867 pro-hibited the employment of children under the age of eight, and they were discontinued as day schools after the passing of the Education Act of 1871. In the East Midlands, lace-making continued to be taught in ordinary schools and in lace-schools held in the evenings, but it was impossible for workers to reach a high standard with so limited a training. The result was that, as the older lace-workers in each area died off, there were few or none to replace them.

At the end of the nineteenth century, as a result of a general reaction against machines and all their works, there was a resurgence of interest in some quarters in dying rural industries and many philanthropic ladies of the upper classes devoted a great deal of time and attention to endeavouring to revitalize lace-making in both the East Midlands and Devon. Although this initiative brought about a minor revival in the 1890s, it was impossible for it to be sustained for very long or for the hand-lace industry ever to become a flourishing commercial proposition again.

Honiton bobbin lace

The Devonshire bobbin-lace industry was confined to a small area of the county around Sidmouth, Beer, Branscombe, Colyton,

Axminster and, of course, Honiton, after which the lace was named. For much of the eighteenth century it seems to have been in a reasonably flourishing state; writers of that time, indeed, frequently extol Honiton lace as equal in quality to that of Brussels. The techniques of both laces were exactly the same and it is, therefore, very difficult to identify Honiton lace of the eighteenth century, although students generally feel safe in ascribing to Honiton bobbin laces in the Brussels technique but of inferior design.

By the early nineteenth century, however, Honiton lace had developed its own distinctive style so that, although the technique remains the same, it is a comparatively easy matter to distinguish Honiton from contemporary Brussels bobbin lace. Perhaps its most notable characteristic is the almost invariable use of ornamental fillings consisting of a network of tiny squares or rectangles, known to the workers as leadworks (Fr. *points d'esprit*). These easily recognizable fillings (Pls. 43, 44) are frequently found in the centres of the flowers which remained the favourite motifs for Honiton lace throughout the century. The flowers are generally executed in a simple, rather naive style, quite different from the precise naturalism or more sophisticated forms of Brussels lace. Prominent among them is the rose; there are very few pieces of mid-nineteenth-century Honiton on which this favourite flower does not appear. Much of the nineteenth-century Honiton lace that has survived to the present day is awkward and clumsy in both design and execution, but there are many pieces of great delicacy, with a simple charm quite different from the opulence of contemporary Continental lace.

Honiton lace suffered a setback during the second decade of the nineteenth century because of the fashion for machine-made nets, both plain and embroidered, and for light blonde lace. This is indicated in an extract from *Magna Britannia* of 1822 (quoted by Mrs. Bury Palliser: *History of Lace*, p. 408): "The manufactory of lace has much declined, although the lace still retains its superiority. Some years ago, at which time it was patronized by the Royal family, the manufacture of Honiton employed 2,400 hands in that town and in the neighbouring villages, but they do not now employ above 300."

Royal patrons were not wanting in the nineteenth century. Queen Adelaide, for example, endeavoured to help the struggling industry by ordering a dress of elaborate design incorporating sprigs of plants, the initials of which spelt out her name—Amaranth, Daphne, Eglantine, Lilac, Auricula, Ivy, Dahlia, Eglantine. This order is said to have been executed by a Mrs. Davey of Honiton (Mrs. Bury Palliser: *History of Lace*, p. 408). The flowers were mounted on machine-made net, a practice which had by this time been adopted in the industry and which was to help it, as it did contemporary Brussels lace, to regain prosperity. The industry was no doubt aided by the establishment in 1816 of a factory in Tiverton by John Heathcoat, inventor of the bobbin-net machine, who left Nottingham in that year.

It was not until Queen Victoria's wedding in 1840, however, that the industry really benefited from royal patronage to any great extent. The Queen was careful to order a trousseau composed entirely of materials of British manufacture and, for her wedding dress and veil, she chose Honiton lace. The work was undertaken by Miss Jane Bidney of Beer, where the workers had always had a high reputation. According to Mrs. Bury Palliser, however (*History of Lace*, p. 409), Miss Bidney had difficulty even in Beer in finding enough skilled workers to carry out the order. The making of this lace was a great occasion, attended with much excitement and remembered long afterwards by those who had helped. The lace on the dress alone cost £1,000, an enormous sum in those days. It was of a complex formal design of eighteenth-century type, quite untypical of most contemporary productions of the lace-makers. The dress may still be seen in the London Museum (Pl. 3).

This order led to a return of Honiton lace to fashionable favour and the industry began to revive. Much of the lace produced during the 1840s was of a high standard, as may be seen from the beautiful bonnet veils and wedding veils which have survived. In the arrangement of their design these pieces resemble Brussels application veils, with rows of sprigs along one or more sides and a border of smaller leaves or flowers forming a scalloped edge, but, as has been noted already, they are simpler and less sophisticated in style (Pl. 43). This type of Honiton lace, with bobbin-made sprigs mounted on a machine-net ground, persisted throughout the middle years of the century. Borders, berthas, collars, cuffs, caps and lappets were made in the same manner.

Honiton lace was shown by G. F. Urling & Co. of Regent Street in their displays of British lace at the exhibitions organized by the

Society of Arts in 1848 and 1849–50. At the latter exhibition there appeared for the first time some examples of coloured lace, known as "Colyton chromatic", produced by W. L. Gill. Further attempts to publicize the manufacture were already in hand. The *Journal of Design and Manufactures* of 1849–50 reported (Vol. II, p. 212): "At the public meeting convened by the Mayor of Honiton . . . a resolution was carried unanimously 'That it is desirable that an effective representation of the Honiton lace manufacture should be secured in the Exhibition of 1851, as tending to revive the trade of that town by exciting attention to the surpassing beauty and excellence of the fabric; and a committee be formed for carrying out the design and co-operating with the Honiton manufacturers.'"

Honiton lace did, indeed, make a very creditable showing at the Exhibition, eliciting the following favourable comment from the Jury (*Report*, p. 1013): "during the past twenty years considerable progress has been made, resulting in the manufacture of fabrics displaying not only extreme delicacy of execution, but also beauty and taste in design". Typical of pieces produced expressly for the exhibition was one shown by Daniel Biddle, 81 Oxford Street: "Specimen of Honiton lace, representing the arms of Her Majesty the Queen and H.R.H. Prince Albert, encircled with wreaths of palm and olive branches, around which the rose, thistle and shamrock are entwined, and the whole enclosed in a border of oak. Designed by T. Sharp and manufactured by John Tucker." This house also showed examples of more normal products, including a bridal scarf and flounce with a "pattern composed of natural flowers", a shawl, bertha collar, handkerchief, coiffure, collar and baby's cap. Two items, a mantle and a flounce, were in a new technique known as Honiton guipure which was to become increasingly important in years to come. In this type of lace the motifs, instead of being mounted on net, were united by bobbin-made bars or *brides* (see Pl. 44).

Other London houses which showed a similar range of products were Groucock, Copestake, Moore & Co. of 5 Bow Churchyard, Howell & James of 5, 7 and 9 Regent Street, and Laugher & Cosens of 97 Oxford Street. Prominent local manufacturers who exhibited were W. L. Gill of Colyton, who showed a collection of lace including his "Colyton chromatic", and Esther Clarke of 18A Margaret Street, London (this lady went on to win a second-class medal at the

Paris Exhibition of 1855, and to exhibit again at the International
Exhibition of 1862). She was described in the catalogue as manufacturer and designer and she showed a "flounce of Honiton lace,
five yards long, in the manufacture of which forty women were
employed during eight months".

The Honiton lace in the Exhibition aroused the admiration of the
critical French expert, Félix Aubry, who described it enthusiastically
in his report published in Paris in 1854, adding the surprising information that the best pieces of Honiton lace were more expensive
than comparable Brussels lace. M. Aubry's enthusiasm was shared
by many of his compatriots, for Honiton lace enjoyed a vogue in
France during this decade, and lace in imitation of Honiton was
produced at Mirecourt in Lorraine (see p. 83).

But although everyone united to praise the workmanship of
Honiton lace, many critics commented on its deficiencies in design,
in which it lagged far behind French and Belgian laces. The Jury
(*Report*, p. 1013) expressed "the conviction that the more the
British manufacture becomes assimilated to the characteristics of the
foreign (which are chiefly suitable, beautiful and clearly-defined
patterns, with refinement of execution) the more the demand for
this lace will extend". Richard Redgrave, in a supplementary
report on design which was published with the Jury Reports, also
noted the superiority of French and Belgian designs and added, "The
patterns of Honiton lace are generally too heavy, the form rather too
large and overcrowded, and the whole effect a little too solid and
equal, although this partly arises from the mode of manufacture."

Efforts had already been made to remedy this state of affairs,
notably by Mrs. C. E. Treadwin, who was to be one of the most
influential figures in the Honiton lace industry in the third quarter
of the century. Mrs. Treadwin had had some designs specially
made for her at the Government School of Design at Somerset House,
notably by C. P. Slocombe and T. Rawlings. Some of these she
had carried out by workers under her own supervision, others were
done by Mr. Gill of Colyton, and the resulting laces were shown
together with the designs in 1851. Richard Redgrave commented:
"The designs are novel but a little too architectural in their general
arrangement, resulting in a slight degree of stiffness, and a want of
that flowing ease which should characterize the ornament of the
material." Mrs. Treadwin had, indeed, experienced difficulty

37. Border of Tape Lace with Needlepoint Fillings, *guipure de Flandre,* Belgian, last quarter of the 19th century. *Victoria and Albert Museum* (No. T.8-1963).

38. Enlarged Detail of Brussels Needlepoint Lace, *point de gaze. Rijksmuseum, Amsterdam.*

39. Border of Brussels Needlepoint Lace, *point de gaze*, made by Verdé-Delisle & Cie. (Compagnie des Indes), Belgian, c. 1867. *The Metropolitan Museum of Art, New York* (No.43-37.1, the gift of Mrs. Edward S. Harkness, 1943).

40. Fan mount, Brussels needlepoint lace, *point de gaze*, designed by Léon Sacré, Belgian, *c.* 1883-4. *Musées Royaux d'Art et d'Histoire, Brussels* (No.2283).

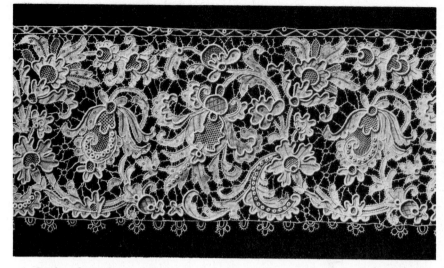

41. Border of Venetian Needlepoint Lace, Belgian, c. 1880. *Musées Royaux d'Art et d'Histoire, Brussels* (No.1604).

42. Handkerchief of Needlepoint Lace, *point d'Alençon,* probably Belgian, last quarter of the 19th century. *Musées Royaux d'Art et d'Histoire, Brussels* (No.3280).

43. Corner of a Veil, Honiton bobbin lace applied to machine-made net, English, mid 19th century. *Victoria and Albert Museum* (No. T.15-1963).

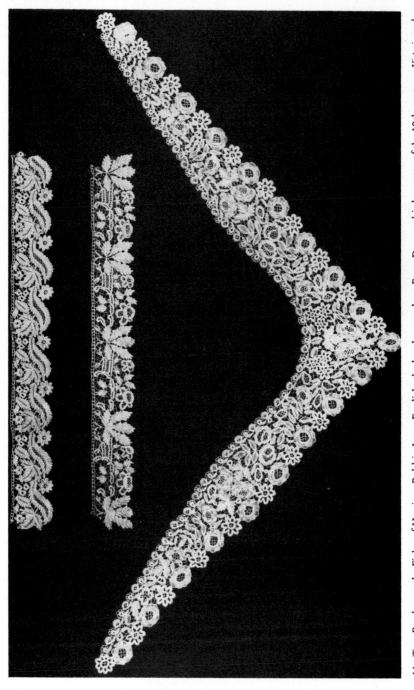

44. Two Borders and a Fichu of Honiton Bobbin Lace, English, the borders made at Beer, Devon, third quarter of the 19th century. *Victoria and Albert Museum* (Nos. T.8, 9-1917; T.196-1929).

45. Handkerchief, Honiton Bobbin Lace, worked by Miss S. Sansom after a design by Lady Trevelyan, English, *c.* 1864. *Victoria and Albert Museum* (No.785-1864).

46. Bobbin Lace Borders; *the top border,* "baby lace", *the others,* "Bucks point", East Midlands of England, first half of the 19th century. *Luton Museum and Art Gallery.*

47. Shawl of East Midlands Bobbin Lace, English, c. 1840-50. *Victoria and Albert Museum* (No.489-1887).

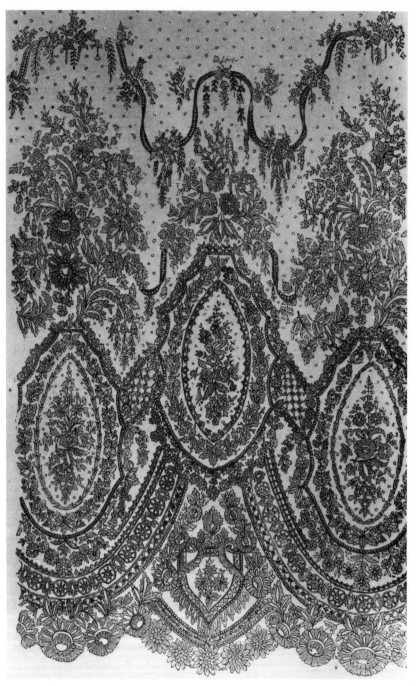

48. Black Silk Lace Shawl manufactured by E. Godfroy of Buckingham, shown by Debenham & Freebody at the International Exhibition of 1862. *Art Journal Catalogue,* p. 81.

in getting the student designers to comply with the requirements of the lace-making technique.

The Jury noted that at this period about seven or eight thousand workers were employed in making Honiton lace. The industry was in a fairly flourishing state, therefore, and the pattern was set which was to endure until the end of the century. On the one hand were a small number of very skilled workers, capable of producing the finest types of lace and those pieces expressly designed for royal orders; on the other were the majority of the workers who were content to turn out lace of moderate or poor quality, for which there was a steady market at any rate in the third quarter of the century. Mrs. Treadwin gave her own account of this position in her little book *Antique Point: Honiton Lace*, which was published in about 1874: "The demand for the lace had so much increased that in 1850 the quality of the work was much deteriorated, for the work-people, finding that whatever was made met with a ready sale, were not desirous of improving their patterns. They preferred common work that could easily be executed to better but more difficult designs, requiring more taste and care, and not even when tempted by a higher rate of pay would they undertake the higher class of work." This "common work" is often innocent of any design at all, consisting of collections of motifs, some traditional, others copied by the workers from objects they saw around them, arranged in a haphazard fashion to form the shape of cap, lappet or collar required.

During the 1850s the demand for application lace began to fall off, while Honiton guipure steadily gained in popularity. It virtually superseded application altogether for normal use, with the exception of wedding veils, by the end of the 1860s. Much of this guipure lace features the favourite stylized roses which almost amounted to a trade-mark of Honiton lace, but there were also attempts to produce more sophisticated designs based on those of contemporary Continental laces. The two borders on Pl. 44 were obviously designed by someone who had studied *point Duchesse*, in contrast to the more traditional collar shown on the same plate.

The results of attempts to improve design were plainly visible in much of the Honiton lace shown at the International Exhibition of 1862. A typically elaborate example was a wide border exhibited by Howell & James of Regent Street (Fig. 6). Here the familiar Honiton flowers have been marshalled into order within a frame-

work of ornament that still seems but a tame version of the bold
designs of contemporary Continental lace. Other examples illustrated in the *Art Journal* Catalogue of the Exhibition show various
attempts to introduce strapwork to give form to the designs. The
style persisted to a certain extent, as may be seen from a shawl
shown by Mrs. Treadwin at Paris in 1867 (Fig. 7) (Mrs. Treadwin
had been awarded a first-class medal at the Paris Exhibition of 1855

FIG. 6. Flounce of Honiton bobbin lace shown by
Howell & James of Regent Street at the International
Exhibition of 1862. (*Art Journal Catalogue*, p. 46.)

for her efforts to improve Honiton lace). This design, "by an
artist of Nottingham", still has an amateurish look when compared
with French or Belgian lace.

It might, perhaps, be considered that these attempts, though well-
meaning, were a little misguided, for it must be admitted that
English designers and workers alike were more at ease with naturalistic
floral designs and it was in these that their happiest effects were
produced. A flounce shown by Debenham & Freebody at the
1862 Exhibition seems to be a successful compromise between old

and new styles (Fig. 8).   Perhaps this may have been one of the
pieces produced by John Tucker of Branscombe whom the Jury
noted as being responsible for the best Honiton lace exhibited.

FIG. 7. Shawl of Honiton bobbin lace, designed by a
Nottingham artist and produced under the super-
vision of Mrs. Treadwin of Exeter; shown at the
Paris International Exhibition of 1867.   (*Art Journal
Catalogue.*)

Naturalism seemed indeed the most profitable line to follow to
many of those concerned with improving the standard of Honiton
lace in the 1860s and later.   Mrs. Bury Palliser (*History of Lace*,
p. 410) speaks of the efforts of Captain Marryat who "took much
pains during a residence at Sidmouth to procure for the lace-makers
new patterns of flowers, insects and other natural objects".   She

also describes a competition held at the Bath and West of England Society's Agricultural Show for lace "worked either in Flowers, Fruits, Leaves or Insects, strictly designed from nature". A handkerchief, worked by Miss Sansom to a design by Lady Trevelyan, is typical of this new, careful naturalism that persisted in Honiton lace to the end of the century (Pl. 45).

The prosperity the industry had enjoyed in the 1850s was not destined to be very enduring. Already in 1862 the Jury of the

FIG. 8. Flounce of Honiton bobbin lace shown by Debenham & Freebody at the International Exhibition of 1862. (*Art Journal Catalogue*, p. 47.)

International Exhibition noted that trade was falling off and that Honiton lace could not compete with Belgian productions as far as price was concerned. How much less, therefore, could it compete with the rising ride of machine production. Mrs. Bury Palliser attributed the decline in part to the attempts of many lace-workers to engage in this fruitless competition (*History of Lace*, pp. 415–6): "Ever since the Great Exhibition of 1851 drew attention to the industry, different persons have been trying to encourage both better design and better manufacture, but the majority of people have sought a livelihood by meeting the extensive demand for cheap laces. Good patterns, good thread and good work have all been thrown aside, the workers and small dealers recking little of the fact that they themselves were undermining the trade as much as

FIG. 9. Veil and handkerchief in Honiton bobbin lace made for Princess Louise on her marriage to the Marquis of Lorne (the veil designed after a sketch by the princess); shown by Howell & James of Regent Street at the International Exhibition, South Kensington, 1871. (*Art Journal Catalogue*, p. 12.)

the competition of machinery and machine-made lace, and tarnishing the fair name of Honiton throughout the world, among those able to love and appreciate a beautiful art."

Good-quality lace was still made, however, particularly to fulfil the royal orders which continued to crop up every few years (Fig. 9). The Princess Royal, Princess Alice and the Princess of Wales all went to the altar attired in Honiton lace in naturalistic designs featuring the national flowers.   Mrs. Treadwin and her workers added to their efforts to improve design by introducing the imitation of older forms of lace—a form of eclecticism that was infecting lace manufacture everywhere at that time.   In the 1860s the making of a kind of tape lace with needlepoint fillings in imitation of seventeenth-century laces was introduced, and in the 1870s copies or adaptations of eighteenth-century Brussels laces were worked in mixed bobbin and needlepoint lace.

In the 1870s, too, a new field was opened up: "A new branch of industry has lately opened to the Devonshire lacemaker—that of restoring or remaking the old lace.   The splendid mantles, tunics and flounces which enrich the shop-windows of the great lace-dealers of London are mostly concocted from old fragments by the Devonshire lace-workers.   It is curious to see the ingenuity they display in re-arranging the old 'rags'—and such they are—sent from London for restoration.   Carefully cutting out the designs of the old work, they sew them upon a paper pattern of the required shape.   The 'modes' or fancy stitches, are dexterously restored, and deficient flowers supplied, and the whole joined together on the pillow" (*History of Lace*, pp. 411–12).   Much of the lace subjected to this renovation was Venetian needlepoint of the seventeenth century.

In spite of all these expedients, however, the Honiton lace industry continued to decline.   In 1887, Alan S. Cole visited Devonshire to report on the condition of the industry to the House of Commons. His report is full of detailed indications of the decay of the lace trade. Mrs. Treadwin, still holding the fort at Exeter, told him of the reduced demand for the lace which meant only intermittent work so that the workers could not sustain their technique by regular practice, of the closing of lace schools, of the dying off of old workers —facts which were corroborated again and again by others to whom he spoke.   She herself was still managing to obtain good work by means of constant supervision.   Her best workers were those who had been trained at lace-making schools she herself had set up in the 1850s; some of them had even managed to produce passable imitations of seventeenth-century Venetian needlepoint, amongst other reproductions of old laces.   Other dealers commented on the lack of good workers and the difficulty of obtaining good new designs.   Everywhere the number of workers was reduced to a pitiful few: in Beer only sixty or seventy were left of the 400 workers of the 1850s, in Branscombe only twenty or thirty workers remained, in Sidbury thirty to forty, and so on.

Still the industry managed to remain in existence, albeit on this very reduced basis, to the end of the century. The mantle of Mrs. Treadwin fell on other shoulders. Her work was taken up by Miss Audrey Trevelyan of Beer (great niece of Lady Trevelyan), by Mrs. Fowler of Honiton and by Miss Radford of Sidmouth, who won prizes at the Chicago Exhibition of 1893 for their work. Their success led to a small scale revival of the industry at the very end of the century, principally directed at the American market. The best work of this time was either extremely naturalistic or very eclectic and it was distinguished by a careful, rather mechanically fine, technique, like much of the best Continental lace of the same period.

There was still a sharp contrast, however, between the good and inferior types of lace produced. For the latter, of which the worst sort was known even to the workers themselves as "rag lace", all too often expedients such as that described by one worker to Alan Cole were adopted. "Sometimes", she said, "we sees a new wall-paper, and prick a pattern off it, changing a bit here, or leave a little or add a little". Another typical method of procedure was described by A. Penderel Moody in her book, *Devon Pillow Lace*, published in 1907. "The small cottage agents still put out work on the same lines as was customary 50 years ago. A customer will order a collar to cost 30*s*., and the agent will begin to figure out what can be done for that sum. For a bordering, perhaps 24 turkey's tails at so much each; an elaborate rose spray for the centre of the back; four sunflowers will fill in the vacant spaces on either shoulder, sprays of ivy leaves will be massed together for the points. So far, in spite of the varied assortment, there is a certain quaintness about the collar, and filled in at this point it might have escaped severe criticism. Unluckily, there still remains a small sum to be accounted for, so some flies, frying-pans, and cats'-paws are intro-duced, and if the customer happens to be specially favoured, a cock-robin may sit erect amid the general confusion."

East Midlands bobbin lace

During the eighteenth century there existed in the East Midlands a flourishing industry producing trimming laces, insertions and borders, often of a modest nature. This industry never had any great pretensions. It had never, like that of Devonshire, attempted to cater for the rich public that bought the most expensive Continental laces, but was, instead, content to find a steady market amongst the middle classes. One of its staple products was, indeed, "baby lace", very narrow lace for trimming babies' clothes and little lace crowns for their caps. East Midlands lace was bobbin-made in the same techniques as those Continental laces which were cheap varieties of Mechlin. Like them it featured Lille or *point de Paris* grounds and airy motifs outlined with a thicker thread to give definition (Pl. 46). This type of lace was often referred to in the nineteenth century as "Bucks point", although it was made throughout the lace-making area which included Bedfordshire, Oxfordshire and Northamptonshire as well as Buckinghamshire. Indeed, in times of prosperity when the industry expanded, it spread into adjacent parts of Hertfordshire, Huntingdonshire and Cambridgeshire.

The early nineteenth century was one of this industry's most prosperous periods: light laces were very fashionable, the important American market had reopened after the end of the War of Independence, and imports of lace from the Continent were temporarily disrupted because of the war with France. As a result the East Midlands lace-makers extended their range to produce large items such as scarves, shawls (cf. Pl. 47) and veils in an attempt to satisfy home demand. Most of the designs normally in use among the lace-makers were of a rather simple, traditional type, but attempts were made at this time to improve the standard of design. James Millward, of Olney, Buckinghamshire, who came of a family that had been in the lace trade for several generations, spoke of his own efforts in this direction years later, in 1836, when he gave evidence to the Select Committee on Arts and Manufactures: "I had many specimens of beautiful French lace sent me for imitation; and after some practice in imitation, I ventured in altering, varying and redrawing some of the patterns." (*Minutes of Evidence*, Part II, paragraph 147.) Millward also mentioned the fact that expensive laces costing one or two guineas a yard were in quite general production at this time.

Nevertheless, lace of a humbler kind still remained the principal product of the majority of the East Midlands workers. Furthermore their lace was, on the whole, declining in quality rather than improving. Designs gradually became more and more debased through constant copying by workers who had little or no knowledge of drawing, and the quality of the lace was by no means enhanced by the changeover from linen to cotton thread which occurred during the first quarter of the century.

Unfortunately for the East Midlands lace-makers, the end of the Napoleonic Wars in 1815 and the consequent freeing of imports of Continental lace coincided with the rise of the machine-lace industry. Nottingham was, indeed, a much more serious rival to an industry specializing in cheap laces than any of the Continental industries with their superior products. Millward, in 1836, stated that the general demand for lace had decreased, but noted (*Minutes of Evidence*, paragraph 152): "the cheapness of the machine lace does still find a market for it, where ours would be excluded by the price; and as an extensive and flourishing trade is sure to prompt to greater exertions, the Nottingham manufacture goes on steadily improving, while ours is constantly deteriorating".

A lack of good designers seems to have been one of the main causes of this deterioration. Millward stated in 1836 (*ibid.*, paragraph 191): "There are only two or three persons who draw lace patterns, and they do very little." A similar state of affairs was commented on in 1853 by Octavius Hudson (*Report on Lace-making*, Appendix VII, e, of *The First Report of the Department of Practical Art*, p. 368): "On my visit to the pillow lace districts, I was told that in the more prosperous times lace-buyers employed pattern drawers or designers; but since the decline of the manufacture, they have discontinued to do so; and I had great difficulty in finding a designer for pillow lace—I only succeeded, indeed, in obtaining the names of two." Hudson noted that these designers only concerned themselves with the better types of lace and that "the greater quantity of lace is made from very inferior parchments".

However, although decline was apparent in the industry by the middle of the century, the manufacture was by no means defunct as yet, and East Midlands lace made a creditable showing at the Great Exhibition of 1851. Indeed, there were signs that the industry was trying to win back some of its former prosperity by adopting new modes and trying new products in order to cater for current fashion. The *Jury Report* noted (p. 1013): "Not many years since, a very considerable number of women and children were employed in its manufacture [white lace] throughout the counties of Bedford, Buckingham, Northampton and Oxford; but the demand having fallen off (being subject to fluctuation like all articles dependent on fashion), has caused this branch of the trade to suffer severely. Contemporary, however, with the diminution in the making of white thread lace, an increased requirement for black lace occurred; the manufacture of which was introduced into the districts enumerated, and has been attended with marked success." The manufacture of black silk laces seems to have been introduced particularly successfully into South Buckinghamshire.

Laces of the best quality, including wide borders, veils and scarves in both black and white, were shown at the Exhibition by the London house of Groucock, Copestake, Moore & Co., by Elizabeth Rose of Pauler's Pury, Northants., Richard Viccars of Padbury, Bucks., and Thomas Lester of Bedford. Both the last-mentioned firms showed quantities of "baby lace", while others, such as C. & T. Cardwell of Northampton, J. T. Knightley of Northampton, and Benjamin Hill of Olney, showed the trimmings and insertions that were still the staple products of the industry. Other manufacturers who exhibited were Elizabeth Frewen of Marlow, Bucks., who showed lace made of cotton mixed with silk to improve its appearance, G. Hurst of High Street, Bedford, who was clearly striving after novelty, for he exhibited "pillow-lace with glass introduced into the figure", Rebecca Phillips of Swanborne, Winslow, Bucks., C. J. Sim of High Street, Bedford, Samuel Vincent of Turvey, near Olney, and William Ayers of Newport Pagnell, Bucks.

The French lace manufacturer, Félix Aubry, noted in his report on the lace in the Exhibition (published in Paris in 1854), that the East Midlands made black silk and white cotton laces which were reasonably good in quality with regular *réseaux*, but poor in design. He bluntly said, in fact, that the designs of these laces were twenty-five years behind the times.

Some attempt to remedy this state of affairs was to be made in the decade following the exhibition, an attempt which met with only a small temporary success. The prime mover was a Frenchman, Edmund Godfroy. According to Thomas Wright, whose book, *The Romance of the Lace-Pillow*, published at Olney in 1919, is a mine of information and popular folk-lore about this industry, Godfroy settled in Buckingham in the 1840s. He attempted to introduce French methods and French designs into this branch of the English lace industry. He taught the workers how to join pieces of lace by *point de raccroc* so that large articles could be made in accordance with current taste (in 1862 the Jury of the International Exhibition in London noted that none of the East Midlands lace shown in 1851 had been more than eight inches wide), and generally endeavoured to improve the quality of their work. It was to his efforts that the Jury of 1862 attributed the great progress of the industry in Buckinghamshire which "may be readily perceived by an examination of piece goods, including shawls, tunics, flouncings, veils, etc., which are exhibited this year". A flounce produced by Godfroy and shown by Debenham & Freebody (Pl. 48) was illustrated in the *Art Journal Catalogue* (p. 81) with the following comment: "It is only within the last three or four years that large articles in fine lace have been made in Buckinghamshire; the workers there have not only improved their fabric... their designs are of a higher character than they used to be." The design is, indeed, obviously a French one and bears out the Jury's remark that "at present the best patterns are taken from designs prepared in France or Belgium". The venture was, however, only a small-scale one and it never had any lasting success. By the time of the Paris Exhibition of 1867, only five years later, it seems to have collapsed. In its report on lace, the Jury noted that no East Midlands firms had sent exhibits. They pointed out the cause of the failure of Godfroy's venture: the Buckinghamshire workers could not hope to compete in the production of black silk lace with those of Grammont in Belgium whose work was far better and much cheaper.

Godfroy's venture seems, in fact, to have been a somewhat isolated one. Most of the East Midlands firms, faced with increasingly serious competition from machine-made lace, chose to adopt the disastrous course of trying to make cheaper laces more quickly than the machines. This process began after the Great Exhibition of 1851. The Maltese lace shown there had had a considerable success, and this type of coarse bobbin lace was quickly taken up by the East Midlands workers. It was much easier and quicker to make than the "Bucks point" and enjoyed a considerable vogue in the 1850s and 1860s (Pl. 49).

At the International Exhibition of 1862, nearly all the lace shown by East Midlands manufacturers was Maltese, showing the extent to which this coarser lace had come to dominate the industry. Amongst those who exhibited it were Copestake, Moore, Crampton & Co. of 5 Bow Church Yard, London, Joseph Hornsey of Bedford, Lester & Sons of Bedford, and Richard Viccars of Padbury, Bucks. The lace was, in fact, adapted for use in quite large articles such as shawls and parasol covers and was made in both black silk and white cotton. The designs sometimes included motifs such as small leaves and flowers as well as the geometric ornament more commonly associated with this kind of lace. A variant of Maltese lace known as "plaited lace", which had a background of *brides* (bars) or of a mesh of *points d'esprit*, was also made (Pl. 50). The adoption of these techniques for a time brought back a certain temporary prosperity to the industry. The Jury noted in 1862 (*Report*, p. 3): "The introduction, since 1851, of black and white Maltese lace into England, has been of great service to this branch of trade, and has added considerably to the number of workers, as well as improved their wages."

But the new, easier technique also served to coarsen the workers' skill and to oust the manufacture of better types of lace. The story of the industry for the rest of the century is one of continuing decline. The workers turned to other coarse types of lace in their efforts to counteract machine competition but these, at best, only enjoyed a short vogue. A catalogue of such laces may be compiled from the pages of Thomas Wright's book mentioned above. The first to follow Maltese, in England, as well as in France and Belgium, was the even simpler plaited Cluny lace (Pl. 50), with another development of Maltese known as Auvergne lace. Then, about 1870, a kind of coarse worsted lace known as "Yak" lace (though it seems never to have been made of yak hair) came into vogue (Pl. 50). This, too, was characterized by simple geometric designs and was made in a technique resembling the plaited laces of the sixteenth and seventeenth centuries. Newport Pagnell and High Wycombe seem to have been particular centres for this lace, and a certain design made in High Wycombe came to be known as the Town Trot. At the same time various experiments were made in producing coloured worsted laces of all widths, narrow for dress trimmings, wider for furnishings. This worsted lace did not remain popular for long, however, and was more or less extinct by the end of the century.

It is clear that the East Midlands industry was endeavouring to follow the example of Le Puy in France (see pp. 77–82) in adapting itself to cater for a changing market by quick, cheap production. It could only lag far behind the French and Belgian industries, however, for the lack of organization and control made it impossible to produce work of a high quality. As always, too, English designs were far inferior to Continental ones.

By the 1890s the industry was at a very low ebb, with the number of workers greatly reduced: 3,376 in the Census of 1891 as compared with 26,670 in 1851. Only four buyers, including the Lester family, were left in business in Bedford, two in Buckinghamshire and one in Northamptonshire. The workers were now producing mainly Maltese, Cluny and torchon laces (Pl. 50), with a very few still carrying on with inferior types of "Bucks point". Alan S. Cole, in a *Report on Northampton, Bucks. and Beds. Lace-Making* (Department of Science and Art, 1891), commented: "Commercial influence is insufficient to foster the higher possibilities of lace-making: as commercial influence in England arises from the commercial working of supply and demand, differing therefore in character and quality from commercial influence in France, which is flavoured with artistic taste and perception of the value of technical instruction."

It was in an effort to supply these deficiencies that various associations were formed in the 1890s and the early years of the present century. Some of these, such as the Midland Counties Lace Association founded in 1891 with its headquarters in Northampton, simply endeavoured to help the workers to sell their lace; others, such as the Buckinghamshire Lace Association founded in 1897, aimed at improving the quality of the lace as well. Numerous public-spirited ladies in the lace-making districts took the industry under their wing, too, and tried to help the workers by encouraging them to improve their products. Attempts at improvement consisted in the main in endeavouring to wean workers away from making Cluny and Maltese laces back to the finer designs of the early nineteenth century. A prominent worker in this field was Mrs. Effie Bruce-Clarke, who, in addition to reviving old patterns, designed new ones herself and encouraged art students to provide others. She showed the results of her work at the various Home Arts and Industries Exhibitions of the late 1890s.

Although, as a result of these efforts, there was a slight resurgence

of activity in the 1890s, this could only be shortlived, for the industry
was by now in too feeble a state to recover. Commenting on the
examples of East Midlands lace shown at the Chicago Exhibition of
1893 (*Art Journal*, 1893, Supplement. *The Chicago Exhibition: Lace
and other personal decoration*, p. xxvi), Florence Fenwick Miller put
her finger on the real reason for the industry's demise: "it can never
compete with machine-made lace, the resemblance being so close
in all points except price".

Miscellaneous centres and types

A few other centres of lace-making, on a very small scale indeed,
existed in England in the nineteenth century, but were of little or no
significance. Lace-making had been carried on to some considerable extent in Wiltshire in the eighteenth century, but this activity
was virtually extinct by the beginning of the nineteenth century,
except in Downton and Malmesbury, where it persisted on a very
minor scale until about 1850. The lace made there seems to have
been similar to "Bucks point". Some attempt was made to revive
the industry in these two places at the very end of the century.
    In 1849 the *Journal of Design and Manufactures* (Vol. I, pp. 47–9)
reported on a lace-school set up in Norwich by Miss Stanley, daughter
of the Bishop of Norwich, and Miss Chamberlain. At first they
hoped to teach the making of Valenciennes, but this proved both too
difficult and insufficiently remunerative, so, after two years, Honiton
lace was substituted. The lace made was rather coarser than that of
Devonshire, but it seems to have had a minor success for a while
and examples were shown in exhibitions held by the Society of Arts
in 1848 and 1849. The lace was sold by E. Blakeley of Norwich.
The making of Honiton in Norfolk lingered on to the end of the
century when the Diss Lace Association was set up to encourage it,
but it was never more than a very minor cottage industry.
    Among the many cottage industries for producing embroidery
which were set up towards the end of the nineteenth century, in the
current wave of enthusiasm for fostering country crafts, was the
Langdale Linen Industry, established by a Mrs. Pepper originally
to revive the old linen-weaving of the Lake District. The linen
was embroidered too and the products of the industry achieved
considerable success at the Home Arts and Industries exhibitions.
The embroideries included *reticella* work, sometimes known as

Greek lace. The designs were mainly geometric in character, though occasionally more ambitious patterns were attempted.

Lace-making was considered a suitable branch of fancy work for amateurs with an interest in needlework, and in the late 1860s and 1870s books were published giving instructions on how to make Honiton lace in particular (see p. 32). For the less ambitious, easier modes were invented and enjoyed a considerable vogue. The most popular of these, to judge by the quantities that have survived, was a type of tape lace with needlepoint fillings which went by the name of "Modern point lace". It seems to have been popular

Fig. 10. Pattern for a point lace collar, 1870. (*The Young Englishwoman*, 1870, p. 277.)

from the middle of the century onwards. Examples were shown in the Exhibitions of 1851 and 1862 by Mme. Riego de la Branchardière of 1 Princes Street, Cavendish Square, London, who also published books of instructions and sold patterns and materials for making the lace. The pattern, usually vaguely seventeenth century in character, was generally printed on prepared linen ready for the amateur worker, who proceeded to tack down tapes over the main lines of the design, afterwards filling in the spaces with needlepoint stitches, mostly of a rather coarse nature. Designs were also published in many books of the period such as *The Dictionary of Needlework* of 1882, as well as magazines (Fig. 10). This lace remained popular among amateurs to the end of the century, when, indeed, it enjoyed a considerable fashionable vogue. An article entitled *The Height of Fashion in the Revived Art of Lace-Making*, which appeared in *The Queen* on July 1st, 1899, described it as follows: "Overskirts to be worn this year are made in various patterns with lace braid and lace-stitches, carried out either in white thread, or in rust-coloured thread with white braid. The work is quite easy. It is correct to use a multiplicity of stitches of endless variety; but in lieu of these it is simply necessary to carry the thread from one point to another on the design and twist it, emphasising it here and there with wheels, or with those raised circles made by twisting several strands of the cotton over the points of scissors, buttonholing them, and then sewing them on where the pattern most requires them. The truth is, it is almost a waste of time to lavish too minute stitches on these patterns, because it is effect that is most aimed at, and lace is used in such liberal folds that any intricacies of detail are lost." Readers will recognize here a domestic version of the Luxueil being made commercially in Belgium at that time. There are few collections of nineteenth-century lace that do not include at least one example of this type of work.

Another type of lace made by amateurs was known as "Guipure d'Art". This was really a nineteenth-century version of the old *lacis* or darned netting which had been such a popular form of needlework in the sixteenth century. The worker either made for herself or purchased a foundation of square-meshed network in linen thread on which she then proceeded to embroider geometric patterns by means of a number of simple darning stitches. Designs for guipure d'art appeared in numerous publications of the second half of the century. It was used for collars and cuffs as well as for furnishing purposes.

49. Cuff and Borders of Bobbin Lace of Bedfordshire Maltese Type,
East Midlands of England, second half of the 19th century. *Luton
Museum and Art Gallery.*

50. *Top to bottom:* two torchon borders; border of plaited lace;
insertion of Cluny lace; border of black worsted Yak lace; East
Midlands of England, second half of the 19th century. *Luton Museum
and Art Gallery.*

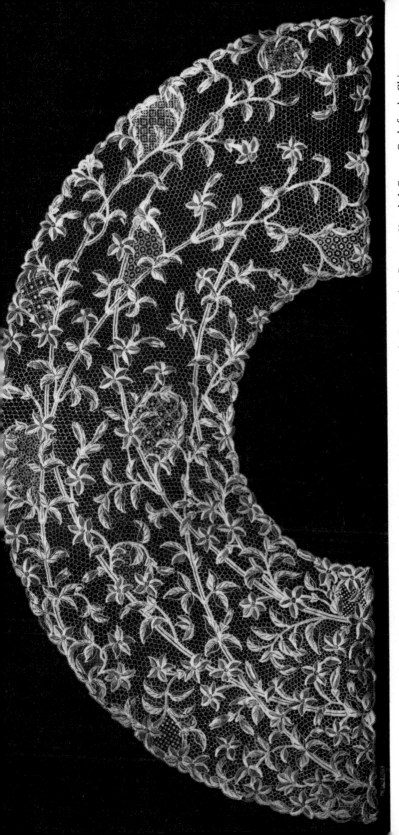

51. Fan Mount, Needlepoint Lace, made from a design by Sister Mary Regis at the Presentation Convent, Youghal, County Cork, for the Chicago Exhibition of 1893. *Victoria and Albert Museum photograph.*

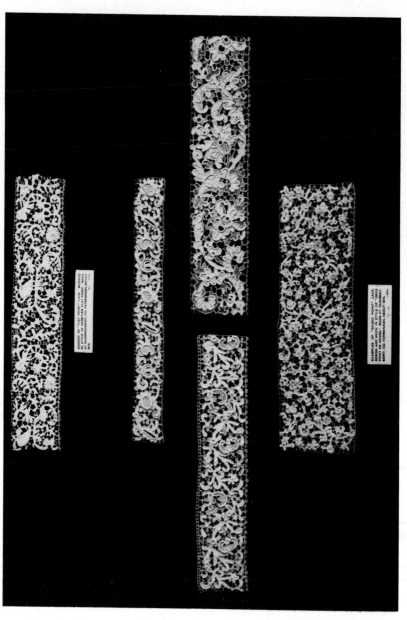

52. Border of Venetian Needlepoint Lace, made at Innishmacsaint, County Fermanagh, Irish, c. 1876. *National Museum of Ireland* (Nos.796 to 800-1880).

53. Border of Carrickmacross Guipure, Irish, late 19th century. *Victoria and Albert Museum* (No.847A-1883).

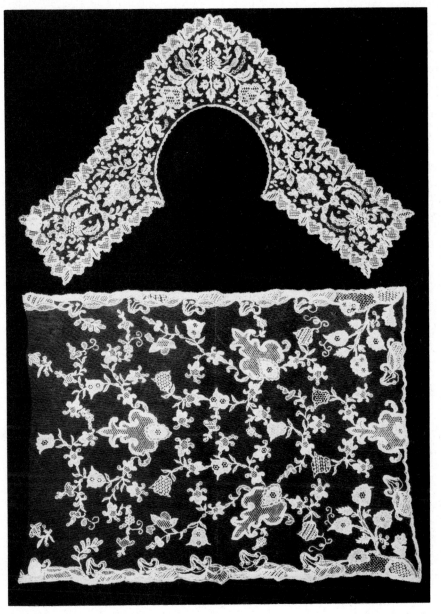

55. Collar and Scarf-end of Needlerun Net, Irish (Limerick), *c.* 1840. *National Museum of Ireland* (Nos.841-1883, 1171-1888).

56. Matching Borders of Chain-stitch Embroidered Net, made from prize-winning designs by Miss B.M. Brophy of London, under the supervision of Mrs. R. Vere O'Brien, Limerick, Irish, *c.* 1887. *Victoria and Albert Museum photograph.*

57. Five Borders of Crochet, made at Clones, Irish, *c.* 1860. *National Museum of Ireland* (Nos.791 to 5-1880).

58. Borders and Insertion of Crochet, designed by Michael Holland for Dwyer & Co. of Cork, Irish, late 19th century. *Victoria and Albert Museum photograph.*

59. Border of Tatting, made at Ardee, County Louth, Irish, c. 1880. *Victoria and Albert Museum* (No.845A-1883).

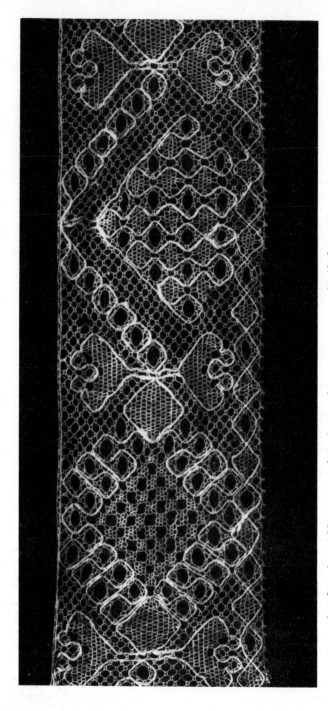

60. Border of Torchon Bobbin Lace, made in the Erzgebirge, German, second half of the 19th century. *Victoria and Albert Museum.*

CHAPTER 5

IRELAND

"THE lace industry of Ireland is the successor to no ancient
school, nor can Erin boast of any laces of her own invention. . . .
Poverty is the mother of the Irish lace industry; for Irish lace existed,
and still exists, not to supply the commercial demand for it, but to
enable a poverty-stricken population to earn a meal of porridge or
potatoes." (Mabel F. Robinson: *Irish Lace* in *Art Journal*, 1887,
p. 145.) It seems paradoxical that in the century when hand-made
lace was on the decline, the industry should have been introduced
into Ireland as a measure of famine relief, to enable peasant women
to earn a pittance to feed themselves and their families, but this fact
is, indeed, a reminder of the extremely depressed state of Ireland at
this period.

There are a few records of lace-making in Ireland during the
eighteenth century, but it is clear that the occupation was never
very widespread and never gained an established foothold in the
country. A similar situation prevailed in the early part of the
nineteenth century, until rather more impetus was given to this kind
of activity by the beginning of the manufacture of Carrickmacross
work and Limerick lace in the late 1820s. Both of these products
were really varieties of needlework and not true lace, but they have
always been treated as types of lace as they were intended to fulfil
the same decorative functions as true lace while being easier and
quicker to make.

The lace industry in Ireland did not, however, become widespread
until the famine years of the late 1840s. At that time philanthropic
ladies and religious orders introduced the making of needlepoint and
pillow laces and, above all, of crochet lace, which they taught local
peasant women how to make in an effort to alleviate their distress.
Lace-making spread rapidly and, thanks to the devoted labours and
enthusiasm of those ladies who had started the industry, was well
enough established by 1851 to make a creditable showing at the
Great Exhibition.

Two societies, the Irish Work Society of 233 Regent Street, London, and the Ladies' Industrial Society of 76 Grafton Street, Dublin, were set up to help to find a market for these laces. The latter was frankly a charitable organization "whose announced object was to correspond with English and foreign acquaintances to induce them to sell, free of charge, any Irish work sent to them, and to remit to the owners the full amount that their work realized. With a programme so innocent of commercial conditions it is not surprising that the Ladies' Society did not live many years." (Alan S. Cole: "Lace-making in Ireland" in *The English Illustrated Magazine*, June, 1890.) Some commercial firms also assisted the venture. A firm which played a major part in promoting Irish lace of all types in the middle of the nineteenth century was Forrest & Sons of 101 Grafton Street, Dublin, while later on H. Goblet of Milk Street, London, and the big lace firms of Copestake, Moore, Crampton & Co. and Haywards all took an interest in Irish products. The last-mentioned firms all showed Irish lace at the International Exhibition of 1862.

The lace industry was, however, largely in the hands of amateurs, and no amount of devoted enthusiasm on their part could take the place of the expertise needed to ensure the success of a luxury industry of this kind. The drawbacks of their system, or rather lack of system, were pointed out in the *Catalogue of the Dublin Exhibition of 1853* (p. 335) where it was stated that the lace industry of Ireland had been greatly extended "through the intervention of private individuals, who took up the matter more with the benevolent object of finding employment for the female peasantry around them, than with that of introducing a branch of trade on any secure basis. In such cases, the degree of success attained has been in proportion to the energy displayed on the part of the patrons, and also on the extent to which they had influential connections through whom the sales of the produce could be made. An appeal from an influential lady on behalf of native industry, partaking somewhat of a charitable nature, and seeking to dispose of articles really beautiful in themselves, was not likely to be often unsuccessful; and hence some Irish ladies have been able to obtain high prices for all the work which their dependents could turn out. And so long as the presiding care which brought matters to this state was continued, all went right; but even on its temporary cessation great inconvenience cannot fail to be felt. The work not being executed with a view to profit further than the wages of labour, the producers get the whole return, however high; and it is often more than double what they would receive if working for a person in the trade, from the lower price at which he would be obliged to sell his goods, and from the necessity of making a profit on his transactions. But parties accustomed to work in this manner can scarcely get on in any other. Their services are of little avail to the legitimate lace manufacturer, and such a system of training, though set about with the best and most philanthropic intentions, practically interposes difficulties in the way of trade being carried on. . . . In the preliminary stage of the introduction of any branch of industry, no very strict regard to economic rules need be enforced; but a resort to such rules should take place at as early a period as possible, to impart to it those features by which alone it can be made self-supporting."

Not only was Irish lace expensive, but the organizers of the industry had little or no idea of catering to the demands of fashion by ensuring a regular supply of new designs and by keeping up standards of work through constant supervision. So the quality of the work declined and sales also diminished. By the 1860s the initial impetus had died away and the industry was in a state of decline. The Jury of the Paris Exhibition of 1867 noted that Irish lace had found its principal markets in England and the United States but that even this trade was much reduced of recent years.

In spite of these disadvantages and setbacks, however, it seemed that the industry had taken a reasonably firm hold in Ireland. Considerable quantities of lace of all types continued to be produced and some new centres of lace-making were established in the 1860s. At the beginning of the following decade there was even a considerable boom in certain types of lace, particularly crochet, when supplies of Continental lace were disrupted as a result of the Franco-Prussian War. But still the Irish lace industry continued to languish as too much cheap lace of inferior quality was produced which could not find a market, until strenuous efforts were made in the 1880s to increase the prosperity of the industry and bring about a revival.

The efforts began with the holding of an exhibition of Irish lace in 1883 at the Mansion House in London by several firms which dealt in it. Here it was apparent that though much of the work was of a reasonable standard of skill, the designs were poor and uninterest-ing.　As a result of an appeal by some Irish M.P.s, Alan S. Cole, of the Department of Science and Art in South Kensington, began to take an interest in the industry.　In 1884 a committee was set up under his chairmanship to promote a revival of Irish lace.　Its aims and methods were set out in a series of propositions:

"I. The making of lace in Ireland is a domestic industry, prac-tised by some hundreds of peasants in their homes, by communities in Convents, by children in Industrial and other schools, and by others.　Great skill in the work has been developed since the earlier part of the present century when the industry was introduced to the country through the efforts of Philanthropists.

"II. But the development of this skill has not been accompanied with the production and use of well-designed patterns.　The merits of the Irish lace, through which a considerable trade has been established, rest upon excellent workmanship applied to a few forms of somewhat stereotyped and poor design.

"III. Consequently the fluctuating success of Irish lace-making is traceable to an evanescent and uncertain fancy of consumers for something 'quaint and original', or to a sentimental desire for what is rather detrimentally called a 'National Production'.　The absence of a regulated supply of well-drawn and composed patterns seems to prevent the industry from becoming established upon either an artistic or a sound commercial basis.

"IV. The means of organizing a supply of such patterns exist in the Schools of Art of the United Kingdom.　But an incentive is necessary to call these means into operation and to induce the lace-workers to feel that it is in their interest to adopt improved designs. Looking to the social advantages of developing this domestic industry in the midst of a considerable agricultural and fishing population, similar in some important respects to those of France and Belgium, it is proposed to raise a fund for the distribution of new patterns amongst the scattered lace-workers of Ireland."

Thus was inaugurated a period of considerable activity.　Patterns were commissioned, competitions held, new schools were established and Irish lace was shown regularly at exhibitions in Ireland, England and elsewhere.　Cole himself made annual tours of Ireland to report on progress and to encourage further endeavours.　Much of the work was, of course, still bedevilled by the fact of its being largely in the hands of amateurs and philanthropists. Mabel Robinson wrote in 1887 (*Art Journal*, p. 145): "The northern lace schools, depending chiefly for their organization on the ability and zeal of one person, are apt to degenerate and flag when death or circumstance removes that inspiring spirit, and it is probably for this reason that we find such a much larger number of lace-makers in the southern provinces where the schools are all under the direction of convents."

There were some central organizations dealing with the work, however, notably the Irish Lace Depot and the Irish Industries Association, and Haywards of Oxford Street also took an active part towards the end of the century. Irish lace was sold in many of the big stores in London, such as Robinson & Cleaver, and by this time it seems to have established a certain market for itself in France as well as maintaining its older market in the U.S.A. The fashion at the end of the century for heavier laces also favoured the Irish industry, which had made a speciality of work of this type, and enabled it to survive against increasing competition from machine-made goods. By the end of the century, in fact, the Irish lace industry, though still tiny and weak compared with those of France and Belgium and far less securely based, was on a reasonably strong footing and seemed about to enter a new period of prosperity.

Needlepoint

The making of needlepoint lace began in Ireland in several areas independently in the later 1840s as a famine relief measure. One of the first ladies to devise this industry seems to have been Mrs. Jane Maclean, the wife of the rector of Tynan in County Armagh. Mrs. Maclean had some seventeenth-century Venetian needlepoint in her possession and she determined to discover how it was made in order that she might learn the skill and impart it to the local peasant women. This she did by painstakingly examining and unravelling the lace. By 1849 she was able to begin teaching needlepoint lace-making, a task in which she succeeded so well that in 1851 she was able to show at the Great Exhibition an "Imitation guipure lace flounce, worked by the children of Tynan Glebe School". This flounce had been bought by Lord John George Beresford, Archbishop of Armagh and Primate of Ireland and, as a result of its being shown in the Exhibition, a considerable number of orders were obtained by Mrs. Maclean. The Archbishop himself and his nieces also helped to find buyers for this lace. So the venture prospered for a while. Its end came in 1865 when the Rev. Maclean died. His family then left the area and, without their support and encouragement, the industry could not survive.

A similar shortlived venture was that of Miss Jane Clarke of 170 Regent Street, London, who set up a lace school at Belfast in the late 1840s. She showed a collection of Irish needlepoint made in imitation of seventeenth century Italian needle laces at the Great Exhibition of 1851. According to Mrs. Bury Palliser (*History of Lace*, p. 443, note), these laces were of high quality and so, indeed, they must have been, for in 1855 Miss Clarke was awarded a second-class medal at the Paris Exhibition. She seems to have died in the late 1850s or early 1860s, however, for her name ceases to appear in exhibition catalogues at that time, and with her died the needlepoint industry of Belfast.

More important than either of these two ventures was the establishment of a needlepoint lace school at the Presentation Convent in Youghal, County Cork. The beginnings of this school recall the efforts of Mrs. Maclean of Tynan, for its inception may be said to date from the moment when a piece of Venetian needlepoint came into the hands of Mother Mary Ann Smith. Like Mrs. Maclean, she unravelled the lace to learn the secrets of its manufacture and then taught the technique to some of the best needleworkers at the Convent School. In 1852 the convent lace school proper was opened. It seems to have enjoyed a reasonable degree of prosperity right from the start and it exerted an influence far beyond the convent itself, for needlepoint lace-making quickly spread from there to many other centres in Ireland. Youghal itself, moreover, remained to the end of the century the most renowned centre for the production of Irish needlepoint and much of the finest lace of this type came from there.

The lace made was the flat point usually considered as typically Irish, and characterized by stitches which, though more widely spaced and larger in size than those of their seventeenth-century models, nevertheless give a firm fabric of strong texture. At first Italian models were relied on for inspiration, but later on designs of a more contemporary flavour were chosen. These are often rather large scale and frequently include a reference to the national emblem, the shamrock. The lace is coarse compared with contemporary French or Belgian needlepoint, but it has a certain bold charm and is often of a good standard of execution.

The industry at Youghal suffered something of a decline in the 1870s, but it was endowed with new life in the following decade thanks to the readiness of the nuns to profit by the advice of Alan S. Cole and to try new designs. In 1887 Cole noted an improvement in trade and stated that the workers at Youghal had begun to make lace from some of the new designs that had won prizes at the competition held the previous year. The nuns had also begun to study the designs of old laces with a view to making copies of them. At the end of the 1880s the convent had the good fortune to number amongst its community a certain Sister Mary Regis, who proved to be an excellent lace designer. She did a great deal to raise the general standard of the work and it was thanks to her that the convent was able to make a very creditable showing at the Chicago Exhibition of 1893 (Pl. 51). Alan Cole's comment on the state of affairs after her death illustrates the utter reliance of even the best Irish lacemakers on an individual of enterprise and skill: "She is now dead, and from the drawings and lace that I saw, I am afraid that there is no immediate chance of anyone really succeeding her. This has a serious effect on the artistic side of the industry, and I was sorry to have found a tendency to fall back upon designs with poor forms and ill-considered contrasts in them" (*Report upon Visits to Irish Lace-Making and Embroidery Schools in 1897*, p. 5). Still, even so, at this time the Youghal industry was reasonably thriving. About seventy workers were employed, now organized on the basis of a co-operative society with the workers directly concerned in the administration. All the Youghal lace was sold through the Irish Lace Depot in Dublin.

The second most important needlepoint lace centre in Ireland was an offshoot of Youghal. This was the Convent of the Poor Clares at Kenmare in County Kerry, where needlepoint lace-making was established in 1861 by the Abbess O'Hagan. Like those of Youghal, the Kenmare workers made flat needlepoint, though they claimed always to use linen thread, unlike Youghal where cotton was sometimes employed. If anything, the Poor Clares were more enterprising as regards design and they seem to have found several competent designers amongst members of the community. Cole noted in 1887 that the convent made lace from new designs only, a rare occurrence at this time. It was in that year that lace was made for the Papal Jubilee by the Youghal convent to a design supplied by the Poor Clares. The lace industry at Kenmare flourished during the 1880s and 1890s. All Cole's reports of those years speak of steady progress and regular sales, thanks to the continuing energy and resourcefulness of the sisters. Cole notes that most of their sales were made to tourists.

Another important offshoot of Youghal was the lace industry of the Carmelite convent of New Ross, County Wexford. Here the Youghal flat-point was taught first of all, but soon the skill of the workers was turned to making imitations of Venetian *gros point*. This new product did not enjoy much success, so around 1865 *gros point* was given up in favour of lighter types of lace. The story is told that at that period the Prioress, Mother Augustine Dalton, bought a piece of rose point from a travelling Jewish pedlar. This she studied to learn the technique. As a result of her efforts, New Ross was, for many years, noted for its fine imitations of rose point. Rose point was produced too in designs of a more contemporary flavour, often incorporating the favourite shamrock. In spite of fluctuations of trade, the convent maintained the lace industry in its neighbourhood to the end of the century. Cole noted that it sold many of its products direct to a French firm.

In 1865, needlepoint lace-making was established at Innishmacsaint in County Fermanagh as a result of the initiative of the rector, the Rev. George Tottenham, who persuaded his sister-in-law, Miss L. Maclean (one of the Maclean family of Tynan, mentioned above), to teach there. After an uncertain start the industry took hold and was maintained until the end of the century. It concentrated on producing raised needlepoint laces in direct imitation of Venetian *gros point* and rose point (Pl. 52). The lace was sold through a Dublin merchant who procured regular orders.

In addition to these centres, needlepoint lace was also made on a smaller scale at the Convent of Mercy in Killarney, at another convent at Merrion, near Dublin, and by classes organized by private individuals at Ardee and Borris. *Reticella* laces of sixteenth-century type were made in the 1880s and 1890s at Cappoquin, County Waterford. This industry was run by a Miss Kean. A similar industry, under a Mrs. Montgomery, existed at Strabane,

County Tyrone, and *reticella* was also made at the Presentation Convent, Killarney.

An offshoot of the needlepoint lace industry was the making of tape laces joined by needlepoint stitches. References to such lace occur in exhibition catalogues of the 1850s and 1860s, but it never seems to have been a very extensive manufacture.

Bobbin lace

Bobbin lace was made in Ireland to a limited extent in the eighteenth century, but it was never a very popular trade. In the middle of the nineteenth century there was a minor revival of bobbin lace-making in various areas, mainly as a famine relief measure. The Dublin Normal Lace School, for example, was noted in the 1850s for its silk and cotton lace borders in the style of Buckinghamshire lace. These it sold through a London dealer, Mr. Goblet of Milk Street.

Most of the bobbin lace produced in Ireland, however, was rather poor-quality lace of Honiton type. Irish Honiton was shown at the Dublin Exhibition of 1853 by the Industrial School of the Convent of Mercy, Dublin, the Belfast Industrial School, the Convent of Mercy, Kinsale, and by the Misses Digges Latouche of Killmaule, County Tipperary. The latter seem to have established a small local industry in the late 1840s. They also showed lace at the Great Exhibition of 1851. None of this activity seems to have been very long lasting, however, for in the last decades of the century the only centres of production of Honiton lace in Ireland seem to have been Birr, and the Convent of Mercy at Parsonstown.

The latter institution also produced a small amount of lace in imitation of Brussels application, though of far inferior quality. According to Mrs. Bury Palliser (*History of Lace*, p. 443, note), lace of this type, known as "Irish" or "Curragh" point, was also made in the middle of the nineteenth century at Curragh in County Limerick, under the auspices of Lady de Vere.

Small amounts of lace of Valenciennes type were made in the mid-nineteenth century at the Convent of the Good Shepherd and other centres in Limerick, and at the Belfast Industrial School. Examples were shown at the Dublin Exhibition of 1853. The lace was not of a very high standard, however, and the manufacture soon died out as it could not hope to compete with machine-made Valenciennes.

Alan S. Cole noted in an article on lace-making in Ireland, which appeared in the *English Illustrated Magazine* in June, 1890, that a small amount of torchon lace was made at the Industrial School of the Convent of Mercy, Dublin and in a few other centres in Galway and the west of Ireland, and that the organizers of the Donegal Industrial Fund were trying to introduce the manufacture of coloured laces in Russian and Bohemian styles.

Carrickmacross work

The remaining "laces" associated with Ireland are not, in fact, true laces at all in the technical sense. The earliest type to become established was Carrickmacross work, a variety of cut-work embroidery on fine muslin. Two types were made: Carrickmacross *appliqué* and Carrickmacross guipure. To make the latter, motifs were drawn on muslin, outlined with embroidery, cut out and united by needlepoint bars (Pl. 53). In *appliqué* (Pl. 54) the motifs were made in a similar manner but, after being cut out, were applied to machine-made net. Sometimes both techniques may be found in the same piece. Quite often the work would be further enriched with needle-made filling stitches similar to those used in Limerick lace.

This type of imitation lace is said to have been introduced in the Carrickmacross area in about 1820. The story goes that a Mrs. Grey Porter, wife of the rector of Dunnamoyne, taught her maid and various other peasant women in the area to make cut-work in imitation of a piece of Italian cut-work in her possession. She succeeded so well that a Miss Reid, in the neighbouring village of Rahans, followed her example. The industry seems to have expanded quite rapidly around these two little centres, and for a while all went well. It depended entirely, however, on such orders as the two ladies could obtain by their own efforts, and thus inevitably languished after a while when too much lace was produced and found very little sale.

It was not entirely forgotten, however. Carrickmacross work was seized on eagerly after the great famine of 1846 as a possible means of relieving distress. A school for teaching this type of needlework was established by Mr. Tristram Kennedy, the agent of the Bath Estate, and by Captain Morant, agent of the Shirley Estate, at Carrickmacross. This was the origin of the celebrated Bath and Shirley School, which was to remain one of the chief centres of production of Carrickmacross work until the end of the century. The organizers seem to have been a good deal more businesslike in their approach than the originators of the industry. They arranged for some examples of Brussels and guipure laces to be given to the teacher at the school as a source of design ideas, and also succeeded in arousing the interest of Messrs. Forrest of Dublin in their products. This firm showed Carrickmacross work at the exhibitions of the 1850s and 1860s held in London, Dublin and Paris. At London in 1862 another Dublin firm, Charles Allen of 108 Grafton Street, also exhibited this type of imitation lace.

The designs used were mainly floral in character, often incorporating ornamental motifs such as scallops and scrolling strapwork characteristic of the mid-nineteenth century. A typical design is shown on Pl. 53. As well as borders and insertions, large articles were frequently made in Carrickmacross work, especially in the guipure variety, and it enjoyed a considerable vogue in the 1850s and 1860s. At this time the manufacture spread to other areas in Ireland.

In the later 1860s and in the 1870s, however, the industry declined as fashions changed and less attention was paid to keeping up the supply of new designs and good quality work. But, like many other Irish lace industries, Carrickmacross enjoyed an upsurge of new activity in the last two decades of the century. For this revival much of the credit must go to the efforts of the nuns of the St. Louis Convent at Carrickmacross itself, who were very active in obtaining better designs. These late designs were often adapted fairly directly from eighteenth-century lace (Pl. 54). The Bath and Shirley School was still productive at this time and there was another school in Carrickmacross itself. A further centre was a school at Crossmaglen, established by Miss Maggie McQuillan. Most of the products of these institutions seem to have been sold through the Dublin Lace Depot. The revival continued into the early years of the present century when the manufacture of Carrickmacross work was again taken up in many other parts of Ireland.

Limerick Lace

The making of the embroidered machine-made net known as Limerick lace represents virtually the only type of lace-making in Ireland in the nineteenth century that was begun purely as a commercial venture. The industry was started in 1829 by Mr. Charles Walker, a native of Oxfordshire who was originally educated for a career in the church. He married the daughter of an Essex lace manufacturer and set up in the lace business himself, working for a wholesale firm in London. On a visit to Ireland he conceived the idea of transferring his business there as it was clear that labour could be obtained there at a much cheaper rate than in England. Accordingly in 1829 he brought over twenty-four girls as teachers and set up a manufacture at Mount Kennet, near Limerick.

From the beginning both tamboured (chain-stitch embroidered) and needlerun net were made at Limerick, both techniques being frequently used on the same piece so as to achieve a delicate effect of light and shade. Further variety was given to the work by the use of many fancy filling stitches. The designs were adapted from those of blonde and other laces currently popular (Pl. 55). The industry prospered, as embroidered net was extremely fashionable at this period. At first Walker sold his products to a London firm in St. Paul's Churchyard, but after 1834, when this house failed, he employed his own travellers to collect orders from all over the British Isles. After Walker's death in 1842, many of his original workers returned to England, but the industry still continued to flourish in Limerick.

The two principal firms in the 1840s and 1850s were Messrs. Lambert & Bury of 77 Aldermanbury, London, who had a factory in Limerick, and Messrs. Forrest & Sons of Grafton Street, Dublin, who ran the Abbey Court Works in Limerick. Both exhibited their products whenever occasion permitted: Lambert & Bury at the Society of Arts Exhibition of 1849–50, at the Great Exhibition of 1851 and at the Dublin Exhibition of 1853, while Forrest & Sons showed at London in 1851 and 1862, at Dublin in 1853 and Paris in 1855. Another Limerick firm showing lace in 1853 at Dublin was that of J. Bannister, Sir Harry's Mall, Limerick. Some idea of the range of products may be gained from the catalogue entry for Forrest & Sons in 1851: "Lace dresses, flouncings, squares, scarfs, mantles, polkas, veils, berthas, handkerchiefs, sleeves, baby's robes, robings, lappets, lace collars, etc.", while in 1853 their display at Dublin included: "Limerick lace bridal dress and veil, ball and court dresses, etc." In the *Catalogue of the Dublin Exhibition* it was noted (pp. 334–5): "the excellence of many of the productions in the Exhibition bore testimony to the admirable quality of the work, the fact of there being now over 1500 individuals so employed in that city Limerick shows the progress which it has made. The firm of Lambert & Bury employ over 600 hands and they have for a length of time done a large export trade. Mr. Forrest, of Grafton Street in this city, has also done a large trade in Limerick for many years past, producing work of the finest quality of its kind, and we believe that at the present time the number of hands at work in his factory is about 400. The average wages earned by the girls in that locality is about nine-pence per day."

In the 1850s the making of this type of work seems to have spread to a few other areas. The Convent of Mercy at Newry, County Down, for example, began making Limerick lace in about 1850 and continued, albeit on a very limited scale, to the end of the century.

However, all was not as well with the industry as it appeared to be. Although Limerick lace appeared in the International Exhibition of 1862 in the displays of the London firms of Copestake, Moore, Crampton & Co. and Haywards of Oxford Street, as well as of Irish manufacturers, the Jury noted in its report (p. 3) that "the trade in this description of lace has diminished greatly since 1851". The reasons given, which included the production of large quantities of lace of inferior quality and "the neglect manifested by some of the Irish manufacturers to the increasing demand in England for novelty of design and improvement in execution", show that the manufacturers had fallen into the trap of letting standards slide. The fact was that, in spite of the cheapness of labour in Ireland, Limerick lace was expensive when compared with patterned machine-made lace, now coming on to the market in ever increasing quantities. It is clear that the manufacturers had tried to meet this competition by producing the embroidered net more cheaply and quickly and in doing so had not only sacrificed quality but had brought about a slump in the industry.

Throughout the later 1860s and the 1870s the Limerick lace industry was in a sad state of decline, but in the next decade attempts were made to improve the standard of the work and bring about a revival. A prominent figure in this movement was Mrs. R. Vere O'Brien who set up a Training School in George Street, Limerick, and began to try to get good new designs for this type of lace. She induced the nuns of the Convent of the Good Shepherd in Limerick, where this work was also taught, to join her in the endeavour. Designs were commissioned from art students (Pl. 56) and good designers in such places as the Convent of Poor Clares at Kenmare, and a much higher standard of work was insisted upon. Some Carrickmacross *appliqué* was also made in Limerick at this period. Mrs. Vere O'Brien's efforts achieved a considerable measure of success and she received and executed orders for the firm of Haywards in Oxford Street. The new designs were mostly eclectic in inspiration, some of them indeed being taken directly from rubbings of old Brussels and other lace. On a visit to Limerick in 1897, Alan S. Cole noted that the demand for Limerick lace now exceeded the supply, but he could not help adding (*Report*, p. 7): "I felt that the position of the Limerick Lace School is rather precarious, depending so much as it does upon the interest and enterprise of one lady." He also noted that "Limerick lace of less ambitious quality than that from the School is made in the town for the trade. But the influence of the school in George Street does not appear to touch this branch of Limerick lace-making."

As a result of this revival the making of Limerick lace was established at one or two other centres in the late 1880s, notably at the Convent of Mercy at Kinsale, which had forty workers employed in this pursuit by 1889 and seventy by 1897. Designs were obtained from the Dublin Lace Depot and drawn out for the workers by the supervisors. The lace was sold to Marshall & Snelgrove and Haywards of London, as well as to a Dublin dealer. Another smaller centre of this period was the Presentation Convent, Kilkenny.

Crochet

As needlepoint lace developed in the sixteenth century from linen embroidery, so, at some time around the end of the eighteenth and the beginning of the nineteenth century, crochet developed from tambour work, i.e. embroidery in chain stitch done by means of a small hook. It was but a short step from embroidering with a hook to dispensing with the ground material altogether and making a decorative textile by means of a series of linked loops or chains. Crochet was thus added to the varieties of fancy work available to ladies and instructions for making it may be found in manuals from the 1820s onwards, although its exact origin is unknown.

It was not until the famine years of the late 1840s that crochet was introduced into Ireland as a cottage industry. Mrs. Susannah Meredith, one of the ladies who assisted in this work, gave a graphic account of the situation at the time in her book, *The Lacemakers*, published in 1865: "When famine ravaged in Ireland in 1847, women were found inspired with an energy to work that was truly surprising. . . . The eagerness to obtain means of support was so pressing, that a perfect clamour for employment arose. . . . Women of the upper ranks developed an extraordinary skill in needlework, and, also, a great commercial aptitude to turn it to a profitable account. . . . The female children of the poor, all over the land, became the subjects of instruction in the making up of various sorts of articles for sale."

The making of crochet in Ireland seems to have started at the Ursuline Convent, Blackrock, Cork, for in 1845 the nuns there received £90 for the work produced by the children they were teaching in their school. In 1847 Mrs. Meredith established the Adelaide Industrial School in Cork for the teaching of crochet and the industry spread rapidly throughout the south of Ireland. Convents in the area were mainly responsible for teaching the work and for organizing the sale of finished pieces.

In the north of Ireland County Monaghan became the centre of the crochet industry. It started, however, though the efforts of Mrs. W. C. Roberts of Thornton, Kildare, to devise some means of relieving famine distress in her area. At first she taught the poor women to make a living by knitting woollen jackets, but when orders for these garments ceased in 1847, she turned to crochet. Within six months her best workers were scattered abroad throughout the surrounding district teaching their fellows. Even boys were eager to learn the craft at this time. Other areas began to demand teachers from Thornton, and twenty-four of the best workers were sent out to more distant places. One of these went to Clones in County Monaghan at the request of Mrs. C. Hand, the wife of the rector. This lady proved adept at devising new and better methods of work and at finding good models from which to take designs. Thanks to her efforts, Clones rapidly became the centre of crochet-making in the north of Ireland.

Crochet of many different types was made, Clones being noted for finer work (Pl. 57) than Cork in the south. Indeed, at that time, dealers could easily distinguish between the work of the two centres, although it is much more difficult, if not virtually impossible, for modern eyes to do so. The simplest type was plain crochet: edgings and small articles worked all in one piece. This plain crochet was naturally a staple product in the early days of the industry, but soon other methods were adopted to enable more complex pieces of work to be produced. It became customary for motifs to be worked separately and to be joined together by another worker with simple bars or twisted threads, producing an effect of lightness but a rather fragile fabric. In a more complex form known as lace crochet, the motifs were more securely joined by needlepoint lace stitches and the designs were often highlighted by relief areas of buttonhole stitch.

Around Clones there were also made three types of crochet known as guipure. Plain guipure was chiefly composed of bars of crochet very closely arranged, with a few small motifs scattered about. Knotted guipure was a more complex variety of this and most expensive and difficult of all was lifted guipure, in which the threads were also knotted as the work proceeded.

Many of the designs were adapted from Venetian *gros point* or rose point. Clones, especially, was noted for copies of the heavier Venetian laces, which secured a considerable success in Continental markets under the name of *point d'Irlande*. Not all the heavy laces were of such a high standard, however, for there was a fair proportion of crochet produced in which the motifs were large and clumsy and not very carefully arranged (Pl. 4). These contrast sharply with the delicate patterns derived from rose point. Other varieties of crochet, not readily identifiable now, were known as "Spanish lace" and "Jesuit lace".

The industry enjoyed a tremendous success in the early 1850s. The largest number of exhibitors in the lace section at the Dublin Exhibition of 1853 were those showing crochet. They included not only the large organizations and firms referred to at the beginning of this chapter, but also schools such as the Adelaide Industrial School, Cork and the Adare Industrial Schools, County Limerick, convents such as that of the Sisters of Mercy, Kinsale, and a host of private individuals, too numerous to mention here, including, of course, Mrs. Hand of Clones.

There can be no doubt that the success of crochet did a great deal to alleviate distress among the Irish peasantry. Mrs. Meredith's

61. Border of Bobbin Lace, Hungarian, 19th century. *Victorian and Albert Museum.*

62. Part of a Border of Venetian Needlepoint Lace made at the lace school at Burano, Italian, late 19th century. Reproduced from A. Carlier de Lantsheere: *Trésor de l'Art Dentellier,* Pl. 62:3.

63. Border of Silk Bobbin Lace, Maltese, second half of the 19th century. *Victoria and Albert Museum.*

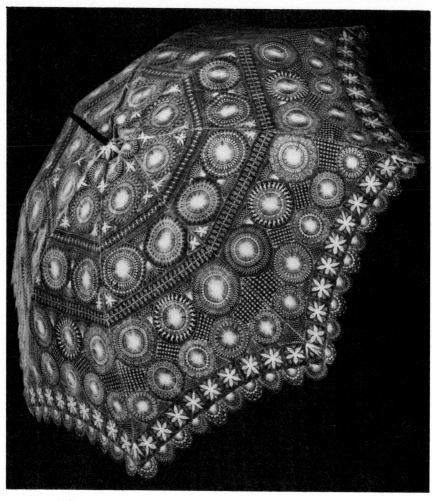

64. Parasol of Needlepoint Lace, *nanduti,* made by Martha Ferreira of Itaguá, Paraguay, end of the 19th century. *Dutch Royal Collection on loan to the Rijksmuseum, Amsterdam* (No. R.B.K.J.358).

65. Part of a Mantilla of Black Silk Bobbin Lace, Spanish (Barcelona), mid 19th century. *Victoria and Albert Museum.*

66. Collar of White Needlepoint Lace, *bibila*, made in Cyprus, shown at the Colonial and Indian Exhibition, 1886. *Victoria and Albert Museum*

67. Samples of Net made on the warp machine and afterwards hand-embroidered by needlerunning, English (Nottingham), *c* 1810-30. *Victoria and Albert Museum.*

68. Part of a Parasol Cover, imitation Chantilly lace made on the pusher machine; the thick outlining threads put in by hand; English (Nottingham), *c.* 1860-70. *The Castle Museum, Nottingham.*

69. Enlarged Detail of Lace made on the Leavers machine. *Rijksmuseum, Amsterdam.*

70. Part of a Scarf, Imitation Valenciennes Lace, made on the Leavers machine, English (Nottingham), 1843. *The Castle Museum, Nottingham.*

account of the industry is full of affecting tales on this theme, of which one example may suffice (*The Lacemakers*, p. 44): "This . . . child, through her exertions, enabled her mother and sisters to come out of the workhouse, where they were when she entered the crochet school, and they all became workers at this trade; the mother a 'washer', one daughter a 'pinner and tacker', and the other two made 'bits' and 'barred'." This extract also illustrates how much division of labour had developed in the industry.

To some people, however, it almost seemed as if crochet introduced more evils than it cured. Alan S. Cole, for example, writing on Irish lacemaking in the *English Illustrated Magazine* of June, 1890, remarked: "Crochet was readily bought up, but it as quickly earned a bad name—not merely on account of its artistic deficiencies, but also because of its socially demoralizing effects. Godly people held the crochet-maker in horror, and as long as travelling agents bought the work freely, and enabled the demoralized crochet women to thrive, there was no doubt or justification for the outcry made against the vice, which seemed to be inseparable from this branch of industry." (This attitude may be contrasted with that of many French and Belgian manufacturers of the nineteenth century who praised the hand-made lace industry because it kept workers safely at home and away from immoral factory life.)

It does indeed seem that crochet-making had a great appeal for the peasant women, not only because they were free to develop new forms and stitches for themselves, but because they were, on the whole, left to themselves in other respects too. Mrs. Meredith quoted a crochet-maker as saying (*The Lacemakers*, p. 374): "I likes the crochet best, ma'am, because there's hope in it. I *may* get ever so much for what I makes, if I happen to hit on a new stitch, and all the time I'm at it, I don't know but I may have a lot of money coming to me, and I'm kep in spirits like, to the last moment; but that pillow-work, och, 'tis horrid, ma'am! You're made sinsible from the beginning that you're only to get the trifle of a price, no more, nor no less, and no thoughts will help you, you must go on with the thing to your *ordthers*, which is what *I won't do*, until I can't help it, please God."

This freedom, of course, was bound to have an effect on the industry, for most workers soon preferred to spend their time on simple pieces rather than attempt more difficult and complicated work, and standards declined. It was, indeed, difficult to keep them up as the craft had become so widespread and control had largely passed out of the hands of the originators. Most of the work made in outlying districts was bought up by travelling agents for sale in small shops in local towns. The sudden success of the industry was destined to be shortlived. Even by 1855 inferior workmanship was becoming predominant, and by the 1860s the industry was in a state of stagnation.

Many of the crochet schools, including those of the Blackrock, Youghal and Kinsale Convents and the Adelaide School in Cork, were abandoned in the later 1850s. Writing of the closing of the latter, Mrs. Meredith noted (*The Lacemakers*, pp. 15–16): "Some of its pupils continued to produce quanities of very fine goods, and many are still working, but under very adverse circumstances. Almost all the hands in the neighbourhood turned, all at once, to the inferior sorts of the lace, and the production of any of the better kinds is now attended with an expense that absorbs the profits. Even at a premium, it is difficult to induce the lacemakers to take the necessary trouble, the habit of working carelessly is so confirmed.... The grotesque-looking coarseness of the fabric, with which the fluctuating demand has been supplied, bids fair soon to terminate its own existence; and for want of being properly treated, the Irish lace trade threatens to come to an end."

In some areas, indeed, crochet-making did virtually peter out at this time. Mrs. Meredith includes in her book a letter from Mrs. Roberts of Kildare (*ibid.*, p. 47): "It will give me great pleasure to give you any information in my power respecting the crochet trade in times past; but I regret to say, it cannot at present be said to exist in these parts. I do not think for the past eighteen months it has averaged £2 10s. per month; whereas in 1852 and to 1859, my payments were £100 to £300 per month."

In spite of all this, however, crochet had taken a pretty firm hold as a cottage industry in many areas and it was not so easily extinguished. Indeed, in the early 1870s there was a period of revival for a time. The crochet most favoured then was distinguished by small neat patterns. Nevertheless it is clear that some of the better types of work were no longer being made. In an account of the lace shown at the International Exhibition of 1874 in South Kensington, Mrs. Bury Palliser wrote (*Art Journal*, 1874, p. 174):

"Ireland sends her customary contribution of lace, Carrickmacross, tatting, etc.; but why has she given up the very fine crochet (sixty-knotted *guipure* we believe it is called), so superior to her usual handiwork? This fine crochet was first made, we believe, in 1851; but cheap production interposed, introduced a coarser material, and the workers prefer receiving the same amount for six common-made pieces, than for the same time occupied in producing the superior fabrications."

The revival of the 1870s was shortlived. In the following decade the crochet trade of Ireland entered the worst period of decline it had yet faced, as a result of competition from machine-made laces. The discovery of new techniques, which enabled cheap copies of needlepoint laces to be made, proved a serious blow to crochet which was itself a cheap imitation of such laces.

It was not until the very end of the 1880s that the industry began to revive again. That it had by this time become a well-entrenched cottage industry is evident from Alan S. Cole's account of the training of young workers around Clones in 1897 (*Report*, p. 11): "The teaching of young workers is carried on chiefly in cottages by the older workers, who under the pressure of demands from the trade find it worth their while to train the children mostly on the lines of the old grooves." This made it difficult to introduce new designs, but none the less many efforts were made in this direction in the last decade of the century. The movement for the revival of crochet was much assisted by the fact that heavy laces of this type enjoyed a great vogue at this period and it thus became worth the while of important lace firms to exert themselves to obtain a product of higher quality.

Messrs. Hayward of Oxford Street, for example, took a direct interest in crochet and invented a new variety called "Royal Irish Guipure" which was made in silk. In this crochet the old practice of joining the motifs by needlepoint stitches was revived. Irish dealers, too, worked hard to improve standards of design. Messrs. Dwyer of Cork were active in the Cork and New Ross areas, with the result that the number of workers was rapidly increased from 60 to 600, all of whom were maintained in employment. Examples of their products, showing the influence of sixteenth-century geometric laces, are illustrated on Pl. 58. The Carmelite Convent of New Ross improved the crochet of their workers to such an extent that they were able to enter into direct relations with a Paris dealer. Indeed, Cole noted that France and the U.S.A. were the two best markets for southern Irish crochet at this period. In the area around Clones a great deal was done to improve the work by Mr. Ben Lindsey, a Dublin lace dealer. Crochet continued to be made at this time around Ardara and a new industry was started at Lisnaskea, County Fermanagh.

Tatting

The most minor branch of the Irish lace industry was tatting, a technique in which a lacy openwork fabric is created by means of a thread manoeuvred with a shuttle or with a ring attached to a pin. This was introduced into Ireland by Miss Sophia Ellis, one of the daughters of the rector of Ardee, County Louth, who began to teach the craft to local children in 1847 as a famine relief measure. She secured a certain success at first and raised considerable sums of money to help the distressed peasants of the neighbourhood. Miss Ellis publicized the tatting of Ardee by showing it at the Great Exhibition of 1851 and the Dublin Exhibition of 1853. The craft continued to be practised around Ardee (examples of Irish tatting were shown at the International Exhibition of 1862 by H. Goblet of Milk Street, London) and also near Ballintubber, but it never became very important. The designs were repetitive and mostly of a geometric character, being based on circles of varying sizes (Pl. 59). Some attempts to improve them were made in the 1880s when new designs were commissioned from art students.

CHAPTER 6

MISCELLANEOUS

L ACE was made in the nineteenth century in many areas other than those already discussed. In most of them, however, the industry was either of a purely local nature, such as that of peasants making lace for their own use, or it was introduced or revived during the second half of the century. Very little of this lace, therefore, had any commercial importance. In this chapter a brief review of lace-making in such areas will be given, the countries being treated in alphabetical order.

Austria and Bohemia

At the beginning of the nineteenth century, lace-making flourished as a cottage industry in the mountainous regions of the Erzgebirge and the Reisengebirge in Bohemia, then part of Austria. According to Verhaegen (*La Dentelle et la Broderie sur Tulle*, 1902, Vol. II, p. 191) over 60,000 persons were engaged in this work. The laces produced seem to have been mainly simple torchons with some coarse Valenciennes and laces of Lille and *point de Paris* types. Similar laces were made in parts of Austria itself, including the Tyrol. The industry declined during the first half of the century and by 1862 there were only about 12,000 workers left.

In the 1870s there was great distress in these regions as a result of an economic crisis, and steps were taken to revive and improve the lace industry as a means of relief. The lead was taken by the Prague Chamber of Commerce and by the ladies of the aristocracy, headed by the Austrian Empress herself. A committee was formed to encourage the sale of lace and to set up schools in which lace-making could be taught. The most important of these was the School of Industrial Arts in Prague where there was established a course in lace design and a model workroom. Here instruction was given in making various types of lace currently prevalent in France and Belgium, including *point de gaze*. Selected lace-makers came to this workshop to learn the techniques and then returned to their country homes to teach them to others. Thanks to the work of this school and to the energy displayed by aristocratic ladies in buying up the lace and selling it again, a reasonably flourishing industry was established in the last quarter of the century. The lace produced seems to have been of a high standard as care was taken to procure good designs. It was publicized in exhibitions, examples being shown at the International Exhibition of 1874 in South Kensington, for example. A notable showing was made at the Paris Exhibition of 1878 by Franz Bollaerth of Vienna who exhibited a complete *toilette*, including a parasol cover designed by J. Storck, and produced at the request of the Empress expressly for the exhibition. The design is accomplished and original and shows the fine quality of the best work produced in Austria and Bohemia at this time. Unfortunately the technique of the lace is not indicated in the catalogue. Perhaps it was as a result of this encouraging success that a lace centre was established at Vienna itself in 1879.

China

Bobbin lace-making was introduced into China in the nineteenth century by mission schools in large cities such as Peking, Hangkow and Shanghai. None of the writers who mention this lace state what kind was made. It was all sold to Europeans and never became popular amongst the Chinese themselves.

Denmark

Lace-making in Denmark was principally carried on in North Schleswig, with Tondërn, after which the lace was named, as the centre of the industry. Here in the late eighteenth and early nineteenth centuries a flourishing manufacture was carried on of bobbin laces of Mechlin type. The laces were cheaper than Mechlin and enjoyed a certain success at that time when considerable quantities were exported to England. In 1801 about 20,000 workers were engaged in the industry. In the second quarter of the century, however, the industry entered a long period of decline. In about 1830, cotton thread was introduced and the quality of the lace deteriorated. Little attempt seems to have been made to keep abreast of current fashions, for the designs popular in the late eighteenth and early nineteenth centuries continued to be copied in a slavish manner. It seems, however, that some laces of Valenciennes type were made as well as Mechlin, and that attempts to broaden the base of the industry included the introduction of laces of Lille type in the 1840s and of Maltese type during the following decade. The firm of Jens Wulf & Son showed examples of Tondërn lace at the Great Exhibition of 1851, but it is clear that the industry was already much reduced, for Félix Aubry noted in his report on the lace in the Exhibition that there were only about 5,000 workers left. Part of the decline of the industry may be attributed to the flourishing state of agriculture in that area which made lace-making a comparatively unprofitable occupation. Two Danish exhibitors of lace were awarded medals at the Paris Exhibition of 1855, but after that time Tondërn lace became a minor industry of local interest only.

Germany

Saxony was the principal lace-making area in Germany in the nineteenth century. The industry was centred on Dresden and it was here that the finest laces were made. At the Great Exhibition of 1851, Madam Schreiber of Dresden showed some imitations of old Brussels bobbin lace in a fine technique with a background of bobbin-made mesh—the *vrai réseau*. The making of copies of old laces seems, in fact, to have become a speciality of Dresden in the second half of the nineteenth century. They were frequently sold as actual old laces, so good was the quality, and although they were extremely expensive, considerable quantities were sold in Paris as well as in the cities of Germany. The most perfect laces, according to Verhaegen (*La Dentelle et la Broderie sur Tulle*, Vol. II, p. 187), were produced in the model lace school at Schneeburg, established under the patronage of the King of Saxony. The imitation Brussels bobbin lace made there towards the end of the century was often enriched with relief work in needlepoint which gave it a very opulent appearance.

There was also a very extensive cottage lace industry in the mountainous area of the Erzgebirge and Voigteland. Men and boys worked at lace-making as well as women and girls, and it is even said (Mrs. Bury Palliser: *History of Lace*, p. 263) that the lace produced by the men was superior to the women's work. The workers were paid very little and their laces were thus very cheap. Various types were produced. Aubry, in his report of 1854 on the Great Exhibition of 1851, enumerates those in contemporary production:

white cotton laces of the types made at Le Puy, a very rough kind of Valenciennes, a poor imitation of Mechlin, bobbin-made lace flowers for application, silk blonde laces of ordinary quality and black silk lace of a rather better sort. It is clear that the industry was not dissimilar to that of Le Puy, though far less well organized and producing laces of far inferior quality. The German lace-makers could not hope to compete with those of Le Puy, and their lace steadily declined to the end of the century. The better types of lace gradually ceased to be made, their place being taken by coarser laces of Maltese type and by wide torchon laces (Pl. 60).

A certain amount of needlepoint lace was also made in Germany at this period.

Greece and the Greek Islands

The making of *reticella* needlepoint spread to Greece and the Greek Islands from Italy. Indeed, the coarser types are sometimes referred to as "Greek lace". A certain amount of heavy *reticella* seems to have continued to be made in Greece and the islands in the nineteenth century. According to Mrs. Bury Palliser some black silk lace of Maltese type was also made in the Greek Islands, while a limited amount of white silk lace for use in Jewish Synagogues was made in Athens and other parts of mainland Greece. Crete was noted for simple bobbin laces of torchon type in which coloured threads were often used.

Hungary

In Hungary the peasants made coarse bobbin laces for their own use in thick linen thread or yellow silk. The laces, which often have a scalloped lower edge, are characterized by debased floral or vermicular designs of bold execution, little or no use being made of decorative filling devices (Pl. 61).

India and Ceylon

The making of laces of Bedfordshire Maltese and other East Midlands varieties was introduced into Ceylon and parts of India, including Travancore and Madras, by missionaries in the second half of the nineteenth century. Some examples of this lace were shown in London at the International Exhibition of 1862.

Italy

Lace-making in Italy had dwindled almost to nothing by the beginning of the nineteenth century. A certain amount of needle-point was still being made then on the island of Burano near Venice. This lace was an inferior imitation of the Alençon needlepoint of the late eighteenth century. In this lace the threads outlining details of the design were merely sewn down into place and not covered by overcasting or buttonhole stitch. The mesh of the ground net-work was square but it had a cloudy appearance owing to the uneven quality of the thread used. It was made by passing a thread across the whole width of the lace as a foundation for a row of looped meshes. The designs usually consisted of borders of small flowers with other small floral or leafy motifs dotted about the ground above. Burano needlepoint had none of the subtleties of other needlepoint laces. The whole piece of lace was generally made by one worker who employed a pillow with a small wooden cylinder on it across which the parchment pattern was stretched. Lace-making lingered on in Burano until the 1840s when it seemed to have become virtually extinct.

Elsewhere in Italy a certain amount of bobbin lace was still made. At Venice small quantities of blonde lace of inferior quality were made at the beginning of the century, while at Pellestrina, a fishing village on the Lido, a rough kind of torchon was produced. It was described by Mrs. Bury Palliser (*History of Lace*, p. 62) as "an inextricable labyrinth of threads with vaguely distinguishable lines and occasional holes". Even coarser bobbin laces were made by the peasant women of the Abruzzi and the Province of the Marche. These were worked over a geometrically perforated card instead of a parchment pattern.

In Genoa, bobbin lace-making was still carried on to a limited extent. The laces made were derived from the Genoese guipures of the seventeenth century. A small collection of Genoese bobbin lace was shown at the Great Exhibition of 1851, but Aubry noted in his report that it was very much behind the times as far as fashion was concerned and that the industry was in a state of complete decadence. The type of knotting known as *macramé* was also made in and around Genoa.

The lace industry in Genoa and the Riviera was revived to a

certain extent in the 1850s.   The making of tape lace with needlepoint or crochet fillings was introduced and guipure laces in black
silk were also made for the French market.   According to Mrs.
Bury Palliser, in 1862 there were 2,210 lace-workers in Santa
Margherita and 1,494 in Rapallo as well as those in Genoa itself.
There was a revival of *macramé*, too, at this time, particularly of the
more elaborate designs.   This revival, which began in the 1840s, is
attributed to the endeavours of the Baroness A. d'Asti, who unravelled
and studied old pieces of *macramé* to learn the secrets of their
technique.   Another centre which enjoyed a revival of lace-
making at this period was Cantu near Lake Como, where black and
white laces of simple torchon type were made in both silk and cotton.

It was not until 1872 that the revival of the Burano industry began.
That year the inhabitants suffered great distress owing to an
unusually severe winter, during which the lagoons became frozen
and the fishermen were unable to earn their living.   A fund was
started to relieve the near-starvation conditions of the peasants and
it was decided that some permanent alternative means of livelihood
should be introduced.   At first the making of fishing-nets was tried,
but when this proved impracticable, the idea grew up of reviving the
old lace industry.

Two ladies, Princess Chigi-Giovanelli and Countess Adriana
Marcello, were asked to become patrons of a lace school (later
Queen Margherita of Italy became the President of the Burano
lace school).   The Countess Marcello discovered an old woman,
Cencia Scarpariola, who still remembered how to make needlepoint
lace and, indeed, had never ceased to make it herself.   The art was
acquired from her by Anne Bellorio d'Este, a teacher at Burano,
who in turn taught it to eight pupils of the school there.   The
venture prospered from the start and by 1878 the school was able
to show some of its products at the Paris Exhibition (Fig. 11).   It is
clear that these consisted mainly of reproductions of the old Burano
designs and technique, both in patterns of the early nineteenth
century and in others borrowed from the eighteenth century.   But
from the lower piece in the illustration it is obvious that even at this
early stage an attempt was being made to broaden the scope of the
Burano workers by setting them to produce other types of needlepoint lace.   By the end of the century, copies of Venetian *gros point*
and rose point had joined Burano needlepoint as staple products of

the industry, and a certain amount of lace was also made in the Alençon and Argentan techniques. It is not easy to distinguish Burano copies of seventeenth-century Italian laces from those made in

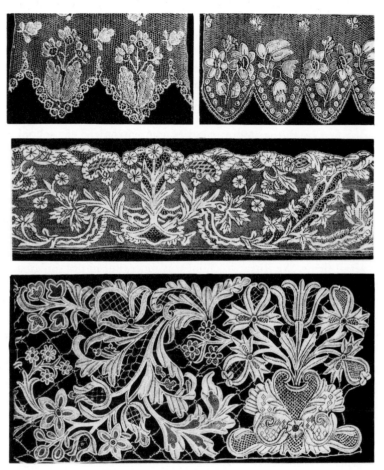

FIG. 11. Needlepoint lace made at the lace school at Burano, shown at the Paris International Exhibition of 1878. (*Art Journal Catalogue*, p. 100.)

France and Belgium, but it seems that a rather stiff and slavish copying of old designs was often combined in them with an over-elaboration of decorative features such as little *picots* and relief areas (Pl. 6a). This often gives the lace a fussy though mechanical appearance.

By the end of the century there were over 400 needlepoint lace-makers at Burano. Great care was taken to ensure a high standard of work. Much of the lace was made in workrooms under super-vision; the best workers were trained by professional artists and a collection of antique lace was formed for study purposes. It seems, indeed, that by this time there was no type of design or technique that the workers could not faithfully copy. Each lace-maker specialized in a different part of the work, according to her capacity, and this made for cheaper and more efficient production.

By the end of the century the lace-making concern had been formed into a limited company. The sale of the lace was greatly aided at first by the aristocratic ladies who patronized the school and secured orders for it from among their friends and acquaintances, and later by those who ran the company. Ambassadors and consuls in foreign countries were asked to assist in publicizing Burano lace, each piece of which bore a trademark (on one side a doge's cap, on the other a trefoil with the initials SMB for Scuola Merletti Burano) which was registered in all the principal towns of Europe. As well as maintaining a steady sale to private individuals and to wholesale and retail firms, the Burano school was successful in obtaining many commissions from royalty and high ecclesiastical dignitaries, as well as selling its products to Paris couturiers such as Worth and Paquin.

Another successful venture in the Venice area was that a Cavalier Michelangelo Jesurum, who set about reviving the bobbin lace-industry of Pellestrina in the 1870s. He studied old designs to improve the technique and founded a lace school. His efforts quickly bore fruit and he was able to introduce new types of lace which enjoyed a considerable success. Among these was a type of poly-chrome bobbin lace, introduced in 1877, which featured designs of flowers, fruit, foliage and animals. In the Victoria and Albert Museum Library there is a catalogue of M. Jesurum & Co., dated December, 1883, which gives a good indication of the range of products offered for sale. These included various types of bobbin lace of eclectic design which were given fancy names such as Doge point, rococo, mosaic point, as well as polychrome bobbin lace, black and white silk lace and laces of Cluny and Maltese types. Jesurum also sold all the types of needlepoint lace made at Burano, as well as offering to repair or reproduce any kind of antique lace.

In the latter years of the nineteenth century, attempts were made to found lace schools in various parts of Italy in an effort to resuscitate dying peasant crafts or to create small local industries. None of these seems to have enjoyed any very lasting success. They included efforts to revive the making of torchon bobbin lace and darned netting (*lacis*) in Sicily, and the foundation of schools at Udine, Naples, Pisa, Florence and elsewhere. In Bologna a society known as Aemilia Ars was founded in 1900. The workers there specialized in making *reticella* needlepoint, for which they used the designs of old sixteenth-century pattern books such as those of Vecellio, Vinciolo and Parasole.

Japan

In the 1870s, as a very minor part of the westernization of Japan, a government-sponsored lace school was set up at Yokohama. Here the making of Honiton lace was taught under the guidance of an Englishwoman. The lace was made in silk as well as cotton. An example of 1885 in the Victoria and Albert Museum is of a fine technique and in a floral style with a distinctly Japanese flavour.

Madeira

In Madeira, blonde lace of Spanish type was made in the mid-nineteenth century. The examples shown at the Great Exhibition of 1851, where Madeira exhibited with Portugal, excited the admiration of Félix Aubry. The making of this lace seems to have died out later in the 1850s in favour of silk lace of Maltese type and narrow borders of bobbin lace of a rather coarse variety. Examples of these were shown at the Paris Exhibition of 1867.

Malta

Bobbin lace-making was introduced into Malta in 1833 by Lady Hamilton Chichester who brought over some lace-makers from Genoa. The lace made was a guipure type bearing some resemblance to earlier Genoese lace, particularly in the little wheat-ear ornaments which are one of its principal characteristics. The lace was made mainly in black and cream-coloured silk in geometric designs in which the Maltese cross frequently figures (Pl. 63). The latter might, indeed, almost be regarded as a trademark. Some examples of Maltese lace were shown at the Great Exhibition of 1851, where they were much admired. Lace of this type became very fashionable in the decades following the Exhibition, and the manufacture was taken up in many of the important lace-making areas of Europe.

The industry in Malta itself enjoyed a great expansion in the 1850s and 1860s. The Jury of the International Exhibition of 1862 in London commented on this in its report (p. 4), noting that Malta had sent "a large display of flouncings, shawls, veils and coiffures, showing the very great improvement made in the manufacture, and giving reason to expect that with perseverance and attention to some few points, a high order of excellence may be obtained. Some of the smaller articles especially are remarkable for their beautiful quality." The Jury went on to complain, however, of "the sameness in the designs of Maltese lace", and indeed, the same few ideas were repeated endlessly over and over again. It is thus very difficult to date Maltese lace unless the shape of the piece gives some clue. The lace continued to be popular until the end of the century.

The Netherlands

In the second half of the nineteenth century, attempts were made to establish a lace industry in the Netherlands. The earliest of these seems to have been the foundation of a lace school at Sluis in 1850 under the patronage of Queen Sophie. Some workers were brought over from Bruges to teach the making of *Duchesse* and application laces. Other lace schools were set up at a later period at Apeldoorn, The Hague, Hoorn and 's-Gravenmoer. They seem to have produced lace similar to that of Sluis.

Paraguay

The former Spanish colonies in Central and Southern America relied mainly on European sources for their lace, but certain types were made locally as well. In Brazil, for example, a coarse type of narrow bobbin lace was made. The most notable lace of these areas was, however, the so-called Tenerife lace or "nanduti", to give it its local name. The finest variety seems to have been that produced in Paraguay. It is a needlepoint lace characterized by circular motifs resembling spiders' webs. The rayed foundation was made first and afterwards decorated, mainly with geometric patterns (Pl. 64). This lace, made in cotton or silk, often has a very delicate appearance. A certain amount seems to have found its way to

Europe in the late nineteenth century for objects such as handkerchiefs decorated with it sometimes occur in assemblages of nineteenth-century lace.

Portugal

The lace industry of Portugal was centred on the Péniche penin-
sula, north of Lisbon. Here were made white silk laces similar to
those of Spain but somewhat inferior in design and quality. A
small amount of black silk lace was also made. The industry seems
to have been reasonably successful in the mid-nineteenth century for
two Portuguese firms were awarded medals for their white silk lace
at the Paris Exhibition of 1855. In Lisbon itself, one firm made
border laces of Mechlin type into which Portuguese designs were
introduced in an attempt to give the lace a national flavour. The
amount of this lace produced was very small as it was only made for
orders from the court and aristocracy.

Russia

The peasants of north-eastern Russia made lace for their own use
throughout the nineteenth century. These were coarse bobbin
laces in vermicular or floral patterns, into which red and blue
threads were sometimes introduced. The best lace was said to be
that from the Nizhniy Novgorod (Gorkiy) area. Some attempts to
exploit this lace commercially were made in the late nineteenth
century. Examples of it were, for instance, sent to the International
Exhibition held in South Kensington in 1874.

At the very end of the century, a school of needlepoint lace was
set up in Moscow under the patronage of the Tsarina. Here were
produced copies of Venetian needlepoint and laces of oriental
design which were known as *point de Moscou*.

Spain

Most of the vast quantities of black and white silk lace consumed in
Spain and the former Spanish colonies in Central and South
America were produced in France or Belgium. There was, however, a blonde lace industry in Spain itself, principally in Catalonia
and in La Mancha, a part of Castile. Although the industry was
on a small scale, it seems to have prospered, at any rate in the middle
of the nineteenth century, as it met the needs of a steady home

demand. The silk used in this manufacture was of a very high quality, produced at a spinning factory not far from Barcelona.

Spanish lace was shown at many of the international exhibitions of the nineteenth century. Commenting on the display in 1851, Félix Aubry noted that it mainly comprised large pieces such as dresses, mantillas, veils and shawls in a heavy style of design popular in Spain but which would never do for the French market. The workmanship was less good than that of French silk lace too. Among the firms who exhibited were José Fites and Magarit & Cie., both of Vich. Included in the display were some examples of net embroidered with floral designs in brightly coloured silks. At this time, too, a small amount of white bobbin lace of Lille type was also made in Barcelona.

Aubry noted in 1851 that some of the mantillas had designs in an oriental style, featuring little scenes with houses, pagodas, rivers and people, and in 1855 at the Paris Exhibition the two firms mentioned above were awarded medals for their displays of lace in this manner. Mainly, however, floral designs or patterns with an eighteenth-century flavour (Pl. 65) were chosen. In 1867 the Jury of the Paris Exhibition noted that there was a slight falling-off in the prosperity of the Spanish lace industry, although the customary display of dresses, mantillas and veils had been sent. The Jury noted that these goods were made exclusively for home consumption or for export to Central and Southern America. They attributed the decline in the industry to deficiencies in its management. Nevertheless it seems to have been able to survive to the end of the century.

Elsewhere in Spain torchon and other coarse bobbin laces, including some of Maltese type, were made by peasants for their own use.

Sweden

In Sweden in the nineteenth century there existed a small-scale lace industry at Vadstena. Here were made guipure and torchon laces in black and white thread. The industry seems to have been quite flourishing up to about 1830 and small amounts of this lace were even exported as well as being sold all over Sweden. After the middle of the century, however the industry declined.

In Scania and Dalecarlia the peasant women made coarse bobbin

71. Border of Furnishing Lace made on the lace curtain machine, English (Nottingham), second half of the 19th century. *The Castle Museum, Nottingham.*

72. Border of Furnishing Lace made on the warp machine, English (Nottingham), *c.* 1855-65. *The Castle Museum, Nottingham.*

73. Shawls of Black Lace made on the pusher machine by W. Vickers of Nottingham, shown at the International Exhibition of 1862. *Art Journal Catalogue,* p.48.

74. Borders of Lace of Spanish Type made on the Leavers machine, English (Nottingham); *top,* 1868-72; *bottom,* made by Brooksbank & Sanby, *c.* 1883. *The Castle Museum, Nottingham.*

laces for their own use, mainly of thick unbleached linen threads in geometric patterns. Attempts were made in the late nineteenth century to revive all these types of lace by a society set up for the promotion of peasant crafts, Handarbetets Vänner. As well as encouraging the production of lace, the society attempted to secure a wider market for it by opening a shop for peasant crafts in Stockholm.

Switzerland

The lace industry in Switzerland was centred on Neufchâtel. Here in the early nineteenth century were made blonde laces and narrow borders of Lille and Mechlin types. In 1840 an attempt was made to establish lace-making in Geneva with the introduction of Brussels bobbin lace there. The Swiss lace industry was, however, never able to compete with the products of Mirecourt in France in either design or quality of workmanship, and it ceased to be of any importance after the middle of the nineteenth century.

Turkey

In Asia Minor and some of the islands of the eastern Mediterranean, such as Rhodes and Cyprus, a type of lace was made with the needle or tambour hook. This lace, known as "bibila", has a closely-worked knotted texture. The designs usually consisted of small flowers worked in bright colours or in white (Pl. 66), and the lace was often used to trim embroidered covers and garments. A display of bibila lace appeared at the Paris Exhibition of 1867, and some of it seems to have found its way to western Europe in the latter half of the nineteenth century.

The United States of America

Although there seem to have been many amateur needlewomen in the United States in the nineteenth century who delighted in working embroidered net or in making easy varieties of tape and bobbin lace, lace-making never became established on a commercial basis in the United States. One curious instance of an attempt at its introduction there may be noted, however. At some of the schools set up in the Indian Reservations lace-making was taught. The Indian girls proved clever lace-makers but "their work is the most servile and mechanical imitation of their pattern; and resembles machine-lace in its showing a faultless regularity that is less pleasing than the little inequalities of the true artistic workwomen of the traditional lace-making countries" (Florence Fenwick Miller: *The Chicago Exhibition: Lace and other personal decoration* in *Art Journal*, 1893, Supplement).

CHAPTER 7

MACHINE-MADE LACE IN ENGLAND

IN the previous chapters on the hand-made lace industry, machine-made lace has figured prominently as the villain of the piece, presenting hand-made lace with severe and determined competition and leading eventually to its decline. Now it is time for the machine-lace industry to take the centre of the stage. In tracing its history we shall see that it, too, suffered many vicissitudes during the course of the nineteenth century and that its path to success was by no means without obstacles.

The fullest account of the industry in England, its country of origin, is to be found in a monumental work: *The History of the Machine-wrought Lace and Hosiery Manufactures*, published in 1867 by William Felkin, a Nottingham lace manufacturer who had personally participated in the development of the industry since 1808. The book contains a wealth of information amidst a daunting mass of technical details about the highly complicated lace machines. Most students will no doubt find the excellent survey: *Nottingham Lace* by Zillah Halls, published in 1964 by the Castle Museum, Nottingham, much easier to cope with and far more comprehensible. This publication contains many references to records and pattern books, preserved at Nottingham largely through the interest of Felkin himself. It is not necessary here to discuss the details of the actual lace machinery except in so far as they help towards an understanding of the finished product, though some comprehension of the techniques employed is essential for those wishing to be able to distinguish machine-made from hand-made lace.

Machines derived from the stocking-frame and the beginning of the embroidered net industry

The stocking-frame was invented in the late sixteenth century by the Rev. William Lee. Since then the stocking industry had been established in the area centring on Nottingham, Derby and Leicester, but it was not until the second half of the eighteenth century that inventors began to try to produce a lace-like fabric on the machine. These attempts were inspired no doubt by other contemporary developments in the field of textile machinery, as well as by the fact that the currently fashionable simple, net-like laces with sparse ornamentation seemed more susceptible to imitation by machinery than the more complex laces of earlier times.

The first patent for making a type of net on the stocking-frame was taken out in 1764, and patterned net was made five years later, in 1769, by Robert Frost of Nottingham. Very few pieces of this early stocking-frame lace have survived, for it was made in the same way as knitted stockings and, like them, exhibited a tendency to unravel when a thread was broken. Samples in both cotton and silk preserved at Nottingham have designs in plain knitting against a mesh ground. The patterns are outlined by threads put in by hand, a practice that was to continue throughout the first half of the nineteenth century. In 1777 Frost took out another patent, this time for "square net", a more durable though expensive fabric, which continued to be made until the 1830s.

By the 1780s a much better type of net had been developed. This was known as "point net". It had a hexagonal mesh and patterns could be made in it by changing the positions of some of the looped stitches to leave holes which were then outlined by a thick thread put in by hand. The point net machine was patented in 1778 by Thomas Taylor of Nottingham, while in 1786 John Rogers of Mansfield altered the machines to enable them to make a fast stitch in the net at intervals, thus greatly increasing its durability. Point net quickly became popular. By 1790 there were more than 200 machines producing it, and the industry had spread to other centres in Europe. Much of the net produced in Nottingham was ornamented by designs worked by hand with the needle, the beginning of an industry which was to employ a very large number of women and children in and around Nottingham in the first half of the nineteenth century. The designs of such pieces as survive at Nottingham are mainly of a light floral type, sometimes with classical key or vase motifs added. According to Felkin, the chief manufacturers of point net were W. & T. Hayne, Maltby & Brewitt, Wilson, Burnside & Watson, Robert & Thomas Frost.

Although point net enjoyed a great vogue in the first decade of the nineteenth century, it was clear that the possibilities of making lace on the stocking-frame were now exhausted and that other ideas must be tried if a really good imitation of hand-made lace was to be produced. A new kind of machine, known as the warp machine, originally invented in about 1775, was soon the subject of experimental lace-making. Unlike the stocking-frame, which employed one continuous thread to make a looped fabric, the warp machine used a different thread for each vertical row of loops and the rows were worked in a zigzag formation in order to link them together. It was quite easy to vary this technique either to produce a more closely-knit, durable fabric, by lengthening the connecting threads between the loops so that they extended over two stitches rather than one, or an openwork fabric in which the vertical rows of loops were left unconnected at intervals so as to leave a series of holes. The fabric produced by the warp machine with its many threads was much more stable and less likely to unravel than ordinary knitting.

From about 1795, attempts were made to produce lace on the warp machine, attempts which quickly met with success for, by the opening years of the nineteenth century, the machines had been adapted to produce nets both plain or patterned with holes, sometimes with the addition of a thread run in by hand. A considerable quantity of warp net has survived. It is not too difficult to distinguish from types of net made on later lace machines, for the tiny loops which form the meshes may be seen if the net is examined under a lens. Needlerun designs put in by hand are readily detectable, too, for the threads pass through the holes of the net and are not incorporated into the actual fabric as they are in hand-made laces, or in later lace which is entirely machine-made. Some small samples of warp net with needlerun patterns in the Victoria and Albert Museum (Pl. 67) probably date from the second or third decade of the nineteenth century. These machine-made nets of various types and simple laces in silk and cotton were widely used in the early part of the century, either as trimmings or, mounted on silk, for entire dresses.

The bobbin-net machine and its successors

All through the late eighteenth century and the first decade of the nineteenth, attempts were being made to produce a net with a mesh which would more closely resemble the hexagonal mesh with twisted sides found in Lille and East Midlands laces (cf. Pl. 18), the easiest of the bobbin-made nets to make and thus to imitate. The breakthrough came in 1808 when John Heathcoat took out the first patent for his bobbin-net machine.

Heathcoat, born in 1793, went to work for a framesmith in Nottingham after serving his apprenticeship in the hosiery industry at Derby. He made a very close study of the movements of a bobbin lace-maker and thus discovered the principle he was to employ in his machine. He distinguished amid the multitude of threads a number whose position varied very little, for they travelled longitudinally along the lace while other threads crossed them and twisted round them diagonally to produce the mesh. Heathcoat used the former as the warp threads in his machine while the weft threads were twisted round and carried over them by means of flat circular bobbins, each held in a carriage. When the fabric was released from the machine, the warp threads, hitherto tightly stretched, were relaxed so that the meshes took on the familiar hexagonal shape.

The machine was an extremely complicated affair and was at first capable of making only very narrow strips of net. All the earliest developments were aimed at reducing the number of movements necessary, thus making the machine more efficient, and at increasing the width of the net produced. Heathcoat patented an improved version of his machine in 1809, and further patents were taken out by him in 1813 and 1815. In 1816 he left Loughborough, where he had set up his factory, because of Luddite riots, and settled at Tiverton in Devon, where he continued to make modifications and improvements to the lace machinery.

Meanwhile various other modifications of the machine had been made by other workers, which were destined to have a far-reaching effect on the machine-lace industry, although for most of the second and third decades of the nineteenth century attention was concentrated principally on the improvement of the net-making mechanism. As early as 1811 a patent was taken out for a machine producing a net similar to Heathcoat's, but using the diagonal threads as the warp instead of the longitudinal. This traverse warp machine, invented by John Brown of New Radford near Nottingham, proved most efficient at producing very narrow trimming nets or "quillings" as they were called.

A more significant advance was made by John Leavers who, in 1813, patented the machine that still bears his name. In the Leavers machine the bobbins and carriages carrying the weft threads were made extremely thin, so that they could all be arranged in one row, unlike those on Heathcoat's machine which had to be accommodated on two rows or "tiers". Another very important development of the period was the patenting in 1812 by Samuel Clark and James Mart of Nottingham of the "pusher" machine, so-called because each bobbin and carriage was worked by a separate device known as a pusher. A further improvement in the making of net was brought about by William Morley, who patented his circular comb machine in 1824, incorporating various technical refinements based on Heathcoat's original invention.

Up to the mid-1820s, in fact, the main emphasis in the machine-lace industry was on the production of a really good-quality net. All the machines listed above made net of exactly the same type. At first this had hexagonal meshes, but by 1830 the characteristic light net with diamond-shaped meshes, the type most familiar from its use in application laces (Pl. 25), had made its appearance. The net resembles the Lille mesh with its crossed threads at the corners, but the side threads are all twisted very much more tightly and the finished net has a more regular, light and mechanical appearance than a hand-made net. Moreover, unlike the hand-made grounds of, for example, Chantilly lace, it shows no tendency to split along the joins for it was, of course, made in any width required not, like them, in narrow strips.

The embroidered net industry

The use of machine-made nets as a basis for applied bobbin-made motifs in the lace industries of Devonshire and Belgium has already been described (pp. 103 and 138), as has the production of an imitation lace patterned with applied muslin motifs which originated at Carrickmacross in Ireland (p. 182). In Nottingham the working of patterns on net by needlerun threads had become a well-established industry even before the invention of the bobbin-net machine. The increased production of net led to a very great expansion in this side of the lace industry between 1810 and 1830. By 1831, indeed, there were said to be no less than 150,000 workers engaged in this branch of the trade.

Two different methods of embroidering the net were employed. For needlerun net a darning stitch was used, i.e. the threads were carried in and out of the holes of the net in a regular way to form the main part of the pattern, while the holes were enlarged or ornamented with various needlepoint stitches to imitate the fancy fillings of real lace (Pl. 67). The designs to be embroidered were printed on the net by wood blocks. The net was then stretched in a frame for the attentions of the worker who used her right hand to embroider the design, keeping her left under the net. Net was also "tamboured" or embroidered in chain-stitch (cf. Pl. 56). This technique derives its name from the fact that the material to be worked was often stretched in a circular frame like a drum (Fr. *tambour*). The design was worked by means of a hooked needle, a technique of chain-stitch embroidery introduced into Europe in the second half of the eighteenth century. In all types of net embroidery the meshes of the groundwork may be seen clearly throughout the embroidered areas and the resulting fabric is quite different from bobbin- or needle-made lace.

The designs of hand-made laces were copied and adapted for these embroidered nets, particularly the rows of flower sprigs so popular on the blonde laces of the 1820s and 1830s (see Pls. 19, 20). Contemporary white embroidery also influenced the technique, for it is not uncommon to find embroidered nets of the 1830s and 1840s in which large holes are worked in the manner of *broderie anglaise*. The name "British point lace" was coined for the best varieties of embroidered net. All types enjoyed a tremendous vogue in the years from 1810–1830, vying in popularity with the blondes, whose designs they emulated. Many pelerines, collars, bonnet-veils and smaller pieces survive from this period in both coarse and fine work, in silk or cotton, black or white.

The centre of the English embroidered-net industry was Nottingham itself, but a considerable quantity of better-class work, particularly of the tamboured variety, was produced in London, whilst the industry was carried on too in lesser centres such as Coggleshall in Essex. Limerick lace, an off-shoot of the English embroidered-net industry, has already been described (pp. 103–6). Embroidered nets were made in Scotland also.

The rapid growth of the embroidered-net industry was, however, only one of the results of the invention of the bobbin-net machine.

One of its earliest effects was to drive point net off the market. Felkin notes that the demand for point net began to slacken as early as 1810–11. The owners of point-net machines tried to compete with the superior twist net made on the bobbin-net machines by reverting to the production of the original non-fast variety of point net, which could be made much more quickly and sold much more cheaply (an expedient similar to those later adopted, as has been seen, in some of the hand-lace industries). This was to no avail, however, for demand virtually ceased altogether by 1815, and by the end of the 1820s point-net machines had gone out of use entirely.

Sharp fluctuations of fortune were, indeed, to bedevil the machine-lace industry right through the nineteenth century. Like the hand-lace industries, and perhaps even more than them, machine-lace was subject to the vagaries of fashion. Novelty was the goal endlessly pursued. As soon as some new lace caught the public fancy, as many firms as possible, both large and small, rushed into production with the inevitable result that the market was flooded, demand slackened, and stocks could not be got rid of. This pattern of events occurred time and time again, but it only hindered and did not halt the steady growth of the Nottingham lace trade throughout the nineteenth century.

One of the worst crises in the machine-lace industry occurred at the end of the 1820s. The beginning of that decade had been a boom period. Between 1820 and 1822, most lace machines were adapted to use by steam power and those years saw a great expansion in the industry with many new factories being established. This expansionist movement was heightened in 1823 when Heathcoat's patent expired. A sort of frenzy set in at this time. Everyone in Nottingham with any capital at all set up lace machines, while workers clubbed together to buy machines. The boom lasted until 1826, when over-production of net had the inevitable result of flooding the market. During the slump which followed some attempts were made to prevent the recurrence of such a disaster by making agreements to limit working hours and by trying to keep prices stable. The following decade, however, saw further distress and disruption in the industry when the demand for embroidered net began to decline. At the same time, embroidered nets suffered severe competition from superior foreign products which were smuggled into the country. 1837 was a particularly bad year for the industry, as only half the available machines were able to be kept in production. These difficulties and distresses led to the rapid growth of trade unions amongst the lace-workers, who were pioneers in this activity, as well as further attempts by the employers to regulate the industry.

The development of patterned machine-made lace

It was very clear that a change of direction was necessary if the industry was to maintain itself and to expand further. It was during the 1830s that much of the work was done which resulted in the adaptation of the lace machines for the production of imitations of various types of patterned hand-made lace. It is impossible in a short account to give a true picture of the incredible amounts of ingenuity and labour that were directed towards the invention and adaptation of lace machinery throughout the first half of the nineteenth century. It must suffice to point out that the persons mentioned here form only the tiny successful proportion of the large numbers of individuals who laboured at refining these extremely complex machines. Some of them, indeed, are even said to have gone out of their minds or taken their own lives in despair over the work.

The process of adapting the machines to produce patterns had begun considerably before the 1830s in one branch of the industry. Like the point-net machines, the warp machines were severely hit by Heathcoat's invention. They continued, however, to produce considerable amounts of plain net, mostly in silk, as well as silk nets patterned with holes and needlerunning. The latter were known as blondes and enjoyed a considerable success in the 1810s. In 1824, William Hardy of Nottingham adapted the machine to produce spots in the net. At this period the warp machine branch of the machine-lace industry was less prosperous, but the production of imitation silk blondes was again very successful in the early 1830s. In 1831, royal acknowledgement was made to the machine-lace industry when Queen Adelaide appeared at a court ball in a dress of Nottingham white silk lace. In the middle of the 1830s, however, the competition of bobbin-net machines again began to make itself felt more seriously for these had, by this time, been adapted to produce patterned laces.

The pusher machine was one of the first to be adapted; indeed, it lent itself readily to adaptation by virtue of its construction. In

1825, John Synyer of Sneinton, Nottingham, patented a modification of the pusher machines which enabled them to produce net patterned with large holes. These were known as "bullet-holes" (cf. Pl.'75). Several small pieces of lace patterned in this way have been preserved at Nottingham (Halls: *Nottingham Lace*, p. 25). In 1831 William Sneath invented a modification whereby spotted nets could be made on the circular comb machine. From these beginnings, the tide of inventions flowed on faster and faster, culminating by the end of the 1830s in the final breakthrough, the application of the Jacquard apparatus to the machines so that patterns could be produced purely mechanically. In 1837 Jacquard cards were used with warp machines, in 1839 with pusher machines by James Wright of Radford, Nottingham, and in 1841, after a long period of trial and error by various workers, with the Leavers lace machine by Hooton Deverill. In the same year a further big step forward was taken with the invention by Joseph Wragg of Lenton, Nottingham, of a modification which enabled the Leavers lace machine to incorporate thicker threads into the design during the process of working, thus doing away with the tedious process of hand-running them after the lace came from the machine.

By the early 1840s, in effect, lace machines were producing creditable imitations of various types of hand-made patterned lace. Each type of machine produced its own specialities.

Warp machines were still concentrating largely on the production of silk blondes which remained fashionable as trimmings. At some time during the early 1840s the warp machine was modified so that extra thicker threads, not actually part of the looped formation, could be put in during the process of manufacture. A pattern book of 1846–7 in Nottingham Museum contains many samples of silk warp laces with simple patterns in thicker threads. The threads are now closely incorporated into the loops of the fabric, instead of passing in and out of the holes, as in the hand-run examples, and the finished work has a flatter and much more regular and mechanical appearance (Halls: *Nottingham Lace*, Pl. 2 and p. 14). Increasing competition from other types of machine, however, was now beginning to drive warp machine owners into the constant search for novelty. A symptom of this was the patent taken out in 1845 by Dunnicliffe & Dexter for making warp lace with velvet pile ornamentation.

Pusher machines were used to produce imitations of Chantilly lace in both black silk (Pl. 68) and white cotton. The machines could be made to produce an imitation that resembled the original very closely. However, the thicker outlining threads always had to be inserted by hand, a fact which gives a helpful clue to those trying to distinguish pusher lace from hand-made Chantilly, for in pusher lace the thick threads pass in and out of the holes in the design, whereas in Chantilly they are incorporated into the twists and plaits of the fabric. The thick threads are usually run in more tightly and evenly in machine-lace, too, and sometimes there is also a sewn-on picot edge. Pusher laces often have a somewhat flat and mechanical appearance and the solid parts of the design may show a certain rigidity and regularity of stitch which is alien to hand-made lace.

It was the Leavers lace machines that displayed the greatest versatility in imitation. Already in the 1830s, imitations of East Midlands bobbin lace were being produced. At this period the thicker outlining threads were still being put in by hand, a practice still followed to a certain extent in the 1840s and 1850s. After 1841, however, it was possible for thick outlining threads to be put in by the machine during the course of work. Even so, these threads are still a useful guide to detection of machine-made lace. Not only are they more prominent on the front of the lace than the back (whereas in hand-made lace they appear equally on front and back), but it is also possible to detect cuts in the threads on both sides of any motif (Pl. 69). Since the machines could not go backwards over their work, it was necessary to use a separate thread to outline each side of any given motif. In hand-made lace it is perfectly possible to make a thick thread encircle a motif completely. Again, the solid parts of a patterned lace made on the Leavers machine are characterized by a very distinctive ridged appearance created by the prominence of the longitudinal warp threads across which the other threads go back and forth diagonally. This is quite unlike the muslin-like texture of the solid parts of bobbin lace, which the machines could only produce in very narrow amounts and which thus seldom appears in machine-made lace. Neither does it bear any resemblance to the looped texture of needlepoint lace.

In the 1830s the Leavers machines began to be used to produce imitation Valenciennes. A patent for an imitation Valenciennes mesh was taken out by Thomas Alcock in 1836. The mesh was made by twisting pairs of threads together and joining them at intervals to imitate the diamond-shaped meshes of Valenciennes. Examination with a lens will, of course, reveal the difference between this technique and the closely-plaited threads forming the meshes of hand-made Valenciennes. The patterned areas, too, show the ridges described above. In the 1840s, delicate borders were produced in imitation of the lightly patterned Valenciennes of the late eighteenth and early nineteenth centuries and larger pieces were also produced in the same technique (Pl. 70). In 1838 a method of making a thicker type of mesh, in which a thread was twisted round the warp threads, was invented by J. W. Bagley. This was used to form the groundwork of even closer imitations of Valenciennes, which were known as plat laces, and it was not to be long before even better techniques were perfected.

A technique similar to that patented by Alcock in 1836 was devised in the 1840s to imitate the hexagonal mesh of Mechlin lace. This mesh was patterned with small floral motifs of a very light texture and with simple imitation filling stitches, to produce lace in imitation of delicate Mechlin laces of the late eighteenth and early nineteenth centuries. This lace, known as "Mecklin", had outline threads put in by hand. It enjoyed a considerable vogue in the middle years of the nineteenth century.

A final development of the 1840s was the invention of the lace-curtain machine by John Livesey. This machine produced a basic square mesh. The weft threads on the bobbins were tightly twisted round the longitudinal warp threads and, at intervals, looped round the adjacent line of warp and taken back again, so as to form the horizontal lines of the mesh. Patterns were easily formed by varying the closeness or otherwise of this crossing process. Curtain lace can always be distinguished by the presence of the characteristic twisted longitudinal lines. It is noteworthy, too, for the shaded effects that could easily be introduced into the patterned areas (Pl. 71). Lace curtains made on this machine gained an immediate popularity, retained unabated to the end of the nineteenth century.

Machine-made lace and embroidered net in the Great Exhibition of 1851

By the time of the Great Exhibition of 1851, the machine-lace industry had got into its stride and was able to make a good showing.

In its lengthy report on the industry, the Jury commented on the tremendous progress achieved in the last fifty years (p. 1006): "There have been incredible sums of money expended, many valuable lives sacrificed by intense study, hundreds of patents taken out, and nearly as many differently-constructed machines built for the production of plain and ornamental laces of every description. It has been a matter of astonishment to see how quickly one inventor has succeeded another, and by simplifying or modifying his machines, rendered useless those of his predecessor." One result of all this activity was, of course, a very great cheapening of the price of the finished article. The Jury noted that "A yard of 4-quarter white silk blonde, which in 1830 sold for 2s., is now supplied for 6d."

In the *Report* (p. 1008) four main types of product were listed:

1. "Black silk piece net ornamented, shawls, scarfs, flounces, trimming laces, blondes in white and colours, some wholly finished on the machine, others partly by machinery and embroidered afterwards."

2. "Cotton edgings, laces and insertions, linen laces in imitation of white pillow lace, muslin edgings and laces, fancy piece net, spotted net, plait net in imitation of the costly Valenciennes lace."

3. "Curtains in imitation of the Swiss curtains, bed-covers and blinds."

4. "Silk and cotton, plain net, Mechlin grounds, blonde, Brussels or extra twist." (It is worth noting that vast quantities of plain nets of various types remained in production throughout the century. Heathcoat in 1851 had no less than 300 machines at Tiverton employed in making silk net.)

Amongst the Nottingham firms who exhibited, the following may be noted in particular: Ball, Dunnicliffe & Co., who showed laces made on the warp and bobbin-net machines; Richard Birkin, who showed black silk laces and white blondes, Valenciennes edgings and laces made of mohair (an important pattern book from this firm, dated 1847, is preserved in the Castle Museum, Nottingham); Heymann & Alexander, who showed curtains, counterpanes and antimacassars, various types of net and black silk lace; Thomas Herbert & Co., products of the warp machine; Mallett & Barton, silk pusher laces, imitation Valenciennes, and imitation Mechlin finished off with needlerun threads; Reckless & Hickling, and William Vickers, both showing a large variety of black silk lace made on the pusher machine; and Henry Steegman & Co., lace curtains. The embroidered-net industry, though considerably diminished since the crises of the 1830s, was by no means defunct. Two Nottingham firms, Samuel Hollins and Greasley & Hopcroft, showed articles in needlerun net, whilst a considerable number of London firms also exhibited. According to the *Jury Report* (p. 1014) the superior varieties of embroidered net known as British Point Lace were made in London, particularly in Islington. Displays included "shawls, scarfs, dresses, court trains, flouncings, lappets, etc." Some embroidered net was already being produced in the heavy floral types of design popular in Spain. Amongst the London firms represented at the Exhibition were Fisher & Robinson of 12 Watling Street, Groucock, Copestake, Moore & Co. of 5 Bow Churchyard, Francis Wheedon of Goldsmith Street in the City, Frederick Price Wheedon of 29 Lower Street, Islington, Samuel Towell of 16 Gresham Street West, William Frederick Gard of 268 Regent Street, and George Frederick Urling of 224 Regent Street, who showed a typical exhibition piece: "White scarf in imitation of Brussels point, composed of British plants and flowers in needlework; the date, 1851, encircled with the rose, thistle and shamrock; the straight lines of the border embroidered in gold, and worked upon a fine clear patent net." Embroidered net was also shown by D. Macarthur & Co. of Glasgow, under the name "Hamilton lace".

A final noteworthy exhibitor was S. Turton of 19 Prospect Place, Radford, near Nottingham, who showed a series of designs for machine-made lace of all types. The question of obtaining good designs had long posed a thorny problem to the machine-lace industry. Indeed, many manufacturers in the early days had recourse to France for designs. In 1846 a Government School of Design was set up in Nottingham itself to train lace designers. This project was already beginning to bear fruit by 1851. The Jury noted that several young men were already at work in the industry producing designs of high quality. They noted too that the vast bulk of the lace shown in the Exhibition by no means reached the highest standards of design. This they attributed to the fact that the manufacturers were catering for different markets, including a

vast export market to both North and South America, with widely
differing demands and standards not of the highest.

As has already been indicated, the majority of designs of this
period had a decidedly eighteenth-century flavour about them.
Even those designs which were more contemporary in feeling, such
as those for black pusher lace (Fig. 12), appear a little old-fashioned
compared with the most up-to-date products of the hand-lace

Fig. 12. Flounce of black lace made on the pusher
machine by W. Vickers of Nottingham, 1852. (*Art
Journal*, 1852, p. 125.)

industries. This was perfectly natural in an imitative industry
which to a certain extent tended to follow the lead given by hand-
made laces rather than striking out on any new path of its own. It
must be stressed, however, that much of the machine-made lace of
this period is of very good quality in both design and execution,
compared with lace made later in the century. The manufacturers
had to compete with fine hand-work and they consequently set
themselves a very high standard right from the start.

75. French Machine-made Lace. *Top left:* bullet-hole lace, *c.* 1834. *Top right:* blonde lace by Topham Frères, Calais, 1863. *Bottom left:* silk lace by R. West of Calais, 1891. *Bottom right:* Bourdon lace by E. Davenière of Calais, 1894. Reproduced from Henri Hénon: *Tulles et Dentelles Mecaniques dans le Pas-de-Calais,* 1815-1900.

76. Scarf of Embroidered Machine-made Net, French or Belgian, second quarter of the 19th century. *Rijksmuseum, Amsterdam* (No. R.B.K. 1955-114A).

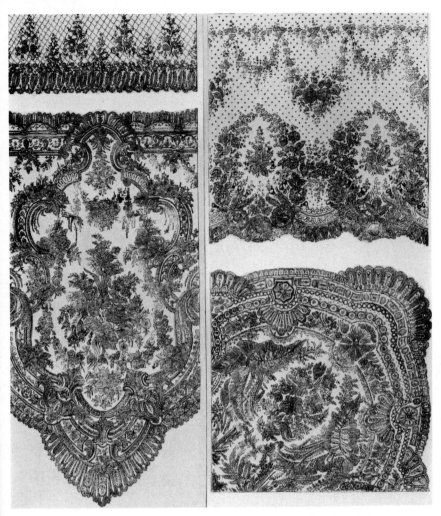

77. Machine-made Silk Lace Shaws shown by Dognin & Cie of Paris and Lyons at the International Exhibition of 1862. *Art Journal Catalogue,* p. 306.

78. Machine-made Silk Lace Shawls shown by Ferguson âiné & Fils, at the International Exhibition of 1862. *Art Journal Catalogue*, p. 167.

Developments from 1851–1862

Throughout the 1850s the potentialities of the various machines continued to be explored. Imitation laces already being made were perfected further. The Chantilly lace made on pusher machines was especially popular at this time. The fabric was refined to the extent that it is often extremely difficult to distinguish machine-made Chantilly from the hand-made variety without a minute examination of the thicker outlining threads, which still continued to be put in by hand. A great deal of attention was paid to improving design in this type of lace also.

Another imitation perfected during this period was the Valenciennes lace made on the Leavers machines. By 1860 the narrow machine-made pieces were so good that it is virtually impossible to distinguish them from similar hand-work. On wider pieces of machine-made Valenciennes, however, the ridged effect is still clearly apparent in the solid parts of the design. Imitation Mechlin declined somewhat in popularity at this time, though it was still made.

Blonde lace, too, fell from favour, but around 1860 a new type of silk lace began to be made on the Leavers machine. In its report the Jury of the International Exhibition of 1862 attributed the introduction of this type of lace to R. & T. Birkin in about 1856. This lace had a hexagonal mesh on which designs were worked in thicker threads. Sometimes parts of the ground were cut away to leave holes, creating an openwork effect, a practice which seems to have gone out of favour after the 1860s (cf. Pl. 75). The lace was made in black, white and cream-coloured silk.

A quite different development of the 1850s was the adaptation of the Leavers machines to produce coarse heavy laces in imitation of the Maltese laces, which became very popular after 1851 and were taken up in many hand lace industries too. Some experiments in making heavier laces had already occurred in the 1840s, when laces were occasionally made with solid designs joined by bars instead of by a net ground, and it has already been noted that laces made of mohair were shown in 1851 by Richard Birkin. His display also included "Guipure à dentelle", a curious name which may refer to these heavier types of lace, which generally had designs of scrolls and leaves. Some early imitations of Maltese lace preserved in a pattern-book at Nottingham probably date from 1854–5 (Halls: *Nottingham Lace*, p. 42). They have a trelliswork ground of little bars like handmade Maltese, though the more solid parts of the design are lighter in texture. Fancy laces made of worsted and known as "yak" or "lama" were also made at this time, while several patents were taken out during the 1850s for the making of Leavers lace patterned with velvet pile, in imitation of that already being produced by warp machines.

The warp machines, increasingly affected by competition from derivatives of the bobbin-net machine, were adapted to produce very light silk nets as well as for making coarser types of lace. After 1850 a type of coarse cotton lace for furnishing purposes was developed (Pl. 72). In this lace great use was made of the extra thick threads which the machine had been able to incorporate into the fabric since the modifications of the mid-1840s. In the cotton furnishing laces these threads became the most prominent part of the fabric and were used to form the design, while the looped threads were made of much thinner cotton and served only to hold the thicker threads in place. Elaborate designs of swags, leaves and flowers were popular for these laces, which continued to be made to the end of the century.

Imitation crochet was also made on the warp machine at this time to rival the currently popular Irish product. Machine-made crochet exhibits many lines of loops, all arranged longitudinally, while the handmade variety is formed basically of one continuous line of loops which may turn and twist in any direction.

Machine-made lace and embroidered net at the International Exhibition of 1862

One of the biggest displays at the International Exhibition of 1862 was that of Copestake, Moore, Crampton & Co. of 5 Bow Churchyard, who showed the products of their Nottingham factory—curtains and pusher laces—as well as embroidered nets and handmade lace from Devonshire and the East Midlands. A steady amount of embroidered net of good quality was still being produced (other examples were shown by Haywards of Oxford Street), though it never again reached the heights of popularity enjoyed in the second quarter of the century. Nottingham firms represented in the exhibition included Thomas Adams & Co., curtains; J. W.

Bagley, imitation Valenciennes, Maltese and Honiton lace; Barnett, Maltby & Co., silk lace; Bradbury, Cullen & Fisher; Dunnicliffe & Smith; Thomas Herbert & Co., crochet, Valenciennes, etc.; Heymann & Alexander, nets, laces and curtains (Fig. 13); M. Jacoby & Co., all types of lace from curtains to Valenciennes; Henry Mallett, Valenciennes and silk laces; Manlove, Aliott & Livesey, velvet laces, etc.; Reckless & Hickling, pusher laces; Sidney

FIG. 13. Machine-made lace curtains, designed by S. W. Oscroft, shown by Heymann & Alexander at the International Exhibition of 1862. (*Art Journal Catalogue*, p. 239.)

Smith; Edward Steegman, curtains; William Vickers, pusher laces (Pl. 73); S. Wills.

In its report, the Jury commented on the marked improvement noticeable in the general standard of design. Patterns were now more contemporary in flavour and more elaborate than they had been before, a fact attributed to the adoption of all firms, by 1862, of machines fitted with the Jacquard mechanism. The Jury particularly commended the improvements made by Mr. Vickers in black pusher lace, by Mr. Bagley in Valenciennes, and by Mr.

Cope in curtain lace. The latter had been very considerably improved since 1851, and was now a much more solid and reliable fabric.

It was noted that the 1850s had not been a period of uninterrupted growth, in spite of all the developments and improvements, for the civil war troubles in the United States had led to a temporary collapse of that particular part of the export market, with the result that a partial slump had followed the boom years 1851–7. By 1862, however, the industry was emerging from these difficulties and, indeed, had hopes of renewed expansion for, from 1860, the French had allowed English lace to be imported on payment of duty, whereas previously it had been wholly prohibited.

Developments from 1862 to the end of the century

By 1862 there were few varieties of hand-made lace that the machines could not imitate. The period of frenzied mechanical invention and adaptation was drawing to a close and attention was now given to perfecting existing manufactures rather than to adapting the machines to new tasks. During the 1860s, for example, the making of Maltese lace on the Leavers machine was perfected, very wide borders in complex patterns being produced. Somewhat later, the coarser Cluny lace, developed from Maltese lace, was also imitated by machinery. Machine-made Cluny, like machine-made Maltese, exhibits both thick and thin threads in its make-up, unlike the uniform threads of the hand-made product. The silk lace made on the Leavers machine was very popular at this period and towards the end of the 1860s a new, heavier variety was developed. This type, known as Spanish lace, exhibited the heavy floral designs long popular in silk laces made for the Spanish market (Pl. 74). In the patterned areas of such lace the characteristic ribbed texture of Leavers lace is very noticeable.

At the Paris Exhibition of 1867, Nottingham manufacturers had to compete with magnificent displays shown by the French machine-lace industry which was now emerging as a formidable rival. The Jury in its report commended the superior Valenciennes shown by M. Jacoby and the magnificent curtains displayed by Heymann & Alexander, but commented that the Nottingham manufacturers showed a rather different range of products from their French rivals, less fine in quality for the most part. It noted in particular that the silk laces produced by both the Leavers and the pusher machines were inferior in design to comparable French machine-laces.

English manufacturers had, in fact, long enjoyed almost a monopoly of a large and secure market, which they were now able to supply with a considerable range of products. Mrs. Bury Palliser's description of the display of the Nottingham manufacturers at the International Exhibition, held in South Kensington in 1874, gives an indication of the scope of the industry: "Nottingham shows all she produces, from the most costly to the commonest article. Nothing has been specially prepared for this exhibition, but all the goods exhibited are regular marketable articles; every description of lace in cotton and silk, such as are selling every day and exporting to all countries—'Pusher' shawls and mantles, tamboured shawls, veils and mantles, Shetland and Spanish shawls; Chantilly flounces and border laces; Brussels, Maltese and Cluny; Valenciennes, Italian, Swiss, Flemish, Mechlin and duchesse lace; Yak, black and coloured, bed and table-covers of heavy tatting-laces, suitable for the South American and West Indian markets; silk nets, Mechlin, Cambrai and Chantilly; Brussels and Paris nets; Shetland and woollen goods made on the lace frame; magnificent flounces and bridal veils, the pattern worked in by hand; and blondes which have much improved in colour, and will bear comparison with the French" (*Art Journal*, 1874, pp. 173–4). This list indicates the trends of the period. It is clear that embroidered nets were still in production; the chain-stitch variety were now often made with the aid of the chain-stitch sewing machine. They did, indeed, enjoy a considerable revival in the last quarter of the century. The designs tended to be somewhat vapid all-over floral patterns, lacking the vigour of earlier work.

In the last quarter of the century it seems to have been left largely to the manufacturers of lace curtains to uphold the honour of the Nottingham industry in the world of international exhibitions. Firms such as M. Jacoby, Heymann & Alexander and Adams & Co. showed splendid and complex designs at exhibitions in Philadelphia in 1876, Paris in 1878 and Chicago in 1893. A typical comment, revealing the current taste in design, was made in the *Art Journal* of 1876, when Heymann & Alexander were congratulated on the "taste, judgment and knowledge displayed in their designs. These are generally, as they ought to be, floral; leaves and flowers gracefully combined, sometimes interlaced with lattice-work, and occasionally presented as pendants over vases. Such Art-aids to our homes are always effective; they refresh the eye and mind, and are suggestive; far more so than designs geometric that, cut up into squares, fail to refresh either."

The silk lace trade also enjoyed an uninterrupted period of prosperity and expansion to the end of the century. The hand-made Chantilly industry virtually collapsed in the early 1870s, but machine-made silk lace continued to be popular and fashionable. Much of the lace of the last quarter of the century was of the heavy

FIG. 14. Machine-made silk lace of Spanish type, shown by Henry Mallett & Sons of Nottingham at the Paris International Exhibition of 1878. (*Art Journal Catalogue*, p. 105.)

Spanish type, patterned with solid floral designs of a monotonous and repetitive type. Examples of silk lace were shown by the Nottingham firm of Henry Mallett at Paris in 1878 (Fig. 14). The only change to be noted before the end of the century was the introduction in the 1880s of much wider silk laces, often with rather more delicate all-over designs. "A decade past the widest width of a pattern was designed principally for dresses, being festooned in flounces down the skirt; but a few years ago a fashion set in which has had a considerable run, of using a single width of lace, from 36 up to 54 inches, for the draping of a skirt" (*Art Journal*, 1891, pp. 87–92, article on the Nottingham lace-trade by C. Lewis Hinde).

The cotton machine-made laces of the last quarter of the century illustrate all too clearly the strictures levelled at English design by the Jury at Paris in 1867. This can be seen from a survey of the machine-lace pattern books preserved in the Castle Museum, Nottingham. Books dating from the 1870s and later contain a stereotyped range of run-of-the-mill products betraying a paucity of design inspiration as well as being less carefully made than laces of the earlier part of the century. It was as if the impetus to good design declined as the great period of mechanical invention ended. By now, too, the cheaper products of the hand-lace industry were generally coarser and markedly inferior to those of the early nineteenth century, so that it seems as if the manufacturers of machine-made lace relaxed their efforts as the product with which they were competing declined in quality.

However, the complacency of manufacturers secure in a settled market was to be severely shaken in the 1880s, when the imitation cotton laces of Nottingham were suddenly subjected to severe competition from new types of imitation lace, produced on embroidery machines in Germany and Switzerland (see Chapter 8). These machine-embroidered laces, made in imitation of seventeenth-century needlepoint, appealed to the taste of the time and by the early 1890s they were seriously challenging cheaper Nottingham lace in the international market.

In spite of temporary setbacks of this nature, however, by the end of the century the machine-lace industry had emerged victorious over its now enfeebled rival. Attempts to revive the latter in these years were doomed to failure in the face of the general attitude of the public, summarized by a remark in the *Art Journal Catalogue of the Paris Exhibition of 1878* (p. 31): "When the machine-made is compared with hand-made lace, the superiority of the latter does not seem to the uninitiated so great as to warrant the enormous difference of cost."

CHAPTER 8

MACHINE-MADE LACE IN FRANCE AND ELSEWHERE

ALTHOUGH the machine-made lace industry spread to many other countries from England in the nineteenth century, England retained her lead for much of this period. It was from France that the most important challenge came, and the French industry will, therefore, be treated first in this chapter, other countries being dealt with afterwards in alphabetical order.

France

The establishment of the machine-lace industry in France followed hard on the heels of that in England. Some details of the early period are given by Felkin whose book is not confined to the English industry alone. It seems that as early as 1774 a fact-finding mission under the Duc de Liancourt was sent over to England to investigate progress in the hosiery and lace industry. As a result of this visit a variant of the stocking-frame known as the "pin" machine (the technical details of this are now lost) was taken over to Lyons by a certain Bonnard and set to producing silk net. This net, made of looped knitting stitches, was known as "Tulle simple et double". Various improvements were made and by the end of the eighteenth century there were 2,000 of these machines in use at Lyons and Nîmes producing vast quantities of silk net. The output was said to be considerably greater than that of the English point-net machines. A large industry for embroidering this net also grew up, chiefly at Courdrieu (Rhône). Continuing improvements included a patent taken out in 1806 by Bonnard for making a fast net that would not run. The machines were still being used in Lyons to a considerable extent when Felkin was writing in the late 1860s. Warp machines were also introduced into Lyons in the 1770s and were used to make silk net in the same way.

Because of the Revolutionary troubles and the Napoleonic Wars there was a long period during which the French were unable to keep up with the latest developments in the English lace industry. Restrictions imposed by governments on both sides of the Channel included a total ban on the importation of English lace into France and on the export of the new lace machinery invented by Heathcoat. After the final overthrow of Napoleon in 1815, however, attempts began to be made to smuggle lace machinery into France. In that year one of Heathcoat's employees, by the name of Cutts, smuggled a bobbin-net machine first to Valenciennes and then to Douay, where he set it up and began to use it. In 1816 he obtained a French patent.

That year there occurred an even more significant development: the first lace machine, a pusher machine, was erected at Calais by James Clark, who started up in business with two partners, Webster and Bonington. Thus began the machine-lace industry at Calais which was to become the most important centre in France, eventually rivalling Nottingham itself. As the Nottingham industry was chronicled by Felkin, so the Calais industry, too, found a historian in a lace manufacturer, Henri Hénon, whose book, *L'Industrie des Tulles et Dentelles Mécaniques dans le Pas-de-Calais, 1815-1900*, published at Paris in 1900, gives not only a most detailed year by year survey of the industry's progress but also contains an incomparable series of illustrations showing the changes in style and fashion in machine-made lace to the end of the century.

In the remaining years of the first quarter of the nineteenth century many other machines were brought to France and with them came numbers of English workmen who set up in business there. Heathcoat himself established a factory in Paris in 1818. He moved in 1826 or 1827 to St. Quentin, where the firm remained until his death in 1861. Like his Tiverton firm, the St. Quentin branch concentrated on producing silk nets. The French at this stage seemed to consider the bobbin-net machine suitable only for making cotton nets, and it was not until 1825 that M. Dognin of Lyons began to produce a heavy kind of silk net known as "grenadine" on a bobbin-net machine he had set up there. This net was often used as a ground for embroidery. Two more centres where the machine-lace industry was established in 1825 were Cambrai and Grand Couronne.

The Calais industry, which from an early period was centred on the suburb of St. Pierre-les-Calais, grew only slowly at first. It was dependent on England for machinery until 1825 when the first machine of entirely French construction was made there. Further difficulties were experienced in obtaining the requisite fine grades of cotton thread for making net, for these could be had only from England and indeed, after a prohibition placed on them in 1819, had to be smuggled in. Consequently for much of the 1820s production of net was slow and expensive. Furthermore English net was allowed into France quite freely. The industry continued to grow, however, and further centres were established during this period at Lille and Amiens.

By 1830 it was estimated that there were about 1,000 machines at work in various parts of France. Embroidered nets of high quality had been displayed in 1827 at a national exhibition held in the Louvre and by 1834, when the next exhibition was held, it was clear that great improvements had been made in this manufacture. The silk-net industry seems to have been in a particularly flourishing state in the early 1830s. Since 1828, Dognin of Lyons had been producing very fine silk nets, known by names such as "zephyr" and "tulle illusion". These and other products of the Lyons industry enjoyed a great vogue in England in the 1830s as they were superior to any silk nets being made there. The cotton-net industry of Calais, on the other hand, was not so prosperous at this period. In 1834, however, the lifting of the prohibition on the import of cotton thread gave a great fillip to the industry which, following the English example, began to develop patterned machine-laces.

Laces patterned with large "bullet-holes" were one of the first innovations. Hénon illustrates a clumsy-looking lace of this type which began to be made about 1834 (Pl. 75). As in Nottingham, these holed laces were enriched by threads put in by hand. Nets embellished with spots of various types were also made in the 1830s, and by about 1837 the step had been taken of applying the Jacquard mechanism to warp lace machines. The first to do this in France was a Nottingham man, S. Ferguson, who came over in 1837 to work in association with Jourdain & Cie. of Cambrai. The firm began to make imitations of white blonde and of black Chantilly lace, the latter being known as "Dentelle de Cambrai". In 1837, too, the firm of Champailler & Pearson at St. Pierre-les-Calais patented a method of making imitations of blonde lace. This was but the first of a series of patents which followed rapidly one after the other.

By 1844 the machine-lace industry was able to put on a considerable display at a national industrial exhibition held in Paris, a display which impressed the public for the first time by the range and quality of the goods shown. In addition to nets, plain, patterned on the machine and embroidered, were shown creditable imitations of narrow Valenciennes laces, and Mechlin laces with thick threads added by hand, as well as a fine range of imitation blonde and Chantilly. The Valenciennes and Mechlin of this period illustrated by Hénon mostly show simple floral patterns of the type popular in the late eighteenth and early nineteenth centuries.

By the end of the 1840s the Calais industry was becoming much stronger and more settled. By 1850, most firms had got rid of their old machines and were using Leavers machines and pusher machines only, while in 1851 the lace curtain machine was introduced by M. Bonsor-Morris. Some idea of the state of the French industry at this time is given in the *Report of the Jury of the Great Exhibition of 1851*. Lyons and Cambrai specialized in the production of silk laces, particularly black lace in imitation of Chantilly, while in Calais some silk lace was made in addition to the types of cotton lace noted above. Félix Aubry noted that while the English industry produced a far wider range of cheap, ordinary laces, French products were very much better designed. This applied particularly to the silk laces which were most faithful and careful copies of the handmade article. Aubry says, too, that the French were now branching out on their own and were no longer content to follow the English lead, a remark which confirms the fact that up till this time the French industry had been heavily dependent on the English. Only one French firm exhibited machine-made lace in 1851: Mallet Frères of Calais, who showed imitation Valenciennes. A firm from St. Pierre-les-Calais showed lace machinery.

In 1851 one Paris firm, F. Audiat, exhibited embroidered nets, but these were often included in displays of embroidery, for the industry had tended to grow up not only around the machine-lace industry but also in other places, such as around Nancy, where white embroidery was an established trade. By 1851 the industry had become stabilized. Lyons was the centre for silk embroidery on silk net. Both the needlerunning and tambour techniques were used here, often on the same piece in order to obtain a rich effect. All grades of work were produced from the most costly to a range of cheap products. Paris specialized in the most elegant articles of costume, dresses, scarves, shawls and so on (cf. Pl. 76), which were often embroidered in colour or in metal threads as well as in black and white. In Lunéville and various towns and villages in Normandy tamboured net for costume was produced, while at Tarare there was an extensive industry in heavy tamboured nets for curtains and furnishings. In the Canton of Vittel in the Vosges, net was embroidered in chain and satin stitch, while Lorraine was noted for tamboured net enriched with needlepoint filling stitches in designs imitative of Brussels application. The French embroidered-net industry seems to have maintained its position to the end of the century. An important innovation of the last quarter of the century was the introduction of the chain-stitch sewing machine for the making of tamboured net.

By the time of the Paris Exhibition of 1855, the French machine-lace industry had expanded enormously. Calais was honoured in 1853 by a visit from Napoleon III and the Empress Eugénie, which was attended with much ceremony. The large order for machine-made nets and laces subsequently placed by the Empress was a great stimulus to the industry. Eugénie felt no compunction about extending her patronage to both the machine- and the hand-lace industries and, indeed, in France at this period there was not felt to be any serious clash between the two. The 1855 Jury gave it as its opinion that, far from harming the hand-lace industry, the machine industry had done it nothing but good by stimulating renewed enterprise and activity. Indeed, as far as France was concerned this was perfectly true. In France, at any rate, while the machines had brought lace, hitherto one of the most highly-priced luxuries, within the reach of almost everyone, the wealthy were now buying hand-made lace on a scale hitherto unsurpassed. At the Paris Exhibition the Calais display as a whole was awarded a medal of honour, and the following firms were singled out for special praise: Champailler, fils, of St. Pierre-les-Calais, who showed blondes and black silk laces of particular excellence; Herbelot, fils, & Genet-Dufay of Calais, for imitation Chantilly made on pusher machines; Dubout, fils aîné, of Calais, for Valenciennes; L. Rébier & Valois, St. Pierre-les-Calais, for the best machine-made Valenciennes in

France; Veuve Cardon & Watré & Cie., St. Pierre-les-Calais, for Mechlin and "Neuville", a similar type of lace; Mullié-Bernard & Hermont, St. Pierre-les-Calais, for an assortment of silk and cotton laces; Robert Belin & Cie. of Calais, for silk laces. Other firms commended for their blonde laces were Cliff Frères of St. Quentin and Lefont of Grand-Couronne.

It is clear from Hénon's illustrations that as well as making blondes and imitations of Mechlin and Valenciennes (including fine wide lappets of eighteenth-century inspiration as well as narrow borders), like the English manufacturers, the French industry was already beginning to branch out on its own. Hénon illustrates a creditable imitation of *Duchesse de Bruges*, made by the Calais firm of Rébier in 1854, and another imitation Duchesse lace produced by Veuve Cardon in 1855. The French machine-lace industry was now beginning, in fact, to follow hot on the heels of the hand-lace workers, eagerly snatching at any novelty that they could produce. As early as 1852, for example, Ferguson of Cambrai had begun to produce imitations of the worsted laces, "yak" and "lama", made by the workers of Le Puy, and in 1856 Dognin & Isaacs of Calais followed suit.

The latter half of the 1850s saw continued expansion in the industry, particularly in Calais and Lyons. Very great improvements were made in the manufacture of silk blondes and Valenciennes, the two machine-made laces in greatest favour at this time, and numerous patents were taken out in both centres. The spectacular progress made by the French industry during these years is illustrated by the fact that at the International Exhibition of 1862 in London more medals and honours were showered on French manufacturers than on English. The Jury made the following comment on the French exhibits (*Report*, p. 4): "The neat and effective style of the patterns, the excellence of their colours, the well-made and superior finish of their goods, are worthy of the highest praise."

Machine-made shawls of black silk lace exhibited by Dognin of Lyons showed, indeed, designs of a richness fully equalling that of hand-made Chantilly (Pl. 77), as did those of Ferguson of Cambrai (now Ferguson, aîné et fils) (Pl. 78). This lace, like similar black silk lace produced in England, had sewn on picot edges and thicker outlining threads put in by hand. Dognin & Cie., in fact, employed many hundreds of peasant women in the Rhône valley and adjacent areas, such as the Dauphiné and Beaujolais, as embroiderers. According to a brochure put out by the firm in 1862 (*Fabrication de la Dentelle dans le Départment du Rhône et les Départments limitrophes*), the work was given out by travelling agents who controlled the cottage industry in a similar fashion to the hand-lace industry of Le Puy. Many of the workers spent only part of their time on embroidery, the rest being devoted to work in the vineyards. The sewing on of picot edges was done in Lyons itself. Shawls, borders, flounces, etc., were made in goats' hair (lama) as well as in silk in the same technique and enjoyed a great vogue at this period. Both Dognin and Ferguson won medals in 1862, whilst among Calais firms so honoured were E. Bemont, Bruno & Lefévre, Cordier frères, Dubout, aîné & fils, Herbelot, fils, & Genet-Dufay, L. Houette, Thomas Léfebure, L'Heureux Frères, Rebier & Valois, Galoppe & Cie., and Topham Frères. Cliff Frères of St. Quentin were again honoured for their black and white silk laces produced very cheaply.

Progress in the French industry was not quite so rapid during the 1860s, partly owing to a swing of fashion away from blonde laces towards heavier plaited laces of Maltese and Cluny type, but the period saw the consolidation of previous advances, and by the time of the Paris Exhibition of 1867, the French industry was fully able to compete with the English in the international market. While English manufacturers produced an immense variety of cheap imitation laces, the French tended to concentrate their efforts on goods of very high quality and, in particular, on silk laces of all types. In Lyons, Dognin & Cie. was still the leading firm, producing immense quantities of black silk lace on pusher machines. In Calais, black, white and coloured silk laces were made on various other types of machine. All these laces had thicker threads added by hand. Many narrow silk laces of most elegant design, dating from the 1860s are illustrated by Hénon. The borders generally have hanging flower or leaf motifs, while insertions are patterned with wavy lines of flowers and leaves and strapwork. Many of these laces have openwork patterns made by cutting holes in the fabric (Pl. 75), a technique found in English machine-made lace of the same date.

The Jury of 1867 singled out Herbelot of St. Pierre-les-Calais for special mention as a leading innovator in the silk lace manufacture.

Many of the firms already mentioned were again honoured, as well as Humbert & Manniez, Bacquet Père & Fils, Valois & Renaud, Hall Frères. New trends were indicated by the fact that Brunot of Calais included "Spanish" silk laces in his display, while Cliff Frères of St. Quentin showed imitation Cluny laces as well as narrow silk laces. Since about 1864, in fact, very creditable imitations of Cluny and Maltese lace had been made in both cotton and silk.

As Hénon's history of the Calais industry comes nearer to his own time, it naturally becomes much fuller. For the last thirty years of the nineteenth century, indeed, he gives a year by year account and it is possible to follow the vicissitudes of the industry in greatest detail. Although it never lost the ground gained by the end of the 1860s, the industry weathered a good many crises before 1900. Some of these were due to changes in fashion but others were the result of the structure of the industry itself which contained, like that of Nottingham, a great many small firms constantly changing hands or amalgamating. As in Nottingham, overproduction of a novelty often resulted in a falling-off of demand, whilst many manufacturers undercut their rivals by selling off surplus stocks at excessively cheap rates. Hénon's account is full of details of attempts to control the industry by regulating prices as well as imports and tariffs. The lace-workers were becoming more militant at this time and Hénon chronicles with much grumbling successive laws reducing hours for women and children and regulating night work. Hénon considered these manœuvres a grievous burden for the manufacturers and occasionally even expresses envy of the hand-lace industry which was not troubled by any such considerations.

In spite of these difficulties the industry continued to the end of the century to pursue its policy of producing high-quality goods. French design became even more markedly elegant at this time and far outshone most contemporary products of English lace machines.

After the prosperity of the late 1860s there followed a period of slump with the economic troubles following on the collapse of the Second Empire and the Franco-Prussian War. Fashions too changed; while Valenciennes and Chantilly remained popular, the lighter blonde laces went out of favour altogether. It was not until the end of the 1870s that the industry fully recovered from this decline, by which time heavier laces such as the silk "Spanish" lace, woollen laces, and thick cotton guipures had become staple products of the industry. Solid designs of stylized flower and leaf motifs were common at this period, while lace made in vermicular designs similar to those found in Eastern European peasant lace, was sold as "Dentelle Russe". Lighter cotton laces included imitations of *point d'Alençon* in early nineteenth-century designs; these were particularly popular in the early 1880s. Imitation Mechlin was revived at this period too.

The early 1880s saw a renewal of great prosperity for the industry but, by 1885, trouble was brewing again, as the market began to be flooded with the new types of machine-made lace being produced on embroidery machines in Germany and Switzerland. These laces were imported into France under fancy names such as "dentelle orientale" (embroidered net) and "guipure d'Irlande" (chemical lace), thus enabling their makers to avoid import duties. The Calais industry was seriously undermined by this competition, and much consideration was given to the possibility of importing embroidery machines and setting up this industry in Calais itself. In the late 1880s, too, attempts were made to imitate these types of lace on the Leavers machine.

This competition affected cotton laces very severely but, fortunately, the silk lace trade continued fairly steady. In the late 1880s and early 1890s some lighter designs were produced again, mostly in a delicate and lively revived rococo style (Pl. 75). Many laces were now patterned with designs of birds and animals or of figures in medieval dress (Pl. 79), motifs which indicate that manufacturers were now branching out on their own and no longer tied to the imitation of the designs of hand-made lace. The influence of *art nouveau* becomes noticeable in floral designs towards the end of the century, eventually superseding to some extent the heavy stylized flowers characteristic of "Spanish" lace. It was not until half way through the 1890s that the cotton lace trade began to recover again. Amongst the products of this period were imitations of Irish crochet, thick imitations of machine-embroidered lace known as "le bourdon" (Pl. 75), heavy guipure and torchon laces and narrow Valenciennes. Towards the end of the century imitation Mechlin became popular again. One enterprising manufacturer, Caron of Calais, secured a steady market by producing imitation laces in traditional designs for the Dutch peasant market.

Throughout the last quarter of the century the industry had

79. Borders of Lace made on the Leavers machine, French (Calais); *top,* made by Houette & Butler, 1883; *bottom, c.* 1890. *Victoria and Albert Museum* (Nos. T.45, 46-1963).

80. Lace made on the Embroidery Machine; *left*, embroidered net or "Edelweiss" lace; *right*, "chemical" lace; German, *c.* 1891. Reproduced from the *Art Journal*, 1891, p. 92.

81. Machine-embroidered Machine-made Net, probably German or Swiss, used for a wedding-dress in 1890. *Victoria and Albert Museum* (No. T.157-1964).

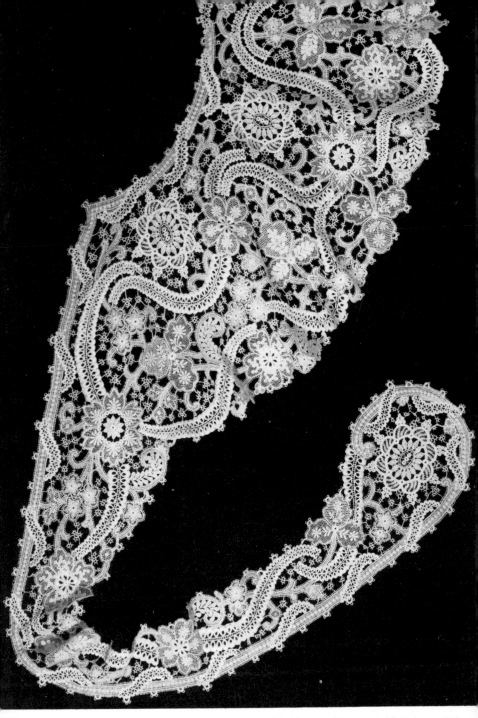

82. Pelerine of "Chemical" Lace, made on the Embroidery Machine, probably Swiss, *c.* 1895-1900. *Victoria and Albert Museum* (No. T.179-1962).

continued to send displays to various international exhibitions, a particularly elaborate selection, including a lace patterned with Columbus's ship *The Golden Hind*, being sent to Chicago in 1893. These publicity manœuvres were becoming less and less important now, however, as the industry became ever more firmly established. Hénon concluded his book, in fact, by stating that the main enemy of the industry by 1900 was not foreign competition, which it had proved itself able to cope with, but overproduction and lack of control within France itself.

It remains only to note one final development. In the 1870s a French engineer, Malhère, invented a machine called "La Dentellière", which imitated the movements of the bobbin lace-maker more exactly than any invention hitherto. The machine consisted basically of a series of bobbins arranged in a semicircle. Malhère himself was not able to make much use of his invention. According to Hénon, he was too ambitious and wasted much time and ingenuity in attempts to enlarge the machine so that it would produce something more than a narrow border or insertion. The idea was taken up again later, however, and an improved version of the machine, known as the Barmen machine, was patented in 1894. It was extensively used in France to produce narrow torchon laces which are indistinguishable from the hand-made variety.

Belgium

In 1801 an Englishman, George Armitage, introduced point-net machines into Belgium, thus inaugurating machine-made net industries in Antwerp and Brussels. The industry later spread to Termonde, Ghent and other centres.

In 1834 eight bobbin-net machines were taken to Brussels by F. Washer for the express purpose of producing nets of the finest quality for Brussels application lace. Washer succeeded in making nets superior in quality to those produced in England, but he was none the less dependent on England for raw materials. In the *Catalogue of the Great Exhibition of 1851* it is stated that he showed "Pieces of table ground work for Brussels lace, the thread spun by Messrs. Nicholls & Ashton, Manchester, and doubled, gassed and finished by Messrs. John Thackeray & Sons, Nottingham." After Washer's death the firm was carried on by his widow. Several other firms were established in the middle of the century. D. M.

Polak of Brussels was awarded a second-class medal at Paris in 1855 and the firm of Lambelin & Cie. of Mechlin exhibited at Paris in 1867, but it seems that all these manufacturers confined themselves to making nets for application and embroidery. Embroidered net was produced in Belgium at Brussels, Antwerp and Lierre. The industry seems to have been very flourishing up to the middle of the century. Four firms showed embroidered net at the Great Exhibition of 1851: Dorteville & Monoury of Brussels and A. Bernhart & Co., M. Paquet and Weil, Meyer & Co., all of Antwerp. Félix Aubry noted that quantities of narrow, needlerun bands were made at Antwerp, much of this work being intended for the Dutch peasant market. Tambour work was produced in quantity too. Buccholtz & Co. of Brussels showed examples in their display at the International Exhibition of 1862 in London. At Paris in 1867, embroidered net was shown by G. H. J. Christiaensen of Antwerp.

When Verhaegen published *La Dentelle et la Broderie sur Tulle* in 1902, the needlerunning industry was much diminished, though some manufacturers were still producing small pieces worked in the hand without a frame for the Dutch peasant market. Tambouring in white or coloured threads, or even metal threads, was still a reasonably profitable industry at Lierre at the end of the nineteenth century. This manufacture still existed to a small extent at Antwerp, too, and it was introduced to Maldegem at the very end of the century. Much tambour work of late nineteenth century date was made with the aid of chain-stitch machines which produced a cheaper, though less durable, fabric more quickly.

Germany

Felkin notes that a small number of bobbin-net machines had been imported into Prussia and Saxony by the middle of the nineteenth century. It was not until much later, however, that Germany entered into the international machine-lace market in any significant way. When she did so it was not with the products of lace machinery, but with imitation lace made on the embroidery machine.

Machine embroidery was introduced into Plauen in Saxony in 1857 from Switzerland. The machines used were improved versions of that invented by the Alsatian, Josué Heilmann, in 1828. Heilmann's machine consisted of a vertical frame, in which the material to be embroidered was stretched and which was connected to a pantograph. As the pantograph was moved to and fro to trace out the required design, so the frame moved up and down. At each movement a row of needles, each with an eye in the centre and each bearing a separate thread, was pushed forward on a carriage to pierce the material. The needles were caught and held on either side of the material as they came through by two rows of pincers. At first, machines of this type made simple satin-stitch embroidery only, but gradually methods of making openwork, scalloped edges and similar ornamentation were developed. In Saxony the industry concentrated on the production of white embroidery and by the 1870s it was competing successfully with similar Swiss products which had hitherto had the lion's share of the market.

Like the machine-lace industry, the machine-embroidery industry was notable for many ingenious inventions and for a constant search after novelty. In Saxony an important breakthrough occurred in about 1881, when Robert Neubauer discovered how to make an openwork embroidery which resembled lace. The method used was ingenious: embroidery was worked in cotton, a vegetable fibre, on silk, an animal fibre, in such a way that it was secure enough to stand on its own when the background was subsequently dissolved by the use of chlorine or caustic soda. The Saxon industry concentrated its attention mainly on the production of imitation lace on a background of machine-made net. Designs varied from delicate floral borders to heavier all-over patterns and the new type of lace enjoyed an instant success which continued unabated to the end of the century. Large quantities found their way into England under the name of "Edelweiss lace" (Pl. 80) and, as has been seen, severely threatened the Nottingham lace industry. This embroidered net was very much cheaper to produce than any other machine-made lace, for it was a good deal simpler to make a design for a pantograph than for a Jacquard mechanism. In these machine-embroidered "chemical" laces the motifs are usually composed of a mass of tiny stitches, giving a muddled appearance to the work when it is looked at through a magnifying glass. The basic satin-stitch technique is also conspicuous.

A great deal of net embroidered by machinery but without openwork effects was produced at this time too (Pl. 81). It is often extremely difficult to distinguish this from hand-work. In the latter part of the 1880s, another machine, the Schifflé machine, patented in the late 1860s by the Swiss, Isaac Groebli, began to be used for this purpose. This machine combined the principles of the embroidery machine and the sewing machine by using one continuous thread instead of separate threads for each needle.

Switzerland

Although lace machinery was introduced into Switzerland by the middle of the nineteenth century, it was the embroidery industry in this country that made the greatest impact in the machine-lace market. The making of white embroidery by machinery was a well-established industry in the St. Gallen region of Switzerland from the 1850s onwards. The development of this industry was chronicled in very great detail in 1931 by a manufacturer, Ernest Iklé, in his book, *La Broderie Mécanique, 1828–1931*, published in Paris. Iklé described how, in 1879, Charles Wetter, a machine embroidery manufacturer, began to experiment with making imitation lace on the embroidery machine. Wetter had taken note of some experiments in which embroidery had been worked on paper which was afterwards washed away. This method was not entirely successful as it was difficult to avoid bits of paper being left in the lace and the paper was not a strong enough ground for embroidery. The use of contrasting fibres and chemicals, described under Germany, was discovered at about the same time as the similar developments in Saxony, and the invention was patented by Jacob Sutter, one of Wetter's employees. The first "chemical lace" was produced in 1883.

At first, imitations of Irish crochet were produced, but it was quickly recognized that this method was ideal for making imitations of Venetian *gros point* and other heavy needlepoint laces which it had hitherto been impossible to imitate. Lace of this type was the height of fashion in the last two decades of the nineteenth century and the Swiss products enjoyed an immediate success. A certain amount of embroidered net was produced in Switzerland on both the old embroidery machine (see p. 259) and the Schifflé machine (see above), but in the main the Swiss left this branch of the industry to the Saxon manufacturers and concentrated on chemical lace.

The Swiss industry had always enjoyed a reputation for high-quality products, and chemical lace was no exception to the rule. On close examination it is not difficult to distinguish chemical lace from real needlepoint, as no trace can be seen in it of the careful rows of looped stitches of varying sizes which combine to produce the many-textured hand-made fabric. From a short distance away however, chemical lace is a very good imitation indeed and easily deceives the unwary. The manufacturers took great care to copy the best examples of seventeenth-century lace. A glance through the illustrations in Iklé's book reveals many excellent pieces which, on a quick glance, look like genuine *gros point de Venise*. Needlepoint laces of the late sixteenth and early seventeenth centuries—*reticella* and *punto in aria*—were imitated too, the pages of pattern books such as those of Vinciolo and Vecellio being ransacked for designs which were faithfully copied. Some designs of a more contemporary flavour were, of course, made as well (Pl. 82), and all types of design were adapted to shapes of collar fashionable in the late nineteenth century. Dress lengths were also made and furnishings such as curtains, tablecloths and antimacassars were decorated with chemical lace, too. The large quantities that survive are an indication of the success of this Swiss product in the latter years of the nineteenth century.

Miscellaneous

The machine-lace industry spread in a minor way into other European countries during the nineteenth century. In Spain and Austria, for example, the variant of the stocking-frame known as the "pin" machine was introduced early in the nineteenth century, to be followed by bobbin-net machines somewhat later (an Austrian manufacturer, M. Schluck of Vienna, was awarded a medal for imitation black lace at the Paris Exhibition of 1855). There seems to have been a small machine-lace industry in Russia by the middle of the century too. In the latter years of the century the machine embroidery industry became fairly widespread also, reaching as far as the United States at this time, when it was introduced into New Jersey by German and Swiss settlers. None of these industries, however, was of more than local importance at this time.

APPENDIX

BASIC TECHNIQUES OF LACE MAKING

Lace is by definition an openwork textile composed of threads plaited or looped together independently of any supporting woven fabric. Most lace, apart from *lacis* or darned netting which does not concern us here, is made in one of two ways.

I. BOBBIN LACE

Basic requirements in making bobbin or pillow lace are, as these names imply, a series of bobbins on which the threads to be used in lace making are wound, and a pillow on which the work is carried out. The lace-maker also needs pins and a pattern.

The basic pattern, usually showing one repeat only of the design to be worked, is marked out in ink on card or vellum and pricked with holes at regular intervals. Copies of such a pattern are readily made by placing parchment or card beneath the original design, pricking the holes through both and inking in details on the under parchment. A parchment thus made for the lace-maker's use generally shows a series of repeats of the design. The pricking of such parchments is a skilled task, requiring much accuracy and precision, for in the holes of the parchment are placed the pins which control the process of lace-making and on which the accuracy and neatness of the finished lace largely depend.

The bobbin lace-maker starts her work by securing the parchment pattern to her pillow, which may be round, square or cylindrical in shape. Pins are placed through the holes at the beginning of the design and to them are attached the requisite number of threads, each wound round a bobbin hanging over the edge of the pillow. Bobbins vary in shape and size according to the variety of lace to be made. The threads thus attached are crossed over one another or twisted together by movements of the bobbins to form the various parts of the pattern, the work being controlled and directed as it proceeds by means of pins stuck through the holes in the pattern.

With these two basic simple movements of twisting and crossing may be built up all the varieties of texture associated with bobbin lace: plaited lines, solid woven areas (*toilé*), joining bars (*brides*), net grounds (*réseaux*) and fancy fillings.

Various terms are used to distinguish different types of bobbin lace:

Plaited laces are composed, as their name implies, principally of interwoven lines of plaited threads. This technique is found in the earliest geometrically-patterned bobbin laces of the sixteenth and early seventeenth centuries and it enjoyed a revival to some extent in the later nineteenth century.

Torchon denotes a very simple type of lace in which elementary geometric patterns are worked against a coarse net ground. This is the easiest type of bobbin lace to make; beginners usually start with it.

Tape lace is bobbin lace in which the design is formed of a continuous tape twisted and stitched into place, the spaces between being joined by bobbin-made bars or, sometimes, by needlepoint stitches.

The term *guipure* is used of laces in which the motifs of the pattern are joined up by connecting bars (*brides*) without any net background.

It was not until the very end of the seventeenth century that lace began to have a regular net ground. During the early eighteenth century, lace underwent a very great refinement with the coming into use of very thin, delicate threads. At this time certain distinctive types of lace, each with its own special characteristics, came into being. They are known by the names of the towns where they originated or which were the centre of their manufacture. These laces fall into two main categories:

(a) *Continuous thread laces*

In making laces of this type the exact number of threads needed to execute the entire design was attached to the pillow at the very beginning of the work, no threads being either added or removed as the work proceeded. Pattern and background were worked simultaneously, the strip of lace growing evenly down its length as the work went on. In all such laces, therefore, the threads in the solid parts of the design (*toilé*) are parallel or at right angles to the long, straight edge of the lace. Normally, only comparatively narrow laces could be made in this way. Continuous thread laces include:

(i) *Valenciennes*, distinguished by its very solidly woven *toilé* set off against a strong net ground of diamond-shaped meshes, all four sides of which were plaited.

(ii) *Binche*, related to Valenciennes but much more cobwebby in appearance, with a rather more loosely woven *toilé* used in less well-defined designs set against a ground known as *fond de neige*, consisting mainly of round spots variously arranged.

(iii) *Mechlin*, in which the motifs of the design were defined by being outlined with a thick thread or gimp and set off against a net of six-sided meshes of which two sides were plaited and the other four twisted (similar to the net of Brussels bobbin lace).

(iv) *Lille*, in which the motifs, again outlined by a thick thread, appear against a light net ground with hexagonal meshes of which the sides are simply twisted and not plaited.

(v) *Point de Paris*, a name given to a net ground, used in laces similar to those of Lille, in which the meshes, worked by twisting and not plaiting, appear to form a series of six-pointed stars.

The laces made in the *East Midlands* exhibit the characteristics of Lille, Mechlin and *Point de Paris*. The cream-coloured silk lace known as *Blonde* is made like Lille or *point de Paris*, and the same characteristics also appear in black silk *Chantilly* lace.

(b) *Lace made in separate parts*

In these laces the motifs are worked separately on the pillow and the threads used therefore follow the twists and turns of the motif and bear no direct relation to the long edge of the finished piece of lace as they do in continuous thread laces. These motifs are joined up when complete by a background of bars or of net worked in each space as required. Fancy fillings are also worked separately. It will be readily understood that there is no limit to the size of a piece of lace made in this way. Such laces include:

(i) *Brussels* bobbin lace, characterized by the use of two varieties of *toilé*, a solid, muslin-like type (whole-stitch) and a more open net-like type (half-stitch), by a little openwork edge which appears around all the motifs, and by a net ground of hexagonal meshes with two sides plaited and four twisted.

(ii) *Honiton*, which shows all the characteristics of Brussels, through the hexagonal net ground is seldom if ever seen.

2. NEEDLEPOINT LACE

The principal items in the equipment of the needlepoint lace-maker are a needle, thread and a parchment pattern. Often this pattern may consist of only a portion of the finished design as there is no limit to size as far as needlepoint lace is concerned. The pattern is first sewn down to two thicknesses of strong material. Then the worker covers the outlines of the design with lines of thread which are secured at regular intervals by another thread passed over them and through the parchment and the two under-lying pieces of material. These outlining threads are called *le tracé*. On the framework thus formed the worker proceeds to fill in the design, some parts worked solidly, others in more open stitches, but all areas built up by the use of the same basic stitch: buttonhole stitch. Further refinements may include the addition of a raised edge (*la brode*) to the motifs, and the inclusion of areas of fancy filling stitches (*les modes*). When the work is complete the lace is detached from the pattern by cutting or breaking the retaining threads between the two pieces of material. The finished motifs may be joined together by needlemade bars (*brides*) which are sometimes enriched by little dots (*picots*), or by mesh grounds of various types; thus, Venetian needlepoint laces have a background of *brides*, Alencon has a ground of square meshes with twisted sides, Argentan a hexagonal mesh of which the sides are entirely covered by buttonhole stitching and Brussels *point de gaze* a very delicate network of simply looped threads.

All needlepoint laces share the same basic technique, though the end-products may differ considerably from each other. In all types, none the less, however different they may appear to the casual eye, the basic looped stitches may readily be detected if the solid parts of the pattern are examined under a lens.

In conclusion it may be pointed out that it is by no means un-common for both techniques to be found in combination in the same piece of lace. Such a lace is known as a "mixed" lace. Examples are tape laces with needlepoint fillings and Brussels needlepoint lace of the eighteenth and early nineteenth centuries which almost invariably has a groundwork of the hexagonal bobbin-made mesh found in Brussels bobbin lace.

BIBLIOGRAPHY

CONTEMPORARY WRITINGS:

Anon. "Lace and Lace-making", from *Chambers' Repository of Instructive and Amusing Tracts, c.* 1878.

Brennan, James. *Report by Mr. J. ... B. ..., R.H.A., Crawford Municipal School of Art, Cork, on a visit to Paris and Belgium in connection with the improvement of the Lace Industry in the South of Ireland,* 1887.

Brennan, James. "The Modern Irish Lace Industry", in *Journal of the Arts and Crafts Society of Ireland,* Vol. 1, No. 2, 1898.

Bury Palliser, Mrs. *History of Lace,* 1st edition, 1869, revised by M. Jourdain and Alice Dryden, 1902.

Caulfeild and Saward: *Dictionary of Needlework,* London, 1882.

Channer, C. C. and Roberts, M. E. *Lace-making in the Midlands,* London, 1900.

Cole, Alan S. *Cantor Lectures on Lace-making,* in *Journal of the Royal Society of Arts,* 1881.

Cole, Alan S. *Reports upon Visits to Convents, Classes, etc., in Ireland,* 1885 and 1887.

Cole, Alan S. *A Renascence of the Irish Art of Lace-making,* 1888.

Cole, Alan S. *Report on the Present Condition and Prospects of the Honiton Lace Industry,* House of Commons, 1888.

Cole, Alan S. *Lecture on Designing Patterns for Various Irish Laces,* 1889.

Cole, Alan S. *Report upon his Visits to Irish Lace-making and Embroidery Schools in 1889,* Department of Science and Art, 1889.

Cole, Alan S. "Lace-making in Ireland", from *The English Illustrated Magazine,* June, 1890.

Cole, Alan S. *Report on Northampton, Bucks. and Beds. Lace-making,* Department of Science and Art, November, 1891.

Cole, Alan S. *Report upon his Visits to Irish Lace-making and Embroidery Schools in 1897,* Department of Science and Art, 1897.

Davydoff, S. *La Dentelle russe,* Leipzig, 1894.

Despierres, Mme. G. *Histoire du Point d'Alençon depuis son origine jusqu'à nos jours,* Paris, 1886.

267

Devonia: *Honiton Lace-making, c.* 1873.

Dognin & Cie.: *Fabrication de la Dentelle dans le Departement du Rhône et les Departements Limitrophes*, Lyons, 1862.

Engerand, Fernand. "L'Industrie de la Dentelle en Normandie", from *Revue des Deux Mondes*, April 1st, 1900.

Felkin, W. *History of Machine-wrought Hosiery and Lace*, 1867.

Goubaud, Madame. *Pillow Lace Patterns and Instructions in Honiton Lace-Making*, 1871.

Hénon, Henri. *L'Industrie des Tulles et Dentelles Mécaniques dans le Pas-de-Calais, 1815–1900*, Paris, 1900.

Hudson, Octavius. "Report on Lace-making", Appendix VII, e, of *The First Report of the Department of Practical Art*, 1853.

Jesurum, M. *A Few Words on Venice and Burano Ancient and Modern Lace. Catalogue and Prices*, Venice, December, 1883.

Lefébure, E. *Broderies et Dentelles*, Paris, 1887.

Meredith, Mrs. Susannah. *The Lacemakers*, 1865.

Murphy, Samuel J. *Report of the Lace Industry at some of the Lacemaking Centres in France and Belgium*, 1887. MS. in Victoria and Albert Museum Library.

Report of the Select Committee on Arts and Manufactures, Minutes of Evidence, Part II, 1836.

A. M. S[harp]. *Point and Pillow Lace*, 1899.

Treadwin, Mrs. *Antique Point, Honiton Lace, c.* 1874.

Turgan, Julien. *Les Grandes Usines. Etudes industrielles en France et à l'Etranger*, Paris, 1866–89.

CONTEMPORARY EXHIBITION CATALOGUES, ETC.:

Catalogues of Exhibitions of Manufactures held at the Society of Arts, 1847, 1848, 1849–50.

Official Descriptive and Illustrated Catalogue of the Great Exhibition of the Works of Industry of All Nations, 1851.

Reports of the Jury of the Great Exhibition of 1851.

Art Journal Catalogue of the Great Exhibition of 1851.

Aubry, Félix. *Rapport sur les dentelles, les blondes, les tulles, etc., 1851*, Paris, 1854.

Illustrated Catalogue of the Art Industry Exhibition, Dublin, 1853.

Catalogue of the Paris International Exhibition, 1855.

Jury Reports of the Paris International Exhibition, 1855.
Official Illustrated Catalogue of the London International Exhibition of 1862.
Reports of the Jury of the London International Exhibition of 1862.
Art Journal Catalogue of the London International Exhibition of 1862.
Catalogue of an Industrial Exhibition at the Palais de l'Industrie, Paris, 1865.
Jury Reports of Paris International Exhibition of 1867.
Art Journal Catalogue of Paris International Exhibition of 1867.
Art Journal Catalogue of Vienna Universal Exhibition, 1873.
Art Journal Catalogue of International Exhibition, South Kensington, 1874.
Art Journal Catalogue of Philadelphia International Exhibition, 1876.
Art Journal Catalogue of Paris International Exhibition, 1878.
Art Journal, 1893, Supplement: *The Chicago Exhibition*.
Elliott, Maud Howe, ed. *Art and Handicraft in the Woman's Building*, Chicago Exhibition, 1893.

CONTEMPORARY PERIODICALS:

Art Journal, 1849–1912.
Journal of Design and Manufactures, 1849–51.
The Englishwoman's Domestic Magazine, 1852–79.
The Ladies' Cabinet, 1832–70.
The Queen, 1861–.
The World of Fashion, 1824–51.
The Young Englishwoman, 1865–77.

MODERN WRITINGS:

Boulard, Félix. *La Dentelle Alençon*, Alençon, 1924.
Boyle, E. "Embroidery and Lace-making in Ulster", in *Ulster Folk-life*, Vol. X, 1964, pp. 5–22.
Buck, Anne. *Victorian Costume and Costume Accessories*, London, 1961.
Carlier de Lantsheere, A. *Les Dentelles à la Main*, Paris, c. 1905.
Carlier de Lantsheere, A. *Trésor de l'Art Dentellier*, Brussels and Paris, 1922.
Czernyánsky, M. *Ungarische Spitzenkunst*, Budapest, 1962.

FitzRandolph, H. E. and Hay M. Doriel. *Rural Industries of England and Wales*, Oxford, 1927.

Iklé, E. *La Broderie Mécanique, 1828–1930*, Paris, 1931.

Lefébure, A. *Dentelles et Guipure*, 1904.

May, F. L. *Hispanic Lace and Lace-making*, New York, 1939.

Morris, Barbara. *Victorian Embroidery*, London, 1962.

Paulis, L. *Pour Connaître la Dentelle*, Antwerp, 1947.

Penderel Moody, A. *Devon Pillow Lace*, 1907.

Ricci, E. *Merletti e ricami della Aemilia Ars*, Rome, 1929.

Vanderpoel, E. N. *American Lace and Lace-makers*, New Haven, 1924.

van Loon, E. *De Kantindustrie in Frankrijk en Italië*, The Hague, 1904.

Verhaegen, P. *La Dentelle et la Broderie sur Tulle*, Brussels, 1902.

Verhaegen, P. *La Dentelle Belge*, 1912.

Wardle, Patricia. "An Exhibition Piece", in *Embroidery*, Vol. 17, No. 4, pp. 107–9, Winter, 1966.

Wright, Thomas. *The Romance of the Lace-pillow*, Olney, 1919.

MUSEUM PUBLICATIONS:

Amsterdam, Rijksmuseum:
  A. M. L. E. Erkelens: *40 Jaar Kantsalet*, 1965.
  A. M. L. E. Erkelens and C. A. Burgers: *Kant uit Koninklijk Bezit*, 1966.
Brussels, Musées Royaux d'Art et d'Histoire:
  L. Paulis: *Les Points à l'Aiguille Belges*, 1947.
  M. Risselin-Steenebrugen: *Les Dentelles Etrangères*.
  M. Risselin-Steenebrugen: *Dentelles Belges, 19e–20e Siècles*.
Dublin, National Museum of Ireland:
  Ada K. Longfield: *Catalogue to the Collection of Lace*.
Luton, City Museum and Art Gallery:
  Charles Freeman: *Pillow Lace in the East Midlands*, 1958.
Nottingham, City Museum and Art Gallery:
  Zillah Halls: *Machine Made Lace in Nottingham*, 1964.
Rotterdam, *Museum Boymans-van Beuningen*:
  Picture Book: *Kant*.

ADDITIONS TO BIBLIOGRAPHY

MODERN WRITINGS:

Elizabeth Boyle, *The Irish Flowerers,* Ulster Folk Museum and Institute of Irish Studies, Belfast, 1971.

Anne Buck, *Thomas Lester, his Lace and the East Midlands Industry, 1820-1905,* Carlton, Bedford, 1981.

M. Coppens-Coppens, 'Dentelles de soie noire de Grammont dites de "Chantilly", *Bulletin des Musées Royaux d'Art et d'Histoire,* Brussels, 47, 1977, pp.153-161.

P. Earnshaw, *The Identification of Lace,* Aylesbury, 1980.

Emil Hannover, *Tonderske Kniplingen,* 1st ed. Copenhagen, 1911, reprinted 1974 with English summary and foreword by Charlotte Portman.

P.L.R. Horn, 'Pillow lacemaking in Victorian England: the experience of Oxfordshire', *Textile History,* III, 1972, pp.100-15.

Alessandra Mottola Molfino and Maria Teresa Binaghi Olivari, exhib. cat. *I Pizzi: Moda e Simbolo,* Museo Poldi Pezzoli, Millan, 1977.

F. Schoher, *Enzyklopädie der Spitzentechniken,* Leipzig, 1980.

G.F.R. Spenceley, The Lace Associations. Philanthropic movements to preserve the production of hand-made lace in Late Victorian and Edwardian England', *Victorian Studies,* XVI, 1973, pp.433-52.

G.F.R. Spenceley, 'The health and discipline of children in the pillow lace industry in the 19th Century', *Textile History,* VII, 1976, pp.154-71.

P. Wardle, 'A late 19th-century lace fan', *Bulletin Museum Boymans-van Beuningen,* Rotterdam, XX, 1969, pp.58-65.

P. Wardle, 'Two late nineteenth-century lace fans', *Embroidery,* XXI, 1970, pp.40-3.

P. Wardle, 'A complete set of Chantilly lace', *Embroidery,* XXIV, 1973, pp.75-7.

P. Wardle, 'A lace society and a lace school', *Lace,* 1977, pp.7-8.

MUSEUM PUBLICATIONS:

Brussels, Musées Royaux d'Art et d'Histoire:
M. Risselin-Steenebrugen, *Les Dentelles Italiennes,* 1973.
M. Risselin-Steenebrugen, *Trois Siècles de Dentelles aux Musées Royaux d'Art et d'Histoire,* 1980.
Burano, Museum of Lace School:
Various authors, *La Scuola dei Merletti di Burano,* 1981.
Exeter Museum:
P.M. Inder, *Honiton Lace,* Exeter Museum Publication No.55, 1971.
Florence, Palazzo Davanzati:
Marina Carmignani, *Merletti a Palazzo Davanzati,* 1981.

INDEX

273

Damières-Petitjean, 107
Damigny, 52
Darned netting (lacis), 32, 86, 164, 209
Dauphiné, 250
Davenière, E., *Pl. 75*
Davey, Mrs., 138
Debenham & Freebody, 134, 150, 159, *Pl. 48*, Figs. 3, 8
De Clippèle, C., 130
Defrenne, Sophie, 107
De Groote, Bernard, 115
Dekeyzer-Weyenberge, J., 115
Delahaye, A., 105, 107, Fig. 5
De L'Arbre, Denis, 115
De L'Arbre Vrancx, 115
Delcambré, L., 68, 69
Delil-Pieret, 115
Demeulemeester-Decrick, P., 115
Demoyer, Victor, 115
De Moyer-Ghysselinck, F., 115
Denblauu-Peel, John, 112
Denmark, 202–3
Dentelle Arabe, 84
Dentelle de Bruges, 109–10
Dentelle de Cambrai, 246
Dentelle Orientale, 252
Dentelle renaissance, 85–6, 127
Dentelle Russe, 252
Department of Science and Art, Reports on Irish Lace Industry, 176, 179, 180, 186, 199
Department of Science and Art, Report on Northants., Bucks. and Beds. Lace-making, 161
Derby, 219, 222
De Ruyter-Vanderdonckt, 115
Deschauwer, Adrien, 115
Designers, 19, 27, 43, 44, 58–9, 63, 64, 79, 88, 89, 90, 106, 116, 127, 139, 140, 150, 156, 157, 161, 176, 179–80, 186, 200, 231, 239
Despierres, Mme G., 45, 60, 61
Destelberghe, 92, 108
De Vere, Lady, 181
Deverill, Hooton, 227
Devonia, 32
Devonshire, 134, 135, 136–40, 149–55, 156, 162, 222, 223, 238

D'Hont, Veuve, 115
Diarville, 83
Dictionary of Needlework, 163
Dieppe, 72
Diericx, Veuve J. B., 115
Digges Latouche, Misses, 181
Diss Lace Association, 162
Doge Point, 208
Dognin & Cie., 245, 246, 249–50
Dognin & Isaacs, 249
Donegal Industrial Fund, 181
Donville, Mme, 57, 60
Dortville & Monoury, 258
Douay, 245
Down, County, 185
Downton, 162
Dresden, 203
Dresses (see also evening dresses, wedding dresses), 24, 25, 26, 31, 32, 37, 38, 66, 68, 69, 128, 132, 137, 160, 164, 184, 212, 221, 231, 242, 248, 261, *Pls. 6, 9, 19, 31*
Dublin, 174, 179, 180, 181, 182, 183, 184, 185, 186, 200
Dublin, Convent of Mercy Industrial School, 181, 182
Dublin, National Museum of Ireland, *Pls. 52, 55, 57*
Dublin, Normal Lace School, 181
Dubout, fils aîné, 248, 250
Duhaijon, B., 107
Duhaijon-Brunfaut, Félix, 111, 112
Dulax, Veuve, 78
Dunnamoyne, 182
Dunnicliffe & Dexter, 227
Dunnicliffe & Smith, 239
Dupré, Mlle, 49
Dutch peasants, lace for, 126, 252, 258
Dutch Royal Lace Collection, *Pls. 21, 26, 30, 33, 64*
Duval, A., 68
Dwyer, Messrs., 199, *Pl. 58*

E

East Midlands, 134, 135, 136, 155–62, 238
East Midlands lace, 24, 28, 32, 155–62, 222, 264, *Pls. 46–50*